Dreamgates

An Explorer's Guide
to the Worlds of Soul,
Imagination,
and Life
Beyond Death

ROBERT MOSS

Three Rivers Press/New York

Published by Three Rivers Press, a division of Crown Publishers, Inc., 201 East 50th Street, New York, NY 10022. Member of the Crown Publishing Group.

Random House, Inc. New York, Toronto, London, Sydney, Auckland

www.randomhouse.com

THREE RIVERS PRESS and colophon are trademarks of Crown Publishers, Inc.

Design by Nancy Singer

Several sections of this book, including the "House of Time" exercise in chapter 6 and the "Journey to Sirius B" in chapter 16, are loosely based on material the author recorded for his audio series *Dream Gates: A Journey into Active Dreaming*. Robert Moss is grateful to the wonderful people at Sounds True for helping him to open the dreamgates for others.

Printed in the United States of America

Library of Congress Cataloging-in-Publication Data
Moss, Robert, 1946–
    Dreamgates : an explorer's guide to the worlds of soul, imagination, and life beyond death / by Robert Moss. — 1st ed.
      p. cm.
    Includes bibliographical references and index.
    1. Dreams.   2. Shamanism.   I. Title.
BF1091.M79   1998
154.6'3—dc21   97-45984
                                         CIP

ISBN 0-609-80216-X

10 9 8 7 6 5 4 3 2 1

First Edition

for the Defenders of the Dreaming

CONTENTS

≋

ACKNOWLEDGMENTS

My students are my teachers. I am deeply indebted to the many adventurers in consciousness who have come to my workshops and Active Dreaming circles in the United States, Australia, and Europe. The journeys we have made together have helped me to develop and refine the techniques explained in this book and have produced many of its best stories.

I am grateful to the many dreamers who have written to me to share their experiences in experimenting with the methods explained in my previous book, *Conscious Dreaming,* and contributed some of the stories included here.

I am grateful for the companionship, encouragement, and example of many fellow explorers, including Wanda Burch, Jean Campbell, Chuck and Shirley Coburn, Trish Corbett, Rita Dwyer, Iain Edgar, Marcia and Jim Emery, Naomi Epel, Myron Eshowsky, Allen Flagg, Patricia Garfield, Jane Gignoux, Robert Gongloff, Michael Harner, Ronald Jan and Monique Heijn, Bob Hoss, Sandra Ingerman, Patricia Keeling, Steve and Wewer Keohane, Stanley Krippner, Marta Macbeth, Fred Olsen, Henry Reed, Joanne Rochon, Carlos Smith, Robert and Faye Spencer, Claire Sylvia, Jeremy Taylor, Aad van Ouwerkerk, Timothy White, Alan Worsley, and Ken Wydro.

I am grateful to the wonderful people who have provided dream settings for group adventures in Active Dreaming: at the Esalen Institute, at the Naropa Institute, at Gaia in Berkeley, at Oibibio in

Amsterdam, at the New York Open Center, at Pumpkin Hollow Farm, at Omega, at the New York Theosophical Society, and many other venues. I give special thanks to Rochelle Brener and Cathy Marcellino Squire at the Mandala Center, a sanctuary for soulwork on my present home ground near Albany, New York; and to Lyna Hanley, a marvelously energetic doorkeeper to the Dreaming in Asheville, North Carolina.

Eagle feathers for the spirited gang at Sounds True in Boulder, especially Tami Simon, Lisa Fitzpatrick, and Andrew Young.

I have been graced with two dream editors, Leslie Meredith and Shaye Areheart, and a dream agent, Stuart Krichevsky. I thank all of them from the heart for helping me to bring my *big* dreams into manifestation. Thanks to many others in the Harmony/Crown family for help and support over the past three years, especially Sherri Rifkin, Joanna Burgess, Brian Belfiglio, and the indefatigable Gail Shanks.

Bear hugs for the "Defenders of the Dreaming" who have brought me such love and humor and shared adventure, especially Cathy, Sara, Carol, Gloria, Paula, Pat, Joanna, Patrick, Susan, Louise, Lonnie, and Suzanne.

Lion purrs for my wife, Marcia, who helps me to join earth and sky, and to my daughters, who share in the limitless adventure and teach me new lessons every day.

My greatest debt is to my teachers in the Real World, whose fierce love recalls me to the paths of soul and spirit.

Unless we attempt the absurd
we cannot achieve the impossible.

Albert Einstein

All day long I have exciting ideas and thoughts.
But I take up in my work only those to which
my dreams direct me.

C. G. Jung

Those who know have wings.

Pancavimsa Brahmana

You Are Born to Fly

In its original state, the soul was feathered all over. So now it is all in a state of ferment and throbbing; in fact the soul of a man who is beginning to grow his feathers has the same sensations of pricking and irritation and itching as children feel in their gums when they are just beginning to cut their teeth.

Plato, Phaedrus

In her dream, Carol is pulling a long drawer out of an immense locker. As the drawer slides out, she realizes it is a safety-deposit box. It is lined with velvet and filled with sparkling jewels—diamonds, sapphires, rubies, emeralds—that reflect and refract the light. The drawer seems endless. As Carol delves deeper, she finds an old book with a blue cover that is written in German. She knows that everything in this safety-deposit box belongs to her, and that knowledge fills her with awe and wonder. She understands that the box has some kind of time release:

"I have the feeling I put these treasures here before this life began, in the hope I would reach the point where I remembered what belongs to me and was ready to use it. A part of me is rejoicing, 'Yeah, she found it!'"

Carol woke charged and energized. In the weeks that followed, she drew strength from this sparkling dream to cope with many challenges in her everyday life. She also went back inside her dreamscape to reopen her safety-deposit box and learn more about its contents. Some of her discoveries led her down paths of research and adventure in waking life. When she talked to family members about the blue book in the drawer, she learned that some of her ancestors on her mother's side had come from Germany. The information she was able to gather about them resonated with her life and offered lessons she found timely and helpful.

Many months later, on the eve of a challenging business meeting, Carol dreamed she opened the box and found a beautiful robe of light inside. A dream guide encouraged her to put on this robe and wear it to her meeting. She woke feeling confident and energized and sailed through the meeting she had previously feared.

Carol's dream discovery of treasure that had always belonged to her in the safety-deposit box with the time release is a beautiful example of how dream exploration is a vital part of soul remembering: recovering knowledge that belonged to us before we came into this life experience.

This book will help you to open your own dreamgates to the realms of soul and to live the deeper story of your life. Both the exercises I suggest and the travelers' tales I report have sprung from my personal practice and teaching, as a lifelong dream explorer. I will encourage you to put everything you find here to the test of your own experience and analysis. I make only one promise: that if you do this, you will never again buy into the notion that dreams are "only" dreams or that imagination is "just" imagination.

Ken Wilber, who has helped us define the varieties of consciousness, rightly insists that "until the full spectrum of knowing is acknowledged, the full spectrum of being—the comprehensive world view—will likewise remain hidden."[1] If we wish to know a certain thing, we must follow a certain way of knowing. Wilber likes the threefold distinction the medieval schoolmen made between three "eyes of knowing": the eye of flesh (i.e., sensory perception), the eye of reason, and the eye of contemplation. Through each of these eyes, we perceive different worlds: the physical world, the world of logic and philosophy, and the spiritual planes.[2]

In tales of shamans and Otherworld journeys, we are struck again and again by the same revelation: to see different orders of reality, you have to change your sight. There is a Scottish tale of a woman who was kind to a fairy and was invited to visit the fairy kingdom under the hill. When she stepped inside, the fairy sprinkled magic dew on her eyelids, which enabled her to see the wonders of Fairyland. When the woman returned to the door between the worlds, the fairy again dropped the magic dew on her eyelid so she was able to switch back from her altered state to the mode of perception appropriate to the physical world.

This is a guidebook that will help you to move into different ways of seeing and knowing in order to see clearly and operate effectively in worlds beyond physical reality. I believe we must look to these realms of spirit and imagination if we are to find the wellsprings of healing, creativity and intuition, and insight into the deeper purpose of our lives. If I had to settle for one of the schoolmen's categories, I would be obliged to say that the whole province of this book falls under the eye of contemplation. But the word *contemplation* is too passive, in contemporary usage, to describe the techniques of Active Dreaming, creative imagination, and shamanic soul-flight offered here. They will take you out of habitual mind-sets and out of the consensual hallucinations of everyday life. They can take you out of your body and make you a traveler between worlds. They can bring you face-to-face with your guardian angel, your personal daimon, your double in heaven. You will learn to see with the eye of the dreamer into universes inconceivably vaster—and arguably *more* real—than those that can be perceived through the outer senses. Active Dreaming is the bridge between dreamwork and shamanism.

My previous book, *Conscious Dreaming,* shows how to harvest and work with the spontaneous guidance and healing of night dreams, how to have fun in the "twilight zone" between sleep and waking, and how to embark on conscious dream journeys. *Dreamgates* takes you on a deeper journey. You will learn to travel through the gateway of dream images to seek insight and healing for yourself and others, to communicate with spiritual guides, and to expand your knowledge of a greater reality. The reality of other worlds can be confirmed and explored *now,* through the arts of Active Dreaming. You can learn to journey between the worlds with the help of the exercises and meditations in this book. *Dreamgates* is a course in human possibility. As you become an active dreamer, you will find you are steadily expanding your horizons of possibility and your personal definitions of reality. You will become familiar with gateways and paths used by previous travelers. You will learn how to journey beyond the maps and recover knowledge that belonged to you before you entered this life experience.

The travel reports in this book come fresh from the travelers themselves, especially from participants in my Active Dreaming workshops, from fellow explorers and frequent fliers who have shared their experiences with me, and from my personal journals. At this stage of our evolution, we are privileged to be able to draw on the collective wisdom of many traditions, including texts that were long held secret by spiritual orders. So I have also borrowed from the experience and sacred teaching stories of many cultures, from the "tobacco shamans" of the Warao to the Kabbalists of Safed and the Orphics of southern Italy.

Part I is a flight manual. It offers simple and effective techniques for shifting consciousness in order to fold time and space and journey beyond the body into hidden orders of reality. You will learn that there are many levels of dreaming. As you explore them, you will discover that the dreamworld is a real world and may even be the source of the events that will take place in your waking life. You will learn how to create a sacred space from which you may safely embark on your journeys, and how to enlist spiritual helpers to guide and protect you during your travels. You will discover how to use dream images as gateways to a larger reality. You will be offered several methods for embarking on intentional journeys beyond the body.

You may wish to tape some of the exercises and meditations, and to experiment with the audiotapes listed in the resources section.

In chapter 4, we go deeper into the dreaming of the shamans. Spiritual science offers many techniques for the expansion of consciousness beyond the physical plane. One of the most primal and powerful is the shaman's conscious dream journey, which is the source of many of humanity's enduring myths and conceptions of the afterlife. Shamanic journeying facilitates intentional out-of-body experiences and routinely increases psychic abilities. You will be invited to practice the arts of shamanic dreaming: shape-shifting, timefolding, dream healing, soul recovery. The dreamworld is the realm of soul. In chapter 5, we will pause to study the core insights of "paleolithic psychology" into the nature of the soul and the reality of spirits. I believe these insights are of urgent relevance to us today, especially in relation to healing, psychic well-being, and our approach to death and dying. They are the gift of *experience*—from ancient shamans to contemporary dream voyagers—and you will be encouraged to put them to the test of your own experience.

In part II, we embark on a series of Otherworld journeys, into realms of imagination, initiation, and healing. Poets and mystics have always known that the world of imagination is a real world, a "Third Kingdom" between the physical universe and the higher realms of spirit—and that it is possible to travel there and bring back extraordinary gifts. We will explore locales in the Imaginal Realm we can visit and revisit for training, initiation, and shared adventures. We will learn how to approach master teachers on these planes and to investigate how collective and personal environments—including heavens and hells—are generated by thought and desire. You will share in powerful personal experiences of training and instruction in "invisible schools" and of journeys into the Celtic Otherworld (among others). We will discuss the understanding of the Imaginal Realm in the works of the medieval Persian philosophers, the Kabbalists, the Neoplatonists, and other schools.

In chapter 8, you will learn how to release blocks and open to creative flow through Active Dreaming. You will be invited to journey to your personal Dream Library to seek inspiration or look up something you need to know.

In chapter 9, we journey deep into the realms of Asklepian dream healing and shamanic soulwork. We see how dream theater is not only a creative and fun-filled way to honor dreams, but a powerful way to release their energy for healing. You will share in moving stories of healing with the aid of the animal helpers, and of journeying to bring back lost soul energy.

In part III, we use the techniques of Active Dreaming to follow the paths of soul and spirit beyond the gates of physical death and develop an art of dying adequate to our needs and yearnings today. Through Active Dreaming, we can visit "ex-physicals" and their guides in their own environments. We can help the dying to prepare for the transitions of spirit, and we can assist people who have become "stuck" on the other side. I report on personal journeys to possible afterlife locales and transition zones, as well as the findings of active dreamers I have led on group explorations of these territories. We will examine the fate of the subtle body after physical death, the challenges of dealing with lost or earthbound spirits, and the reasons why the departed sometimes turn to the living for help and guidance.

In chapter 13, you will be challenged to reach into the place of your deepest fears: to face Death on its own ground and revalue your life and its purpose from this perspective. When we "brave up" enough to confront our personal Death and receive its teaching, we forge an alliance that is a source of power and healing in every aspect of life.

In part IV, we use the tools of Active Dreaming to explore the nature of multidimensional reality and the possible evolution of our species. You will learn the arts of soul remembering, reclaiming knowledge of your life's purpose that belonged to you before you entered your present existence. We will explore the possibility that each of us is born into a spiritual, as well as a biological, family. In later chapters, we investigate the evidence that through "alien encounters" and other anomalies, beings from higher dimensions are breaking through the crust of materialism that has divorced many people in modern society from a larger reality. We share in the journeys of shamanic dreamers who claim to have traveled to other star systems. We explore what our lives might become if we could re-vision our world of physical extension and see the larger pattern.

Finally, we recall that dreaming is about living more richly and generously. As you become an active dreamer, you will learn to navigate by synchronicity. When you view dreams more literally and waking life more symbolically, you enter the flow of natural magic.

As we approach the new millennium, we have the chance to participate in the emergence of a more gifted and generous version of our species, the multidimensional human. To accomplish this, we need to marry the best of contemporary science and scholarship to the techniques of paleolithic psychology: conscious dreaming, hyper-sensory perception, and the care and feeding of *soul*.

I hope that when you have reached the end of your journey through *Dreamgates* you will take with you a flight manual for your own adventures in consciousness, an anatomy and genealogy of soul for healing and self-understanding, working maps of hyperspace that will serve until you draw your own—and wonderful games to play any day of your life.

Dreamgates is for *active* spirits, but not only for people who are already frequent fliers. You are born to fly, and in dreams you remember the soul has wings. If you have ever dreamed of flying, if you have ever sensed that delicious discomfort Plato evokes (the itch and scratch of your wing feathers growing back), then the dreamgates are waiting for you. One caution before you embark on this journey: the side effect may be transformation.

PART I

≈

A Little Course in Dream Travel

Self-projection is the one definite act which
it seems as though a man might perform equally well
before and after bodily death.

Frederic W. H. Myers, Human Personality
and Its Survival of Bodily Death

It may well be a prejudice to restrict the psyche to being
"inside the body." In so far as the psyche has a non-spatial aspect,
there may be a psyche "outside-the-body," a region so utterly
different from "my" psychic sphere that one has to get out of
oneself . . . to get there.

C. G. Jung, Mysterium Conjunctionis

In order to arrive at a place you do not know
you must go by a way you do not know.

St. John of the Cross

CHAPTER 1

Becoming a
Frequent Flier

"Tell me how to dream better, Sebastian."
"My kin, I have waited a long, long time to hear you
ask that question. . . . Simply to dream is not enough.
There are many, many kinds of dreams. They exist
perhaps on different levels."

Dorothy Bryant, The Kin of Ata Are Waiting for You

The Dreamworld Is the Real World

"I came because I don't want to miss the movies," explained a man at the start of one of my dream workshops. He saw his dreams as a nightly film festival. He wanted to make sure he had a good seat and took rich memories home from the show.

Are dream images really projections, like pictures thrown on a movie screen or holographic images dancing between two laser beams?

When she was ten, my daughter Candida presented me with a cardboard figure in a magician's hat she had cut out and painted. "This is Dreamgiver," she informed me. "He has the biggest video library ever! Each night he picks out the movies we are going to watch."

We have dreams (often dreams within dreams) that *are* movies. We watch movies in our dreams, just as we do in waking life. Some of these experiences seem entirely literal and may be a preview of a new release or revival we will later watch at a neighborhood cinema or on a plane. But when a movie comes up on a screen inside a dream, we are not obliged to remain passive spectators. We can step through the screen, as Alice stepped through the looking glass, and become actors (and even directors) in a new adventure. Similarly, the characters who loom up on the screen can jump out and interact with us in our dream reality.

Pay close attention to the spontaneous images that come in the twilight zone between waking and sleep, and you may receive strong impressions of a movielike process of dream projection. You may find yourself looking at lots of still photographs of strangers, random pieces of footage of unrelated events or landscapes, fleeting or blurry pictures reminiscent of someone trying to get a test pattern into focus. Sometimes there is a sense of mechanical difficulties: slides and shorts come up out of sequence, get stuck, or fail to fill up the whole screen.

If dreams are like movies, is waking life any less so?

I sometimes have the impression, on waking from an exciting dream in which I have played an active role, that I am back in the movie theater, where the next installment of a long-running serial is about to unroll. Dreaming, I can enter the projection room and play other episodes—from past or future or alternative scripts. I can wander out into the studio lot where the movie is filmed, sit in on scripting and conferences, and hunt through an immense multimedia library of other productions. Beyond this, I can explore the world in which the movies are made, and the dimensions from which this vast imaginal realm, in turn, is projected. Dreaming, I am like the man in Plato's cave, who turns from watching the shadow play upon the wall and awakens to the source reality beyond appearances.

In dreaming traditions, they say simply that the dreamworld is the real world, and that the most important events in our lives may take place in the dreaming. Anthropologist Irving Hallowell writes of one dreaming people, the Ojibwa, "When we think autobiographically we only include events that happened to us when awake; the Ojibwa include remembered events that have occurred in dreams. And, far from being of subordinate importance, such experiences are for them often of more vital importance than the events of daily waking life. Why is this so? Because it is in dreams that the individual comes into direct communication with the *atiso'kanak,* the powerful 'persons' of the other-than-human class."[1]

From this perspective, to dream well is to live well (and vice versa). An Ojibwa elder tells Hallowell, "You will have a long and good life if you dream well."

Among Australian Aborigines, the Dreaming is the state in which messages and guidance are received from the ancestors. In dreaming, sacred stories, songs, and rituals are transferred from the spirit world to the sphere of mortals. Groups of people who share in the same Dreaming are bonded by a shared link to the spiritual world and its powers. Dreamtime is creation time, when the ancestors descended from the sky, rose from the sea, or pushed up through the ground. But it is also *now*. Humans enter this sacred realm through dreams and visions, ritual, and visits to sacred sites.[2]

All things that will be manifested in physical life are initiated inside the Dreaming.

Dreaming, the souls of unborn children choose their parents and rehearse for the lives that lie ahead.

Walking through Central Park on a brilliant spring morning when the trees were just starting to bloom, I thought about these insights of Australia's First Peoples, which are shared by indigenous peoples wherever the Dreaming is alive. I was on my way to a meeting with a woman television producer who turned out to be eight months pregnant. At nearly forty, she was carrying her first baby and was both elated and nervous.

I asked her if she remembered any dreams about giving birth.

"I've had a recurring dream, of rocking my baby in my arms. It's very sensual. I feel her cheek against my breast. I smell the incredible freshness of her breath, fresher than Irish spring."

She felt wonderful each time she woke from one of these dreams. We both felt confident that holding to the dream would help ease her way through labor and delivery.

"You know, your baby is dreaming inside you now," I remarked.

"But what can she be dreaming about?" the producer asked, intrigued but puzzled. "She hasn't seen the world yet."

"Ah, but maybe she's coming from another world. She remembers the origin of her spirit, which may be starborn. Right now, she's rehearsing for the transfer to a new dimension, the dimension of physical reality. As she grows, she'll continue to rehearse the skills she will need, including language skills."

The producer patted the dolphin swell of her belly.

"So she's rehearsing, too," she said, smiling. "Dreaming her way into her new world."

Open Secrets of the Dreamtime

Here are the open secrets of the Dreamtime, insights shared by many dreaming traditions and indigenous peoples that challenge the ruling paradigms of a culture that confuses the *real* with the *physical*.

1. Dreams are real experiences.

There are big dreams and little dreams. "Bottom-line it for me," bulled a radio host over the phone from North Dakota. "Aren't dreams caused by spicy pizza?" Well, yes, *some* dreams are. But we will not expend much space here on the surface bubbles of the dozing brain and belly.

In big dreams—in what Sri Aurobindo called "the sleep of experiences"[3]—we are dealing with events, encounters, and challenges that are entirely real on their own level of reality. Our dream memories may be garbled or muddy, but the dream is a real experience whose meaning lies within the dreamscape itself. The dream experience, fully remembered, is its own interpretation. But we must do more than interpret dreams; we must manifest their energy and insight in our waking lives.

Shamanic dreamers tend to be quite literal-minded about dreams. If you dreamed you fell off a rock-face, you'd better remember to check your safety harness if there is any chance you might go rock climbing. If you flew with the eagle, you discovered a powerful spiritual ally—and your own ability to transcend the limitations of your physical body. If you dreamed of your dead uncle, before you start asking yourself what part of you he might represent, you should consider the possibility that you had a visit with him. Is he bothering you—maybe trying to cadge a drink or a smoke—or offering you help? If you dreamed you received instruction at a mountain shrine, you should be open to twin possibilities: that you may go there someday, in physical reality; *and* that you may have been called in your dreams to one of the many "invisible schools" where training and initiation on the higher planes are conducted.

2. Dreams are flights of the soul.

During one of the final presentations at a hectic conference in Berkeley, I regretted that I had not taken that Saturday morning off to explore the Bay Area. I closed my eyes, slipped free from my physical focus, and felt myself gliding over the Bay on the wings of an eagle. It was a wholly tactile sensation. I was drawn to a wild, lightly wooded area with intriguing stone formations that looked from the air like volcanic rock. As I dipped into a fold in the hills to examine the area more closely, I saw another interesting formation, shaped by human hands: a circular labyrinth, or spiral, at the edge of a pond.

At lunch, I casually described the scene I had explored. "It could be the Sibley Volcanic Preserve," one of the local conferees piped up. "I can take you out there this afternoon if you have time." She did not know about the spiral path, but we found it fairly easily, at the edge of a swampy pond.

From a shamanic perspective, there was nothing extraordinary about my experience. It was just a routine scout—a Middle World journey—in which I moved beyond the range of my physical senses to check out my environment. I was traveling beyond my body, but I kept a firm connection with it, maintaining awareness of the activity in the lecture room even as I flew across the Bay.

Shamans say that in *real* dreams (waking or sleeping) one of two things is happening. Either you are journeying beyond your body, released from the limits of space-time and the physical senses; or you receive a visitation from a being—god, spirit, or fellow dreamer— who does not suffer from these limitations. In the language of the Makiritare, a dreaming people of Venezuela, the word for dream, *adekato,* means literally a "flight of the soul."[4]

The open secret is that consciousness is *never* confined to the body and brain. We discover this in spontaneous night dreams and intuitive flashes, when our left-brain inhibitions are down. As we become active dreamers, we can hone the ability to make intentional journeys beyond the body at any time of day or night.

3. You have a dreambody as well as a physical body.

I am leading one of my Active Dreaming circles. We are squatting around a centerspread with a white candle. Someone asks whether there is any way to prove that we are not dreaming. I pick up the candle and pour hot wax onto my hand. I feel a sting of pain as the wax sears the web of skin between thumb and forefinger, and I tell the group, "I guess that proves *I'm* not dreaming." Then I wake up.

What was this dream telling me? That I am a nitwit because I can't tell whether I'm dreaming? If so, I will take solace from the fact that in most sleep dreams, most people are completely unaware that they are dreaming. Actually, I think this dream has a more interesting and specific message, related to the theme that dreams are real experiences. In my dreambody, I can know pleasure and pain just as vividly as in my physical body. I have more than one body, or vehicle of consciousness, and when I go into the dreamworld and other worlds, I go embodied. And so do you.

As we will soon discover, the importance of this statement—in relation to our ability to operate in nonordinary reality and to access spiritual sources of insight and healing—can hardly be overstated.

4. Dreams may be memories of the future.

I dreamed of a silly little dog decked out with fake antlers for some kind of Christmas pageant. The dog ran out on the road and was killed, but was magically revived by a dubious, utterly amoral character who seemed remote from the normal range of human emotions.

The dream had a movielike quality. I had no idea what was going on here, but because I had no particular feelings about it, I was content to record it in my journal before rushing off to the airport to catch a plane to Denver.

I missed my connection and later found myself on a different flight from the one scheduled. Whenever my travel planes come unstuck, I am alert for the play of the Trickster. On the "wrong" plane, I found myself seated next to a woman who turned out to be best friends with a person in publishing to whom I had been introduced only the day before, and I was able to glean some useful insights. Our conversation was interrupted by the screening of the in-flight movie. I looked up to see a silly little dog decked out in fake antlers for a

Christmas pageant. Later in the movie, the dog is killed on the road and magically revived—by a low-flying angel portrayed by John Travolta. The title of the movie is *Michael,* and I highly recommend it. What interested me most was that I seemed to have attended an advance screening in my dream the night before.

We dream things before they happen in waking life. If you work with your dreams and scan them for precognitive content, you can develop a superb personal radar system that will help you to navigate in waking life. You can also learn to fold time and travel into the possible future by the methods explained in this book. For even the most active dreamers, however, the meaning of many dreams of the future may be veiled until waking events catch up with the dream.

I dreamed of a garden in Manhattan, modest in size, but beautifully designed. A place for quiet meditation, a refuge from big-city noise and hustle. A place where I felt I could do good work with good people. I was intrigued by this dream, which came to me at a time when I was quite resistant to leading programs in New York City because of the energy required to clear out all the static and psychic clutter and create a safe space for soulwork. The dream left me feeling bright and happy. I was curious about the location of my dream garden. Did it exist in ordinary reality? When I reentered the dream, I found myself on a block in the East Fifties, between Third and Second. This satisfied me that I had visited a locale that existed in physical reality. Lacking an exact address, I forgot about the dream after logging it in my journal. Yet the dream continued to exercise an influence: to my mild surprise, I said yes when several groups subsequently invited me to conduct workshops in New York. Nine months after the dream—the period of an average pregnancy— I entered the meeting room of the New York Theosophical Society, on East Fifty-third Street, for the first time. I stopped short. Through the picture window at the end of the room, I looked out into the garden from my dream. As I stepped out into the garden, an austerely elegant man in a black tunic followed me out. He introduced himself as Alex Sprinkle, the society's program director, who had invited me. He explained that he had also designed and now tended my dream garden.

If dreams are memories of the future, is much of waking life the experiencing in the physical body what we have already lived in the dreambody? What would we become if we participated more consciously in this process? There is an Iroquois story of a great hunter who always scouted ahead, in conscious dream journeys, to locate the game and rehearse the kill. In one of his dream scouts, he located an elk and sought its permission to take its life to feed his extended family. He killed the elk in his dream and noted the red mark on its chest where the arrow had gone in. The following day, he walked to the place he had visited in dreaming and identified *his* elk by the red mark on its chest. He then replayed an event that had already taken place, by killing the elk again with a physical arrow.[5]

5. Dreaming, we choose the events that will be manifested in our waking lives.

The fact that we dream things before they happen does not mean that everything is predetermined. People who are not active dreamers can get quite confused about what is going on when they wake up to the fact that we are dreaming future events, both large and small, all the time. I think it's like this. If you do not remember your dreams, you are condemned to live them. (If you don't know where you're going, you will likely end up where you are headed.) If you remember some of your dreams and screen them for messages about the future, you will find yourself able to make wiser choices. You will discover that by taking appropriate action you can often avoid the enactment of a "bad" dream or bring about the fulfillment of a happy one. As you become a *conscious* dreamer, you will find yourself increasingly able to choose *inside the dreaming* the events that will be manifested in your waking life.

It's not about predestination. It's about the spiritual secrets of manifestation—and your ability to become cocreator of your life.

Meister Eckhart tells us how it is with the razor-sharp clarity of the practical mystic who has seen and experienced for himself: "When the soul wishes to experience something, she throws an image of the experience out before her and enters her own image."

Indigenous peoples tell a recurring story of how the material world is spun from the dream of a deity. For the Guajiro of Ecuador, the physical universe is the product of conscious dreaming. The

Guajiro say that the Creator-god made this world after the divine Dreamgiver, Apusanai, made him aware that he was dreaming and he began to experiment with molding and solidifying the fluid forms he perceived endlessly aborning and transforming on another plane of reality.[6]

It is not merely that we dream things (maybe *everything*) before they happen; dreams *make* them happen.

6. The path of the soul after death is the path of the soul in dreams.

Your dreambody does not die when your physical body loses its vital signs. You will live on in your dreambody for a shorter or greater time, according to your ruling passions and personal evolution. You will find yourself, as you do each night in dreams, in a realm where thoughts are things, and imagination, the great faculty of soul, can create whole worlds.

You come from the Dreaming, and you are released into the Dreaming when you drop your sack of meat and bones.

Conscious dreaming is excellent preparation, not only for the challenges that lie before you on the roads of this life, but for the challenges of the journey you will make after physical death. How do you know for sure? By doing it.

Conditions for Liftoff

You are prepared for these adventures if you are ready to play, if you are able to relax in a protected space, if you are open to the unexpected, and if you are willing to ask for help.

In dreaming traditions, many techniques have been used to facilitate the shift in awareness required for conscious dream journeying. These range from breathwork, meditation, and the use of mantras and mandalas to dancing, fasting, and the ingestion of hallucinogenic drugs. No less important are safety procedures. There are possible hazards in dream travel, as in riding in cars, subways, or airplanes; frequent fliers learn to take the appropriate precautions and keep their vehicles in good working order. In my own practice and teaching,

I find that liftoff is achieved quite smoothly and safely through a combination of these simple techniques:

1. Choose a flight path.   You need to establish your general intention. This may be to seek healing or guidance on a specific issue for yourself or another. It may be to commune with a spiritual teacher, to seek creative inspiration, or to explore the nature of a large reality. Your intention may be to develop your ability to travel outside the physical body or simply to have fun and adventure in the dreaming.

Your point of departure is likely to be an image: an image from a remembered dream or a previous journey, a personal power site or place in nature, a "generic" image (such as a spiral stair or an elevator), a borrowed image or visualization (a mandala, a tarot trump, a pathworking), or a spontaneous image that comes in meditation, in an intuitive flash, or in the twilight zone between waking and sleep. If you are a frequent flier, you may be familiar with a large section of the route you will follow. You may have a specific destination: to go back to your Dream Library or to Merlin's Cave.

Alternatively, you may choose to target a person or place in ordinary reality. This may result in the experience of "remote viewing" or what psychic researchers used to call "traveling clairvoyance."

2. Airport security.   If you are experimenting on your own (or with a partner), you need a quiet place where you will not be interrupted by the phone ringing, the dog barking, or someone walking into the room. This may be your bedroom or another corner of your home, a place in nature, or a specially prepared site.

By lighting a candle, you affirm that you are opening a sacred space. Apart from the candle, you want as little external light around you as possible. It is easiest to see with inner light in conditions of total darkness. When I am journeying in daylight hours, I often wrap a bandanna over my eyes or cover them with my hand. You may wish to cleanse your space by burning sage or sprinkling saltwater, especially if you are using a new space or have never done this before. This helps to remove psychic litter.

Before you embark on a soul journey, you need to ensure that you are protected psychically as well as physically. This involves establishing a psychic boundary. A simple way to do this is to walk the perimeters of your space, and perhaps the whole property. Start facing the east and walk in a sunwise (i.e., clockwise) circle until you return to your starting point. As you walk, see yourself creating a wall of Light around your space. This wall of Light will be a welcoming beacon to those who come to you in love, but will repel and shield you against any unclean or hostile thoughts or presences. After you return to the east, move in an inward spiral until you reach the center of the circle. Now see the circle becoming a sphere of Light that extends beneath you and above you, shielding you on all sides.

When you invest the full force of your will and intention in this mental shielding, it is highly effective. You may see yourself tracing the circle with a sword of fire. You may choose to invoke guardian presences to watch over the four quarters and the above and below. If you are working with power animals—and you will be before long, if you take the shamanic path—you may call them to stand guard over your space. You may call on angelic figures to watch over you. Raphael is traditionally associated with the east, the direction of air; Michael with the south (fire); Gabriel with the west (water); and Uriel with the north (earth).

You should use only the names and the images in which you truly believe. These must come from the heart. It is quite sufficient to invoke the saving power of Love and Light.

Once you have set up your shields around a particular space, you will not have to renew them every time you journey. They should remain effective for a considerable time unless you invite in people and presences that create confusion in your field—in which case, you will need to cleanse your space thoroughly and raise the shields again. But it is *always* advisable to call on spiritual protectors to watch over you and your body when you are preparing to embark on dream travel.

3. Follow your breathing. The simplest relaxation technique—which can also do wonders for your blood pressure and other symptoms of stress—is to focus your attention on the flow of your breath.

Breathwork is central to the practice of dream yoga in Eastern traditions. *Pranayama,* the science of breathwork, teaches methods known as the rising breath, the prolonged breath, the great psychic breath, and cross-breathing, in which you shut off one nostril and then the other. Correct breathing, in all these variants, is from the diaphragm, not the chest.

To get started, all you need do is to sit comfortably, with your back straight, and shift your awareness to the flow of your breathing. Breathe in through your nose, out through your mouth. Notice the passage of the air as it moves through your nostrils, down into your lungs, and into your bloodstream. Feel yourself drawing the air down into the pit of your belly—perhaps all the way down to your feet. Don't be shy of letting your tummy bulge as it fills with air. Hold your breath for as long as is comfortable. Then slowly release it, pushing the air out from the depths of your body until you are completely empty. Hold the moment for as long as is comfortable, then let the air stream back naturally into your lungs and move down through your body.

You may find that prolonging the moment between the in-breath and the out-breath will help you to operate at the junction between different states of consciousness: for example, between sleep and waking.

You may wish to experiment with adjusting the flow of your breathing to different rhythms. To get in tune with the sea and enter its deeper mind, traditional Polynesian navigators adjust their breathing to the rhythms of the ocean swells, breathing in as the vessel rises, out as it dips, drawing the breath in all the way down to their feet. You have probably done something like this quite spontaneously, dozing at the beach. When you do it *intentionally,* you may discover yourself slipping into a gentle rocking motion that will carry you into a conscious dream voyage into oceans of possibility.

If you are lying down, you may find it helpful to combine conscious breathing with *progressive muscle relaxation.* Perhaps the simplest and most effective approach is to tense and relax each part of your body, from your feet to your scalp. Start by curling and uncurling your toes and work your way up your legs, through your abdomen, to your torso, clamping and releasing each group of muscles. Flex your shoulders and then let them go deliciously slack. Work your way down your arms until you are flexing and releasing your fingers. Now stretch and release your neck, tense and release your jaw. Screw up your face and then let it go soft. Raise your eyebrows and feel your hairline go tight before you gently release it. You are becoming comfortable and cushy in your body, fully relaxed, but not at all sleepy: focused on your intention.

4. Baggage check.   You don't want to be burdened by excess baggage, especially if it contains things that are liable to leak or blow up during flight. You should plan to travel light. Any guilt about the past, any anxiety about the future, can only hold you back. In dreaming, past, present, and future are all instantly accessible to you—and may be changed—but only if you are able to give yourself to the moment without fear and self-limitation. Your only time is *now*.

As you continue to follow the cycle of your breathing, scan your body and your whole state of being. Notice any areas where you feel blocked. Notice any negative thoughts and feelings that may be holding you back and preventing you from relaxing into the opportunity and adventure of the moment. As your breath flows into your body, feel it loosening and releasing any blockages, any areas of pain or weakness or stress. As you breathe out, make it your intention to release from yourself, and put out of your space altogether, any of those negative thoughts and emotions that are holding you back. *You* know what they are. If they involve issues you will need to come back to, you might see yourself putting them in a closet or a box or a well you can seal up, to be dealt with at the proper time. If you are ready to part company with these negative thoughts and feelings *now,* you might see yourself putting them into a fire and watching the negative energy released and purged by the flame and carried away by the smoke of the cleansing fire.

5. Flight safety.   You have taken steps to protect your space. You need to take further steps to guard your psyche during your dream travels. Calling in light to fill you and surround you with a radiant aura is a powerful safety procedure that works immediately to raise confidence and energy. It is also useful in many situations in waking life. In dream travel, according to your personal evolution, it can help you to move smoothly and naturally beyond the physical plane and the lower levels of the astral plane in your shining body, your

Body of Light. Here is a simple version of the technique that I offer in many of my workshops:

Calling in Light

Sit in a comfortable position, with your back straight and the soles of your feet on the ground. Repeat steps 3 and 4: Follow the flow of your breathing until you are quite relaxed. Release any negative thoughts and feelings you are carrying.

You are ready to shift your awareness to the crown of your head. You are beginning to open yourself to the inexhaustible source of Light energy you see streaming toward you from above and beyond you. You may think of this source as God or All That Is or your own Higher Self. By any name, this Light source is limitless. You may see it as a cone of Light, pointing down toward the crown of your head.

You are opening yourself to the Light. It streams down through the crown of your head, shining. It flows down to your forehead, shining. It rolls down to your throat center, shining. It streams to your heart center, shining . . . and to your solar plexus. It washes down through the lower centers of your body, down to the base of your spine. It rolls on down through your legs . . . and comes out through the soles of your feet . . . and streams up your back and up your neck and up the back of your head . . . to enter you again, at the crown . . .

The Light streams down through all the centers of your body, shining . . . and cycles up your back, and enters you again . . . so that, at this moment, you are within the Light and you are surrounded by the Light . . .

And with each breath, you are stronger and brighter . . .

As you breathe in, see and feel the Light streaming down through you from the crown of your head . . .

As you breathe out, see and feel the Light flowing up your back . . .

Now find the place in your being where you feel strongest and brightest. It might be your heart center, or your solar plexus. Let the Light pool in this place and grow stronger . . . until it is blazing within you like an inner sun.

*Let the Light from your inner sun stream through every fiber
and particle of your being . . . down to the soles of your feet . . .
and across your shoulders and down your arms to the tips of
your fingers. Let the Light flow to the surface of your skin . . .
and beyond the surface of your skin, to glow around you as a
radiant aura . . .*

*You are now inside an egg-shaped cocoon of Light. You are
in a space where you are loved and protected. You can let the
surface of this egg of Light become harder and more solid if
you feel the need for additional protection.*

Frequent fliers may run into situations where other security mea-
sures are required, especially if they are called to help lost souls in the
murkier regions of the astral planes. I will deal with such situations
at the proper time. For now, it is sufficient to offer a few general
guidelines about flight safety:

- *Like attracts like.* The principle is the same as in everyday life.
If you are off on a cosmic power trip, expect clashes with other ego-
maniacs—incarnate or discarnate—who want to count coup or steal
your energy. If you are out for sex and thrills, you may wish you had
insisted on a health inspection before getting involved with some of
your partners. If your intention is to learn and grow and bring gifts
of healing and insight for others, you will rarely be disappointed in
the company you find.

- *At places of passage, you will confront your own fears.* At all
the crossings between the worlds, from your first conscious journey
beyond the body to your discovery of worlds beyond human conceptions of form, there are tests to be passed. These often involve
encounters with the images of your own fears and limitations: surly
gatekeepers or monstrous Dwellers at the Threshold. Though they
often appear terrifying, they are part of your safety net. Their function is to ensure that you do not pass beyond certain limits until you
are fully prepared and it is safe for you to do so.

- *There are bad neighborhoods in the dreamworld,* just as in
ordinary reality. If you choose to hang out at the wrong kind of bar
or the wrong kind of séance or to ramble around in a rough inner-city
neighborhood in the middle of the night, you can expect problems.

The lower levels of the astral—what the occultists use to call the sub-lunary plane—is full of lost souls (of both the dead and the living), people driven by appetite and addiction, zonked out of their minds on drugs. You have no need to linger in these territories unless you are called, perhaps for a rescue mission (which we will get to later)—in which case you will be given special help to come and go safely.

• *It is always appropriate to ask for help, and help is always available.* You are going on a journey, but in all likelihood you are also responding to a call—a call from a deeper aspect of your Self, a call from a spiritual teacher (perhaps even a Master) who has been watching over you and waiting for you to reawaken to the deeper dimensions of reality in which your life and your soul's purpose have their source. Aslan says to the children in *The Silver Chair,* "You would not have called to me unless I had first called to you." You are reaching inward—or upward—to something that has been reaching to you, perhaps unnoticed by your everyday mind. Call for help to that unseen agency that supports your life, or to guides and allies with familiar names, and help *will* be given.

6. Sideline the skeptic.   You are almost ready to voyage. But there is one more character you are likely to encounter who needs to be mentioned now: your inner skeptic. He is hard to get away from because he lives in your head. Even if you have done a good job of releasing your blocks, you will probably find the naysayer who lives in your left brain surfacing from time to time—even in the midst of a thrilling dream journey—saying things like "I'm making this up." "This is just my imagination." "How do I know this is true?"

Be firm with your inner skeptic, but also be fair with him. He has his place. He's the one who will help you to test and verify the reality and value of your experiences—when you come back. The cardinal rule is not to allow your inner skeptic to come between you and your experiences. Put him where he belongs—on the sidelines—while you take flight on your journeys. Afterward, you should be ready to tackle all his questions. You might find it helpful to make a private appointment to dialogue with your skeptic and get these ground rules straight. If you don't explain to your skeptic why he's on the sidelines (for now), he's likely to run out into the field and throw an illegal tackle.

As you become an active dreamer, you will find that your relationship with your skeptic becomes increasingly rewarding. On the one hand, your skeptic will fall silent during your journeys as you travel between different levels of reality and develop the ability to adjust your perception to the conditions of each plane. On the other, when you come back from your journeys, your skeptic will make sure you invest the necessary time and energy to follow up leads and confirm details. This will help you to bring through more of what you have learned to work for you in everyday life. It will also help to resolve the persnickety but perennial problem of *proof*.

7. Fuel the journey with sound.   Monotonous heartbeat shamanic drumming (at four to seven beats per second) is a remarkably efficient tool for powering conscious dream travel, especially in a group setting, with live drummers. The human voice is no less powerful. Chanting, singing, and the repetition of mantras can all be highly effective in facilitating a shift in consciousness that will carry you into other orders of reality. You should be aware that if you are borrowing the chant or mantra from a particular cultural or religious tradition, this will tend to shape your experience—and sometimes to distort or confuse it if you are trying to move outside the parameters of that tradition. It is most inadvisable to "tune in" to chant when you do not know the meaning of the words or the nature of the entities the words are intended to invoke or evoke (i.e, bring into manifestation).

I encourage my students to find their own "power songs" and, while seeking these, to experiment with a line or two from a simple song or lullaby—preferably uplifting, with a driving beat—in words they understand. "This Little Light of Mine" has become quite a favorite. So has a Mohawk cradle song inviting the Bear to come and dance. As a game to play at home, pick a snatch of music that feels right and try to substitute this for whatever is running on your inner sound track. Hum it aloud, then let it hum in your mind. You will probably find, after a time, that it drowns out the clutter—all the chatter and noise in the brain—and gives you fuel for liftoff.

The *sound,* as well as the rhythm, of your breathing also helps, especially when you deliberately increase the volume, letting your breath drag out from the back of your palate through your half-opened mouth. Barbara Brennan calls this "rasp breathing." I think of it as *shamanic snoring*. It sets up a resonance and a driving beat that can easily substitute for the effects of shamanic drumming, and you can do it alone. (Perhaps you had *better* do it alone, unless you have an understanding partner!)

8. Open a visual gateway.   "The doors to the invisible must be visible," as René Daumal says in *Mount Analogue*. The gateway to a conscious dream journey may be a scene from a remembered dream or previous journey: a dreamscape to which you may return. Especially for warm-up purposes, you might choose to focus on a physical image, such as a mandala or a painting, and try to travel through it. You might target a person or place in either physical or imaginal reality and try to pay them a visit. With practice and motivation, you can arrange "dream dates" with partners or whole groups. You might work with a guided visualization (such as the House of Time in chapter 6). In the next chapters, we will explore all these departure gates and the flight paths that lie beyond them. You will be offered a series of exercises and flight instructions that will help you to get airborne and test the wind currents for yourself.

9. Call for a pilot.   We are not alone! This is another of the open secrets of the Dreamtime. Call on your *authentic* spiritual guides and teachers. They are listening. The distance between you is no distance in space, but a difference of frequency.

CHAPTER 2

≋

The Gateway
of Images

The doors to the invisible must be visible.

René Daumal, Mount Analogue

Welcome to the Twilight Zone

Your departure lounge for dream travel is open to you anytime you
are ready for adventure. You can go there with any itinerary that
appeals to you. Do you want to go on a dream vacation or engage in
a steamy romance with an astral lover? Would you like to communicate with a spiritual guide or experiment with your ability to make
intentional journeys beyond the body? Or scout ahead through time
to prepare for the job interview next week? Or get your own close-up
view of the surface of Mars? This is the right place to begin. You will
want to be open to changing your plans, however, because you will
soon discover that the possibilities are limitless. You will also find
that you can draw on the advice of travel consultants who are knowl-
edgeable about territories you never even knew existed.

Your departure lounge is the twilight zone, the half-dream state on
the cusp between waking and sleep, and between sleep and waking.
Frazzled by the pressures of everyday life, many of us tear through
this zone without pausing to notice what is there. We knock ourselves out with sleeping pills, booze, and fatigue. When we still can't
get to sleep right away, instead of recognizing that something might
be goading us to open to something beyond the obvious, we line up
to buy yet another pill from the hustling industry that deals in "sleep
disorders" but not in dreams. We are jolted awake by clock radios,

traffic, caffeine. We lose not only the memory of our nocturnal dream journeys, but the recollection of how we returned from them. We are in the condition of a person who makes a return flight to another city or another country every night of the week but insists that he never left home and has never heard of an airport. You might think that this is a false analogy, since planes and airports are "real," while dream flights and half-dream states are something else. If you are leaning this way, I would ask you simply to be open to the possibility that your definition of reality may be about to shift.

Active dreamers tend to spend a lot of time in the twilight zone, even whole nights. In everyday life, the easiest way to embark on conscious dream journeys is to practice maintaining full awareness as dream images rise and fall during twilight states. The twilight zone offers optimum conditions to develop your ability to make intentional journeys beyond the physical body and to learn the nature and conditions of other orders of reality. As you spend more time in the twilight zone, you will discover a notable increase in both your creativity and your psychic awareness. Going with the flow of spontaneous imagery in the twilight zone puts you into the stream of the creative process. It puts you in league with your creative source, mediated by mentors who appear to you in the half-dream state, or coming through cool and clear as a mountain spring. It is no accident that highly creative people—from Einstein to the romance writer and the powerboat designer I met on recent plane trips—are very much at home in the twilight zone.[1]

In the language of the sleep scientists, the twilight zone is the realm of hypnagogic and hypnopompic experiences. *Hypnagogic* literally means "leading toward sleep"; *hypnopompic* means "leading away from sleep." But these terms do not take us to the heart of the matter. You may enter the twilight zone before and after sleep, but you may also enter it wide awake, with no intention of sleeping. It is not the relationship to sleep that defines the twilight zone; it is its character as border country. It is the junction between sleep and waking, certainly. But more than this, as Mary Watkins writes beautifully, it is "the plane of coexistence of the two worlds."[2] In this borderland, you will find the gates to other worlds opening smoothly and fluidly—if you let them and are prepared for what may follow. When I allow myself to drift through this frontier region with no fixed agenda, I have the sense of leaning through a window or a doorway in space. Sometimes this feels like hanging out of the open hatch of an airplane. I have come to recognize this as the opening of a dreamgate. Depending on circumstances and intention, I can step forward into the next dimension or haul myself back into physical focus.

From this departure lobby, the great explorers of the imaginal realm have used many gates and flight paths. This is why the twilight state has such vital significance in dream yoga, in shamanic training, in the Western Mystery traditions, in the "science of mirrors" of the medieval Persian philosophers, and in other schools of active spirituality.

According to Tantric teachings, it is by learning to prolong this "intermediate state" and to operate with full awareness within it that you achieve dream mastery and, beyond this, the highest level of consciousness attainable for an embodied human. The *Spandakarika* of Vasagupta, which dates from the tenth century, recommends the use of breathing exercises to focus and maintain awareness as you move from waking into the twilight state. The dreamer is urged to place himself "at the junction between inhaled and exhaled breaths, at the very point where he enters into contact with energy in the pure state." This is the entry into conscious dreaming, whose gifts (according to the Tantric text) could be immense: "The Lord of necessity grants him during dreams the ends he pursues, providing that he is profoundly contemplative and places himself at the junction between waking and sleeping."[3]

The aim of the practice is to achieve continuity of consciousness through sleeping, waking, and the intermediate state. When this is attained, the practitioner has ascended to the mystical Fourth State— the *turiya* of the Upanishads. This is the highly evolved consciousness of a person who has awakened to the reality of the Self; it now infuses his awareness at all times.

In the Greco-Roman world, the twilight zone was a place of rendezvous with divine messengers and even the gods themselves. Iamblichus, the author of an important book on the Mysteries, urged the need to pay special attention to "god-sent dreams" in the intermediate state, especially after waking:

"They come when sleep is leaving us, or we are just waking. We may hear a certain voice that tells us concisely what needs to be done. Sometimes we feel surrounded by a presence that cannot be perceived by the sight, but is sensed in other ways. The entrance of the spirit is accompanied by a noise. . . . But sometimes a bright and tranquil light shines forth."[4]

From the ascent to the Fourth State to a walk-in by a spirit or *daimon,* there is clearly no ceiling on possibility in this area. But first and last, experiment in the twilight zone is wonderful *fun.* Think of this as your cosmic playground. If you are ready to play, here's how you might start:

EXERCISE: INTO THE ZONE

Beginner's mind, please. You are simply going to have fun and open yourself to an inexhaustible source of creativity that is available to you any day of your life. If there is any area in your life where you feel blocked, this exercise may help you to get round those blocks by getting into flow.

1.   Lie down or sit comfortably in a quiet, protected space. Follow the flow of your breathing until you are quite relaxed.

2.   Cover your eyes, shutting out all external light.

3.   Notice how long (if at all) your inner screen remains dark.

4.   Allow shapes, patterns, colors, to rise and fall spontaneously. Maybe you'll get the sense of forms shaping in the grainy dark, curving like the wall of a cave, or the eye sockets. Of a tunnel or trapdoor emerging within the dark. Of phosphene patterns flashing off and on.[5] Luminous dust, points of light, spiral whorls, waves, and streamers of color. Of more complex and stable patterns like tree bark or webbing or woven cloth or embroidery. Or waves of color, dancing spots. Perhaps a rush of cartoon images, childlike drawings, photos.

5.   Notice changes in your perception of light. What do you suppose is the source of the light that brings images into resolution and bathes the scenes that emerge?

6.   Notice changes in your perception of depth and texture. After a time (if not immediately) you will probably be looking into scenes that appear to have autonomous life and dimensionality. You can step

into one of these scenes and explore it from within or interact with its characters. You may allow your consciousness to merge with one of the players or stand apart.

7.   You will come to a point where you either pull back into physical focus or go further in, along the path of a developing dream. As you go deeper into the dream—or into dreams within dreams— you may lose the awareness that you are dreaming. But there is a good possibility that, starting from this entry point, you will be able to embark on a conscious dream journey and bring back a full travel report.

Games to Play in the Twilight Zone

1. Scanning your psychic field

Checking what is in your psychic space is important for basic health and well-being. As you practice using your inner senses in the twilight state, you will find you are able to identify the thoughts, emotions, and visitors you are attracting. It is important to establish that any astral guests are there by invitation.

When you are in transitional environments—a motel, a friend's home, a hospital ward—chances are you will pick up a lot of "stuff" that is not related to you but could affect you, for better or worse, unless you are able to draw boundaries and discriminate thoughts and emotions that belong to you from those that do not.

On the first night of my stay at a well-known holistic center on the East Coast, I spent several hours in bed watching the tumble of alien images on my inner screen. I realized that I was viewing leftover clutter from people who had come here to release their burdens—and had left their psychic litter all over the environment. There was dark-side Tibetan stuff, involving the use of human bones. There were painful scenes of men's writhing bodies, naked and bloody, sticky with fluids; I watched some of them dragged screaming into the belly of the beast. After a time, I performed a simple operation to clear the space and shield myself with Light energy. The next day, I was able to put what I had viewed in context when I learned that the center had recently played host to a retreat for gay men with AIDS and to a group of Tibetan Buddhists.

When you start scanning at home, you may notice the presence in your psychic space of many more people than are lodging under your roof. They may include departed relatives, dream visitors (welcome or unwelcome), psychic intruders, or spiritual guides of varying degrees of reliability. Your visitors may be offering help or seeking help from you. When I got into bed one night, I sensed a presence in the room and tuned in to my inner screen. I realized that my visitor was an elderly woman who was close to my family. She was wandering about in her dreambody, frightened and confused. Now in her eighties, she was anxious to know what awaited her after physical death. I tried to reassure her that what she was doing now was an excellent rehearsal. All she needed to do was decide where she wanted to go. I invited her to come flying with me, but she got scared. I asked what she would like to see and explore. She mentioned her childhood home. I was focused on how to get her there when her father—who had passed over many years before—came through, showing himself with pipe and stick, as she remembered him, though he made it clear to me this is not how he normally goes about these days. The old lady sat in his lap, like a little girl, leafing through pictures in an album. The photos that interested her became like TV screens, with living pictures inside—pictures she could enter.

Later I focused on sending her some healing energy and saw a brilliant stream of green light passing through me and beaming to her. When I saw her again, she was in fine form. She told me she wanted to show me an old photograph album.

2. Scouting

In our dreams, we are forever scouting round the corner, rehearsing for challenges that lie ahead in waking life. As you become a more frequent player in the twilight zone, you will find you can play this game in a relaxed state while fully conscious. For example:

Rita's Owl

I am at a hotel in the Washington, D.C., area. In the twilight zone, I decide to check in on Rita, who is hosting a dream workshop for me the next day. I zoom toward her house, noticing various objects in the living room.

An owl flies up so suddenly it startles me.

Then Rita emerges. I look for the owl and find it's turned into something like a small helium balloon. We both find this funny. I suggest to Rita that if she wanted, she could keep her owl-form more focused and durable.

We agree to check out the facilities at the college where my workshop will be held the next day. Microphones are set up on a large movable podium. I point out to Rita that we don't need these and should have the podium removed to clear the space for people to move around freely.

When I met Rita the next day, I shared my impressions. She told me the owl was important to her as a dream companion and chuckled that her family accused her of "going up like a helium balloon." Neither of us had viewed the room where my workshop would take place. Inside, we found the blocky podium from my scout and had it removed.

If you are interested in playing this game, the easiest way to begin is to put yourself into a relaxed state and try to track forward, step by step, along a route you may follow in waking life in the next couple of days. Note any oddities or striking impressions, and check yourself for accuracy when you travel that path in physical reality.

3. Dialogue with the spirits

Like attracts like. My work is greatly assisted by communication with spiritual beings who are interested in helping me to assist other people and to expand my understanding of multidimensional reality. My mode of interaction with these beings is entirely different from that of the passive trance channeler. We have active dialogues, and I am always wary of newcomers (unless they come properly introduced) until I have been able to check their bona fides and verify their information.

I don't *believe* in spirits; I talk with them and interact with them, through communication in the twilight zone as well as through shamanic journeys to the spiritual realms. I also notice that even when they are entirely well-meaning, spirits are often quite unreliable or simply at a limited level of understanding and evolution. For example, when I started working on the section of this book on journeying beyond the body, a lively gypsy woman showed up in the twilight zone, eager to demonstrate her favorite technique for astral projection. This involves sitting in front of a cheval glass—which she charmingly called her "riding glass"—seeing your second self in the mirror, and then transferring consciousness to your projected image. This was all very well, as far as it went. But I would put the gypsy in a very different category from master teachers who have instructed me at "invisible schools" on a higher plane, and from the deep, clear flow from a source that I know is in no way alien to me, but speaks from my larger Self.

To return to our games: You may find that thrilling discoveries flow from inner dialogue with the beings who are easily accessible in twilight states. If you invite them in, be careful what you summon. "I ask for guidance from my true spiritual teachers . . . from my Higher Self . . . from my creative source." These are all formulations that are unlikely to lead you astray.

4. Moving into conscious dreaming

When you are completely at home in the departure lounge, you will find you are able to embark on dream flights without losing consciousness.

Quite often, in the half-dream state I find myself looking at the patterns and textures of what looks like woven cloth or webbing. Sometimes I find myself suspended in the mesh. The following experience was quite tactile:

Through the Net

I floated weightless, looking into a dark, grainy field, textured like hessian, a very palpable depth. I felt I was hanging in this, as in a hammock or net. I was uneasy, to begin with, hanging between the worlds. I did not feel stuck in the net. I realized I could push through the net and travel in any direction. I eventually resolved simply to open myself to my creative source.

The "hessian sacking" opened into a textile bazaar. I examined bolt after bolt of richly textured patterns and designs.

I heard my partner stirring and turning in the bed and realized I was operating with multiple consciousness, fully engaged in dream travel while safely tethered to my body in the bed.

I spent the whole night slipping back and forth between dream locales, meditation, and long study sessions in which I devoured books and memorized material.

One of the dream episodes involved the Egyptian Mysteries, especially the mysterious god Ptah, whose power is associated with the breath and who is said to be the Giver of the Ka.

Another dream episode carried me into the realm of the Kabbalists. I tried out a thronelike chair with a hard wooden strut that stuck out low down at the back of the seat. This guaranteed that you would not get too comfortable or doze off. It was intended to assist Kabbalistic meditation.

These adventures sent me off into a spate of happy research. The palpable resistance of the web or net in which I had hung, and the fact that, once through it, I had access to Mystery teachings in corresponding locales, sparked many thoughts and speculations. The name of the temple of Thoth at Khemennu in ancient Egypt was the House of the Net. This net confined unevolved humans to their lower natures. But to initiates, it became a kind of cosmic trampoline, a springboard to higher realms.[6]

The net I encountered may evoke the web of the human energy field, woven from Faraday's "lines of force." But to me, it suggests something more: the sense of being inside the cell walls of the larger universe, of testing the energy membranes that separate levels or dimensions.

5. Into the matrix

As you become more practiced in maintaining full consciousness at the junction between sleeping and waking, you may find yourself moving beyond the flow of images to a perception of the source of those images—the dream matrix—and the stuff of which they are formed. Here is another excerpt from my journals, describing an experience of entering the dream matrix:

Into the Astral Sea

I am floating in a twilight state, shortly before dawn.

I watch a parade of faces.

I "step forward." I have the impression of immensely tall doors. In the crack between them, I see deep blue-green light. I move through the doorway.

I find myself in the astral sea. It has substance, but this substance is lighter than foam rubber and endlessly malleable. I see temples and palaces rise and dissolve back into the matrix.

I seek clearer understanding. I am told by a higher intelligence that I am in the "high subplanes of the astral." The inhabitants of these realms can create their environments by thought and are aware of this ability. But they still work with the inheritance of earthly lives and memories of form.

I slip into a more vivid scene of construction. I am amazed by the detail of this work. Is it due to the limited understanding of the astral builders—or will it give greater substance and beauty to the finished structure—or is it simply part of their pleasure?

Visual Doorways

The most powerful and effective images you will ever find—for healing, for journeying, for creative inspiration—will be the gift of your personal experience, especially in dreams and half-dream states. But you may find it interesting and helpful to experiment with physical images and guided visualizations.

What follows is a practical meditation that will help you to improve your concentration, to enhance your visual memory, and to shift consciousness beyond the physical plane. In the Western Mystery schools, the tarot trumps are used in developing this technique. This not only leads to a deeper understanding of the symbolism of the cards and their divinatory meanings, but opens gateways to inner teachers and explorations along the paths of the Tree of Life.[7]

To begin your experiments with this technique, all you need is a picture with a border or frame. I suggest that for this particular exercise, you select a representational image rather than an abstract painting or mandala. The picture must arouse your interest or curiosity. If you like travel, you might focus on a photo or postcard of a foreign landscape. You might choose a canvas by a favorite painter; I have had great fun stepping into the surreal worlds of Magritte and De Chirico, and into the gaslit Paris of Toulouse-Lautrec. If you are interested in mythology or ancient civilizations, you may wish to pick a card from Caitlin Matthews's *Celtic Book of the Dead,* which beautifully evokes the landscapes and presiding spirits of the Celtic Otherworld, or the *Book of Doors,* which performs the same service for the Egyptians.[8]

EXERCISE: STEPPING INTO A PICTURE

1.   Spend a few minutes carefully studying the picture you have chosen.

2.   Close your eyes and reproduce the picture on your inner screen.

3.   Open your eyes and examine the picture again. Check how accurately and completely you were able to call it up from your visual memory.

4.   Try again and repeat the process until you are confident you can reproduce the whole image in your mind.

5.   Sit comfortably, with your eyes closed, and follow the flow of your breathing until you are fully relaxed.

6.   Call back the picture. Be sure you see it as a scene *within a border or frame*. Blank out any extraneous details. You may see it hanging or floating against a black background.

7.   When the image is vivid in your mind, pull it gently toward you. The scene is becoming larger. The backdrop falls away. Your inner screen is now entirely filled by the picture, *within its border*.

8.   The border now resembles the edge of a doorway. Step over the doorstep and enter the landscape beyond it.

9.   You are now free to explore and adventure in any direction that takes your fancy. You may want to talk to people you encounter along the way. You will probably find that the country or city you are in is vastly bigger than you could have guessed before you stepped through the door. The landscape and its inhabitants will now appear to you as entirely real. Take your time to travel or linger, whichever way you are drawn.

10.   When you are ready to come back, turn around and look for the doorway through which you entered.

11.   Approach the doorway and look through it, into the room where you are sitting. You will see the room from a different angle than before. You may find yourself looking at the space *behind* your chair. You may see yourself, still seated in meditation. If this happens, it is no cause for alarm—simply confirmation that you have succeeded in shifting awareness beyond the physical plane.

12.   Come back gently through the doorway, back to your body and full awareness of your physical environment. Open your eyes.

13.   Write a brief narrative or draw a sketch-map of your journey.

14.   Do something to ground yourself: jump or stretch, eat a snack, go for a walk.

CHAPTER 3

Through the
Dreamgates

For those who have the symbol, the passage is easy.

Alchemical saying

Traveling Through Dream Images

The gateways to other worlds are already open to you, in the land-scapes and images of your remembered dreams.

Dream reentry is one of the core techniques of Active Dreaming. The basic approach is quite simple. You focus on a scene or image from a remembered dream and travel back into that image with your question or intention. You may use drumming to power the journey. You may take a partner with you to watch over you and scout for additional information—which frequently produces rich experiences of telepathy and shared dreaming.

Dream reentry has four main applications, as follows. The first three are explored in depth in *Conscious Dreaming,* so I will deal with them only briefly here.

1. Getting the message straight

Our dream memories are *not* the dream experience itself. At best, we wake with postcards from a journey. By going back inside the dream, we can fill in some of the gaps and bring back something of the fuller dream experience. In this way, the deeper meaning of dreams emerges and we learn how to manifest their energy and insight in waking life.

For example, if you dream of a plane crash, you need to establish whether you should take this literally or metaphorically. Maybe you are in danger of taking a nosedive at work or in a relationship. But maybe you—or someone relevant to you—could be involved in a literal plane crash. If this seems possible, you don't want to develop a phobia about air travel. You need to see whether you can go back inside the dream and clarify specific details. Which airline? What destination?

The counsel of Artemidorus, the celebrated Greek dream interpreter, is still valid: "You must spare no pains in ascertaining exactly every detail of the dream since sometimes the addition or omission of a tiny detail will change the entire meaning of the dream."[1]

The best way to do this is to get back *inside* the dream and look around. Notice, in particular, where you are. Location, location, location is a motto for dreamworkers as well as real estate brokers. If you find yourself in an unfamiliar but realistic locale, you may be dreaming of a place you will visit in the future in ordinary reality. Joanna dreamed of walking a ceremonial path between stone figures. When she went back in, she counted twelve human and twenty-four animal statues. Two years after the dream, she joined a group tour to China and counted the same number of statues as she walked the Sacred Way to the Ming dynasty tombs.

Alternatively, your dream landscape may prove to be in another order of reality—perhaps a locale in the imaginal realm you can visit again and again for fun or instruction.

The dream message you need to get straight may be vital to your health and well-being. Gina dreamed she was walking along a dusty country road when she noticed with disgust that maggots were crawling over her arm. Some of them were coming out of her flesh. She rushed into a house and asked a man for help. He brought her a drink to help her sleep. She woke up nauseated and frightened.

When she went back inside the dream, she recognized the country house as a place she had been thinking of buying. The man who "put her to sleep" was her current partner. She realized that the strains in this relationship were having an adverse effect on her health, but was unable to take any decisive action before she was diagnosed with lymphoma several months later—in the arm in which the maggots were breeding in her dream.

2. Dreaming the dream onward

You may have been ripped from a dream by a lover's caress, a child's happy squalling, or the shrill of an alarm clock. Or you may have fled from a dream that posed terrors you were unwilling to face. You may want to go back into the dreamscape to pursue the adventure or to face your dream adversaries on their own ground. When nightmare antagonists are confronted in this way, they often prove to be allies in disguise, who resorted to shock tactics to get your attention.

Suzie was terrified for ten years by an enormous serpent that reared up next to her face in dreams and half-dream states. When she found the courage to confront the snake, it became an ally that escorted her on a path of shamanic initiation and training that included an underworld journey to her ancestors.

3. Dialogue with dream characters

You may want to go back inside the dreamscape to ask a dream character to explain himself. You may find yourself dealing with an angel in disguise, or with an unrecognized aspect of yourself. You may discover that a troubling dream visitor is an entity you created through your own thoughts and emotions, who is now goading you to reclaim your energy.

I asked Libby to go back into her dreams to confront a terrifying demon who had been bothering her. Though she was still scared, Libby agreed to do this when I promised I would play bodyguard. When she asked her demon to identify himself, he told her, "I am your own fearsome rage." Dream reentry enabled her to acknowledge her legitimate anger over the abuse she had suffered both as a child and as an adult, and to harness its energy for creative living—instead of leaving it "out there" as an uncontrolled demonic force, dangerous to herself and to others.

4. Opening personal doorways to other dimensions

The gateways you discover in night dreams and twilight states are the best, safest, and most timely starting points for conscious dream journeys, including shamanic soul-flight. With practice, you will find you can have wonderful adventures riding that dream elevator, exploring that dream house (or dream city) or stepping through the hole in the wall or the magic closet, like the children in *The Lion, the Witch and the Wardrobe*. A Montana woman dreams of riding down to a basement in "an elevator that looks like a diving pod." A Louisiana mother encounters a dream guide who leads her upward, toward a "black hole." She is scared of going through it, but she trusts her guide. When she makes the crossing, she finds it is "incredibly beautiful" on the other side:

> *Everything is flying, including me! Clear blue skies, fresh air, pure green on the ground below. We are so high up. The sense of freedom is enormous; it is exhilarating. Then we have to return through the black hole.*
>
> *Since I have learned dream reentry, I have returned to this hole several times by myself just to enjoy the freedom of flight and the beauty of an untouched world. Instead of fearing the black hole, I know it as a gateway to another world.*

Maybe your dream gateway opens into a space in your present home you never knew existed, as in Wanda's dream:

My Dream Library

I am in my present home, but I go through a doorway into a library that does not exist in my house as I know it. The walls are newly painted white, and the marquetry floor has been refinished. There is no furniture yet. But when I open the tall cupboards, I find they are filled with books I did not realize I owned. I am thrilled to discover that this wonderful space is waiting for me. I will come here again and again.

Maybe your gateway is into an imaginal locale. Marcia dreamed she found herself in an "encyclopedia factory." Different rooms were assigned to different topics. Different floors were assigned to different years. What a splendid invitation to research and exploration! Through dream reentry, she was able to return again and again to her encyclopedia factory to gather information on subjects that interested her.

Your dreamgate might be a portal to a different dimension, as in dreams where you discover you can breathe in a different element:

I step outside a spacecraft and find I can breathe and travel about safely among the stars.

Your dreamgate might speed you into a separate reality, as in a San Francisco woman's dream:

Fire on the Lake

I dreamed of a fire in the middle of a lake. The fire itself was not at all threatening. It was about six feet tall, in the center of a dark space, floating on a black and glassy lake. A young moon was reflected in the dark lake, dancing in the moving water. It was utterly beautiful to me. The fire spoke directly to me about dreams and dreaming: "We are the dreams, the dreams are you."

This seemed like the boldest invitation to the life of the spirit I'd ever received. I felt like I was being invited to come back to myself.

Your dreamgate might take you into other life experiences that are relevant to you—from the past, from the future, or from parallel worlds.

I have made many conscious dream journeys—and led others on shared adventures—through the image of a spiral staircase that first came to me in a dream. This image is especially powerful because it is kinesthetic as well as visual. You may find that it will help you to travel beyond the physical body.

EXERCISE: CLIMBING THE SPIRAL STAIR

Quiet your mind in a protected space. Follow the flow of your breathing. When you are fully relaxed, let yourself flow with the following sequence of images:

You are walking toward a staircase with wide flagstone steps. The staircase winds upward, describing a gentle spiral, through an immense stone building.

There is light above you.

The passage narrows. You are moving in tight circles around a central column, whirling faster and faster as you ascend toward the light.

You see it first as a point of light above the top of your head. You have to roll your eyes back into your head to look at it.

As you move higher, circling and spinning, the light grows. It becomes a skylight, a perfectly round skylight.

When you shoot through it, you are out among the stars in the deep blue night.

You will set your own course for the rest of the journey. If you like, you may set your course for another planet or star system.

The Journey to the Sea Cave

The following sequence, from my personal journals, involves many facets of the adventure of Active Dreaming. They include dreaming the future, dream contact with spiritual beings, dream reentry, shared dreaming—and the way that the full meaning of dreams is sometimes impossible to grasp until waking events catch up to them. Around 9 P.M., relaxing at home in early summer, I felt an urgent "tug" of a kind that had long been familiar to me—a call to leave ordinary reality and embark on a dream adventure that was waiting to unfold. I promptly went up to my bedroom. As soon as I lay down, I slid into a series of dreams within dreams. The transition markers included getting in and out of bed (inside the dreams), walking on and off a movie set, and watching scenes switch from color to black and white and back again. For the sake of simplicity, my report of the original dream is confined to the central drama, the innermost and most exciting of the scenes I recall.

DREAM: APPOINTMENT AT THE SEA CAVE
(JULY 9, 1995)

I am going on an expedition in the middle of the night to a sea cave, set among massive cliffs along the coast. I have been attending a dream conference; I tell some of the people who are with me that my journey to the sea cave will bring about a reunion for which I have waited for "fifty thousand years."

A woman is concerned that I may be in danger. She tells me she dreamed that ferocious Native American guardians stand watch over the sea cave: they take the form of spirit bears. With my inner eye, I picture them at the scene, the waves rolling and crashing behind.

I tell her it would be natural for Native Americans to set wards over such a powerful place.

I'm less troubled by the spirit bears than by other guardians who may be stationed in the inner passages leading to the sea cave. I make an analogy with the "curse of the pharaohs." Concealed beneath the rocks is the sanctuary of an immensely powerful being who is other than human. He is one of those the ancients called daimons. He may have made his way here from a distant star system, although some regard him as Atlantean. He has been able to make some humans his servitors. He will have formidable gatekeepers.

Nonetheless, I am fairly sanguine about the looming encounter with the daimon or Atlantean or star master. I half-expect to find he is myself.

DREAM REENTRY: JOURNEY TO THE SEA CAVE
(JULY 9, 1995)

I woke in the early hours in high excitement from this dream. I was eager to go back into it and dream the next installment: to get a close look at the mysterious character in the sea cave.

In a relaxed state, I focused on the image of the spirit bears I had picked up while talking to the woman in my dream. Instantly, I found myself traveling along a rocky coast. The bears were huge—as tall as the cliffs themselves. But they paid no attention to me.

The cliffs were an amazing sight, striated in reds, yellows, and blacks. I found an opening near the top. I found myself looking into a compacted mass of swirling energies. It was rather like looking into a whirlpool. I decided to go in. I was menaced by rather nasty hooks and tentacles. I focused on the light from my own heart. This became a beam of light I could follow, sweeping aside all obstacles.

I came to a doorway where a human form was imprinted in a pinkish surface. I somehow "knew" that I should press my body into this mold, moving my arms to make the sign defined by the imprint. The door yielded, stretching like a membrane until I was through.

I sped along a passage and came out at an extraordinary observatory. There, in the depths of the cave, all conventional ideas about perspective and dimension were suspended. I could survey tremendous vistas, not only seascapes but cities, mountains, and forests.

After a time, the scene reshaped itself into the "sea cave" I had expected; I saw the waves lapping at its mouth. It remained clear to me that this was less a place than a portal through which many scenes could not only be observed, but entered.

I sensed a great presence there. I scanned to locate and identify it and felt a distinct "locking" of minds. I was now in direct communication with another intelligence. It indicated that it could assume any form. We agreed that it would manifest in a shape I could recognize. To my mild surprise, I found myself looking at a lean, immensely tall black man who reminded me of a Masai warrior. He gave me to understand that his life span is immensely longer than that of humans, though he is *not* immortal in the physical sense. He gave me further information that suggested that he did not originate on Earth, though he has long operated from a physical location that is sacred to one of the Native American tribes, who venerate him as a sacred being.

DREAM TRACKING: LOOKING FOR THE DAIMON
(JULY 12, 1995)

A few days later, I led an Active Dreaming workshop in the Washington, D.C., area at the invitation of Rita Dwyer, a wonderfully enthusiastic and spirited dreamer who is the executive officer and past president of the Association for the Study of Dreams. During the partner exercises, I enlisted the help of a man called Bill to go further into my dream of the sea cave. I gave him a brief description of the cave, mentioning the "spirit bears" but not their gigantic size. I asked him to bring me any information he could glean on the nature of the entity I had encountered in the cave.

After the drumming, Bill immediately established that we were on the same page by exclaiming, "Wow! Those bears are *big!* They have to be at least a hundred feet tall."

He had the strong sense that what was in the cave had to do with "ancient religions." He told me, "I felt I was going to discover a gold statue. Instead, I found something like a bronze ceiling, with the shape of a human figure. I looked down on an immense table. It was the size of several city blocks. There were thousands of people there."

All of this provided a tantalizing match with details of my dream that I had not shared with Bill: the imprint of a man, the sense of surveying whole cityscapes, the use of the word *daimon* (associated with "ancient religions") in my original dream.

But I was interested in more than further evidence that we can dream together; I wanted to know why I had been called to the sea cave and its unusual tenant. I did not get anywhere near the bottom of that mystery (I am still not at the bottom!) until waking events caught up with my dream.

DREAM FULFILLMENT: AT MOSHUP'S BEACH
(JULY 31, 1995)

My family had arranged to spend a couple of weeks that summer at Martha's Vineyard. This was my first visit to that beautiful island off Cape Cod. We drove down to Gay Head from our rented house one afternoon and I walked the beach, through a scattering of nude bathers, toward the cliffs, which a friendly neighbor had described as a "must-see."

When I rounded a headland and came into plain view of the cliffs, I froze. I had just walked into my dreamscape. Ablaze with color in the sunlight, there were the cliffs themselves, striped in reds and yellows and blacks—and in pink and orange and ivory. From this angle, in this light, the shapes of two gigantic bears were sharply defined in the folds of the clays.

Black cormorants stood sentinel on rocky outcrops on either side of my dream cliffs. At my feet was a red rock, the length of a man, shaped exactly like a sperm whale with its jaws open.

I walked over ridges of clay that slipped and squelched and remolded underfoot, and I remembered the moment in my dream when I had pressed my body into the imprint of a man on a door that yielded like this rubbery, springy clay.

After my walk, I grabbed for books on Gay Head and the Wampanoag Indians, whose land this is. I learned that the Wampanoag practiced "clay bathing," pushing their whole bodies into the colored clays of these cliffs both for cleansing and as part of their initiation rituals. I learned that these cliffs and that coast are the precinct of Moshup, a godlike being who is said to have come from the sea. As with other sea gods—Manannan or Poseidon or Oannes—it is not always clear, in the telling, whether Moshup's ocean is also the astral sea.[2]

At one of the bookshops I visited in search of the history and mythology of Moshup's beach—Bickerton & Ripley, in Edgartown—I found a copy of Justin Cartwright's beautiful novel *Masai Dreaming*. Naturally I bought it, to honor the form in which the figure in my sea cave had revealed himself. But I felt I needed to do more to honor these dreams.

DREAM ENACTMENT: WRITING FROM THE DREAM (FEBRUARY 1996)

My writing gave me a way to do this. In the climactic sequence in my novel *The Interpreter,* a young man is led by a numinous dream to an encounter with a spiritual being in a sea cave below the cliffs at Gay Head. (Having been a novelist for many years, I still have a tendency to camouflage "true life" experiences as fiction before I report them en clair.) These adventures opened a window on a spiritual landscape and enlarged my sense of what the ancients meant when they used the term genius loci, spirit of place. You may find that you are receiving invitations of a similar kind, if you are willing to work with your dreams and to honor them. Be open to the interplay between inner and outer experience, and especially to the possibility that before you make a trip in ordinary reality, you may be scouting ahead in your dreambody.

If you record your dreams and follow the correspondences between dreams and later events, you will probably find that you are *constantly* dreaming of places you will visit in the future. Since I walked into my dreamscape at Gay Head, I have been more keenly aware that our dream selves not only visit physical locations ahead of time, they scout out the spiritual landscape as well. The night before I traveled to Boulder for the first time, I had a dream in which I explored an unfamiliar locale that included swinging bridges and a railroad line that stopped in the middle of nowhere. In the same dream, I had a jolly encounter with a husky, hard-drinking entrepreneur I described in my journal as the Taipan. He came from Asia—though I did not think of him as specifically Asian—and we got on famously. He told me we were "spiritual brothers" and urged me to stay at his place. Walking around Boulder prior to a recording session at Sounds True, I found myself inside another dreamscape. There were the swinging bridges over the creek (a precaution against flooding); there was the old railroad engine on the tracks that stopped nowhere at the edge of the park. I mentioned my dreams to friends connected with the Naropa Institute. They were more excited about the Taipan than the precognitive stuff about swinging bridges. One of them was convinced I had dreamed of Chogyam Trungpa. "He was very much the entrepreneur, the guru in a business suit. He loved to drink. And he is very much a presence here in Boulder." I cannot say that my friend was right, but I liked the idea that Chogyam Trungpa might have welcomed me to what he once called his "kingdom." And I am sure it is a meaningful coincidence that the workshop I subsequently led at the Naropa Institute, the extraordinary college he founded, is one of my all-time favorites.

Such experiences are not difficult to explain if you remember that in dreams you are not confined to your physical body. As you become an active dreamer, you will develop the ability to embark on intentional dream journeys beyond the body.

The Body Is in the Mind

Among indigenous peoples, the experience of journeying outside the body is regarded as entirely natural and even routine. It's what you do when you have interesting dreams. Strong dreamers do it whenever they feel like it.

Even in mainstream Western society, out-of-body experiences are by no means unusual. Robert Crookall, a British geologist interested in parapsychology, collected and published the undramatic stories of 750 "ordinary people" who reported leaving their bodies under a great variety of circumstances—mostly without chemical assistance or life-threatening crises—in the 1960s.[3] When researchers started polling the general public, they were stunned to discover that one in five adult Americans claimed to have had an out-of-body experience.[4] The experience is probably universal during some phases of sleep. On any night of the week, any of us is likely to make a dream excursion outside the body, even if we wake with no recollection of where we have been.

Go to a certain type of psychiatrist, and he will tell you that an out-of-body experience is a specimen of "distortion of body image" (where the sense of the body's boundaries becomes confused) or "autoscopy" (seeing one's own apparition) or some other disorder he will treat if you have the appropriate insurance coverage. But as you become a conscious dreamer and learn to embark on intentional journeys beyond the body, you will find that it is quite easy to verify that you have traveled beyond your physical environment. For example, you might bring back information on people or places at a distance that you can subsequently check, or you might make a dream date with another journeyer and compare notes afterward.

We will experiment with several techniques for embarking on conscious journeys beyond the body. You will confirm that you can think without your brain and travel without your physical body into worlds that parallel the physical universe and worlds that are utterly remote from it. Trust what works for you. The masters in this area are people who have simply gone and done it. Don't get stuck on the experience of *separation* from the physical body. Western esoteric schools distingish between astral projection, in which there is a clear separation from the physical body, and astral travel, in which there is not. Gareth Knight remarks that "in astral traveling one is always, to a greater or lesser extent, aware of being located in one's own physical body, with its various minor discomforts and distractions. In astral projection one has dissociated consciousness entirely from the physical body." Knight maintains that "all that one normally needs to do of a magical or psychical nature can be effected by astral traveling,"[5] and he may well be right.

Beyond all techniques is another open secret: mind is never confined to the physical. The brain is its instrument for attuning to the physical environment, as are the outer senses, and the transceiver through which we either succeed or fail in bringing back messages from other dimensions. But mind is not contained by the brain and body; rather, the brain and body are contained by mind, by consciousness. Out of habit, we think of consciousness as being located in our heads. The challenge is not so much to move consciousness out of the body as to break the consensual hallucination that it is ever confined to the body.

Journeying Beyond the Body

The basic conditions for journeying beyond the body were explained in chapter 1. As with all inner work, the keys are *intention* and *relaxation*. You need to be able to shift into a state of relaxed attention, or focused relaxation. Breathwork will help. So will monotonous shamanic drumming.

Many books on astral projection and out-of-body experiences suggest techniques for deliberate *separation* from the physical body. You are encouraged to see and feel yourself rolling out, pulling loose, or rising up from your body, and to experience sensory recognition signals such as strong vibrations, humming, buzzing, and flashing lights. A recent author describes himself chanting "I'm out of body now" for a full fifteen minutes![6]

This approach is fine if it works for you—and if you remember to shield yourself and your space—but I feel the emphasis is misplaced. You can easily become diverted by the bumps and grinds and special effects. You may also find your experiences confined to the lowest levels of nonordinary reality. Since consciousness is never confined to the body, the statement "I'm out of the body" seems a self-limiting *mantra*. Frequent fliers discover they can lift off from the physical and return to it quite smoothly, without all the transitional son et lumière. You will find it more helpful to focus on where you are going, and on which vehicle you are using, than on what you might be leaving behind in the bed or the armchair.

THE APPROACH RUN

The twilight zone, once again, is your ideal departure lobby. You may open yourself to a flow of visual or kinesthetic images that will carry you beyond your body focus.

You may see yourself walking, then running, then lifting off the ground.

You may find yourself approaching the mouth of a tunnel, or a trapdoor or keyhole that opens in inner space, and moving through it at increasing speed.

You may start tracking a point of light that appears on your inner screen. Following a point of light upward and backward, beyond your physical line of sight, is an excellent method for projecting consciousness beyond your physical limitations.

CONTACT WITH A FAMILIAR GUIDE

You may simply open yourself to advice and instruction from a spiritual guide—perhaps an aspect of your own Higher Self—who will come through to you in this relaxed state.

The preliminary to much of my own exploration beyond the body is a contact signal from a familiar guide. The initial instruction may be as simple as "Lie on your back" or "Prepare for takeoff." I may be asked to "shift out of your physical focus" or to "shift to the second (or third) attention." Contact with a familiar guide reassures me that conditions are right for journeying, that a source of knowledge that is wiser than my little everyday mind is open to me, and that I will come and go fully protected.

STEPPING INTO THE ROOM

One night, as I rolled onto my left side in bed, an inner voice said, "Lie on your back." I did so and immediately saw a trapdoor open to my inner sight. I stepped through it and became aware of the massive, physical presence of furniture. I realized I had stepped out of my body into my own bedroom and was moving toward the dresser between the windows. As an experiment, I decided to inspect the litter of business cards, matchbooks, and foreign currency on top of the highboy for some detail that might have escaped my waking attention.

Taking a look at—or better, a walk around—your immediate environment from a perspective independent of the physical body is a good warm-up exercise. See if you can imagine yourself looking down at yourself in your present space, as if you were perched on the overhead light.

Better yet, as you lie or sit with your eyes closed, let your consciousness flow forward into your room and begin moving around it, looking at things from different angles.

EXERCISE: THE SECOND SELF TECHNIQUE

One of the oldest and most effective techniques for traveling beyond the physical body is to visualize your second self and then transfer your awareness to it.

When you are fully relaxed in a protected space:

1.   Visualize your second self. If you are lying in bed, you might see your double floating a couple of feet above you. If you are sitting or standing, you might visualize your second self in the same position, just in front of you, so you are looking at the back of your own head.

2.   Notice details of your appearance. These may be novel to you, since you can't ordinarily look at yourself from this perspective: the back of your neck, the lint or stray hair on your clothes.

3.   Let your consciousness flow to your second self. Allow your awareness to shift to the point where you are looking through the eyes of your double.

4.   Scan the space around you from this new perspective.

5.   Move about the room. Look at objects and furnishings from unfamiliar angles.

6.   Consider further explorations. When you are at home in your new vehicle, you are ready for further travels. You may choose to stay close to ordinary reality, moving through other rooms in your house.

You may wish to experiment with your ability to push through walls that are no longer solid and explore the neighborhood. You may target a person or place at a distance and journey to them. Or you may set your course for a destination in a different order of reality.

EXAMPLE: TRAVELING AS MY SECOND SELF

Behind closed eyelids, I could see the patterns of the wallpaper in my bedroom as if looking through a translucent veil. I decided to explore techniques and locales for conscious dream travel that I might report in this book.

I visualized my second self floating up above my physical body in the bed. I bounced up almost to the ceiling. I could see the plaster just above my nose.

I decided to raise my head and shoulders up through the roof and scan my external environment, staying close to ordinary reality. I was able to do this with only the briefest impression of molecular *stretch* as I slipped through the roof. Outside, I was drawn to a family of crows that is nesting in an old maple beyond the terrace at the back of my house. As I glided toward the nest, a huge crow erupted from the tree, flapping his wings and squalling at me.

I wondered if he could see me, traveling in my dreambody.

It seemed that he could. I felt myself shape-shifting to fly with the crows. I became aware that "our" crows had become guardians of my property—especially in warding off unwanted astral visitors. All of this was intensely tactile and physical-seeming.

I now wanted to contact a higher source of guidance. An inner voice reminded me to go straight up the middle pillar, which I perceived as a column of light that shot me upward like a high-speed elevator.

I came to the statue of an immense throned figure, somewhat reminiscent of the Lincoln Memorial, but vastly bigger. I thought of the statues of the pharaohs at Karnak. A door opened in the base, and I entered. There was a "false door" ahead, as in the Egyptian Houses of the Ka. I stepped through it and moved through a series of inner gateways and passages. I came to a space filled with loathsome, creepy figures who grabbed at me. I struggled fiercely with them. They may once have been human, but there was nothing of human mind or feeling left. I fought them without fear or emotion, but the outcome was unresolved until a being from a higher level drove the things back with rays of light that pushed through the murk like fingers.

Now I was up on a higher level, a place of instruction, where I received guidance from spiritual teachers. The work of a whole day was condensed into a few minutes of clock time.

Targeting

Another simple technique for projecting consciousness beyond the body is to focus on a person or place in ordinary reality and try to travel to that environment.

You might hold the image of a friend in your mind. See her face at the end of a tunnel and project yourself through it into her space. You may enlist her help by asking her to focus on *you*.

As an everyday practice, you might experiment before you leave home with traveling the routes you will follow during the day (in your physical body).

EXAMPLE: SCOUTING A ROUTE
YOU WILL TAKE IN WAKING LIFE

I was catching a morning train to New York City to do a TV interview with Fox Channel 5. I had never been to the building on East Sixty-sixth Street. In the hour before dawn—the twilight of the wolf—I decided to scout ahead along my possible path.

A tunnel opened and I flowed through it. I came out in a familiar setting: Penn Station. I noticed the panhandlers and dossers as I glided through the halls. I took the Eighth Avenue exit and moved uptown. When I crossed over to the East Side, I had the strong impression of a curious metal sculpture, tubular, with a big cross-arm and lesser bars or arms coming out at all angles. I could not figure it out: it made me think of a coatrack, but I knew it also had something to do with the church.

Entering the Fox building—big red letters above a largely windowless facade—I studied a black security guard with pleasant, rounded features and a mustache. He was conversing with an Indian or Pakistani woman.

Later that morning, I was able to check the accuracy of these impressions. Walking uptown, I came to a curious metal structure, with bars protruding at all angles. It was a stylized cross in front of St. Peter's Church that I had not previously noticed. When I reached the Fox studios, I recognized the security guard from my scout; he was talking to a Pakistani woman.

TRAVELING TO AN ESOTERIC SCHOOL

Of course, you are not confined to targeting people or places you already know. After reading a book by the leader of a European esoteric school, I decided to see what I could learn by journeying to the school—at a physical location I had never visited. My awareness flowed effortlessly beyond my body. I moved through a kind of tunnel and emerged to find myself approaching a gray stone building with antique vases at the entrance to a vestibule. I noted symbols and inscriptions, wondering whether I had arrived at a literal building in Europe or at an "inner temple" on the astral planes.

I was challenged at the doorway and identified myself by two of my spiritual names. I was given permission to enter. I had a strong sense of contact with the leader of the school. I asked for a special name by which to address her, and she shared one that evoked her love of the opera. Then I embarked on a short tour of the premises, which included a small room with hanging tarot images. I was given to understand that this room was a passage to deeper mysteries.

I was curious to see how much further I could go. I pushed off into an increasingly vivid dream that became so absorbing that I lost the awareness that I was dreaming. I rose charged with excitement with extensive recall of a dream in which I spent what seemed like a full day of intense research, discovery, and acquisition in a library filled with books, prints, tarot decks, and magical tools associated with the school. I filled a personal notebook with elaborate sketches of landscapes filled with symbolic figures, temples, palaces, gates, and gatekeepers—a whole imaginal geography.

This dream journey took me into one of many Clublands in the imaginal realm. You will come to recognize created locales of this kind in the dreamscape and your need to establish your right to be there. If you are entering a school or temple used by a spiritual order, for example, you may be required to pass certain tests—produce certain passwords or sigils—on penalty of incurring the wrath of the gatekeeper. If you have ascended to a level beyond your present evolution and understanding, you may simply find what is being said or transacted there incomprehensible.

Counterpart Reality

In training and honing your ability to fold space and scan the external environment beyond the range of your physical senses, you should remember that what you perceive is often a counterpart, or double, of physical reality. This "counterpart reality" should not be confused with external reality, though there are close correspondences. With practice and discrimination, you will find you can derive rather exact information about external conditions from these sightings.

EXAMPLE: THE CASE OF THE MISSING PORCH

A friend from overseas was staying with her daughter in a house in Pleasantville, New York, that I had never seen. We had agreed that I would drive down to visit her the following day. I decided to pay her a dream visit that evening. I used the targeting technique to embark on my dream journey. I lay down in bed, let my body go slack, and pictured my friend. I repeated her name, and the word *Pleasantville*. Soon a kind of trapdoor opened in inner space, and my consciousness flowed through it. I had the sensation of rushing through the air at increasing speed, until I descended into a pleasant, leafy neighborhood.

I was looking at a tidy white Federal with shutters and flowerpots, and a bench in front of the door. The entrance was slightly marred (I thought) by a porch that had been added on in violation of the original design. The whole scene was quite brightly lit, though there was no sun in the sky—and of course it was nighttime in ordinary reality. I toured the inside of the house, noting that the rooms were overfurnished and overheated. In the guest bedroom, I found my friend's luggage, but there was no trace of my friend herself in the house.

When I drove to Pleasantville the next afternoon, I confirmed all these details, including my friend's absence from the house (she had spent the night in New York City), with one notable exception: there was no porch at the front of the house. The owners told me that when they had purchased the house, it had a porch like the one I described; they had taken it down ten years before.

I found this episode quite instructive. What I had viewed, it seemed, was almost (but not quite) the physical house in Pleasantville. I had viewed its energy double, complete with the missing porch—perhaps in the same way that a clairvoyant or medical intuitive, scanning a person's energy field, might notice the energy pattern of an amputated limb.

Journeys Beyond the Dreambody

When you journey outside the body, you travel in another vehicle. As you journey to higher levels of reality, you may have the experience of moving from one vehicle to another—of using and temporarily discarding a series of subtle bodies. If you slow down the transition, you may notice yourself shifting awareness from the physical body to an energy double that hovers close to your sack of meat and bones. Then you may find yourself journeying beyond familiar locales in a dreambody that may initially replicate your normal appearance but will prove to be highly malleable; in your dreambody, you are not confined to your current age, weight, gender, ethnicity—or species. You may rise beyond the dreambody to travel as a point or curl of light, or as pure thought. We will explore the meaning of these transitions in chapter 5. For now, let me share an excerpt from my personal journals that reflects the experience of moving beyond the dreambody:

In and out of the Dreambody (December 28, 1995)

I perceive a brilliant band of colors at the edge of my energy field.

My awareness flows beyond my physical body. Now I have the sense of rising beyond both my energy double and my astral body.

I enter a sphere of light. My physical body is far below; I look down on it as if I am looking down from an airplane. I see a second body floating above it.

I have a sense of liberation from the tug of feelings and desires.

I am told, "You are now in your mental body." Its form (when separated from the astral body) is that of a point of light.

I am guided through a series of exercises to test the role of Kama, or desire. I descend into the astral body to experience the force of the appetites and desires that live with it. I return to a sphere of light that now embraces the whole scene.

I resolve to practice continuity of consciousness to preserve this experience. I move deeper into dreaming and spend the rest of the night learning and studying.

Shared Adventures

Shared dreaming—which Yeats called "mutual visioning"—is an important practice in shamanic training and has recognized uses in many spiritual traditions.

Rabbi Zalman Schachter-Shalomi relates a wonderful teaching story about interactive dreaming in *The Dream Assembly*.[7] A bunch of Hasidic rabbis are discussing the goals of prayer. Instead of joining the debate, Zalman says, "I would like all of you to join me in a dream tonight." Then he immerses himself in prayer.

The others are confused. How can you join another person in a dream? Then someone remembers tales of rabbis who met each other in a "dream assembly" in former times. They used standard formulas in the prayer upon retiring to synchronize takeoff.

1. "Grant that we lie down in peace, O Lord" = all lie down.
2. "And assist me with thy good counsel" = heads on pillow, ready to listen.
3. "Guard our going out and our coming in" = close eyes, ready to embark on a dream.

Someone remembers the old mystical teaching that "those joined in prayer together will be joined together in a dream."

That night (as the story relates mysteriously) the Hasidim lay down and closed their eyes "just as the Shekhinah turned to face herself in the mirror, and that night they met each other in a dream."

The dream locale is an Otherworldly orchard full of beautiful but unfamiliar fruit, filled with unusual light, as if from an unseen sun. Only one remembers that Rabbi Zalman told them to meet him in a dream, and he does not tell the others for fear they'll wake up. Instead, he simply reminds them they agreed to meet Zalman. They find him under a tree. He's younger and brighter. He refers to the difficulty of bringing all of them together—harder than finding and ascending a ladder to heaven. He speaks of how each generation requires a set of wings to carry its prayers to Sandalphon, who will weave them into garlands for the Holy One on his throne; each generation must create its own mystical dove. In the dream, he assigns his companions the role each will play in creating this mystical bird. They wake with the beautiful echo of birdsong in their minds; it returns every time they pray.

I have conducted many experiments in shared dreaming, both with individual partners and with much larger groups. I once asked the members of a weeklong adventure I was leading at the Esalen Institute to rendezvous in the early hours at a locale none of us had visited in ordinary reality: Ghost Canyon, Utah. We used a colored photograph of the pictographs on the walls of the canyon as a visual focus, passing it around the circle before we retired for the night. The stated intention was to try to understand the meaning of these enigmatic figures—and of course to have fun. The results of this experiment were both thrilling and instructive. More than half the members of the group had vivid recollections of shared adventures. Some reported joining in "aerial acrobatics," swooping low to explore a crevice below the level of the rock paintings. Several brought back overlapping reports both of "Native rituals" and of the sense that this site was regarded as a "landing place" for "star travelers," beings from the Sky World.

Even if you have never had the experience of intentional *shared* dreaming, you probably find yourself engaged from time to time in *interactive* or overlapping dreaming with acquaintances or partners.

Dream Dates and Astral Sex

Where there is shared affection and erotic interest, dream dates can be tremendously happy and fulfilling.

My wife and I agreed to meet for an astral date. Here is a fairly sedate account of the dream experiences we recorded independently:

My dream: I am constellating the gods in the lives of living people. I am feeding the Love Goddess golden and peachy foods: honey, champagne, fruit preserves. This flows into joyful sex with the Goddess—in the dreambody of my wife—in a sacred union.

Marcia's dream: I am making huge quantities of peach conserves with Robert's help. I feel shivers of sensual delight as our fingers and arms interlace and glide over each other. We reach deeper and deeper into the deep, rounded jars until our sexual energy explodes in showers of light and pure joy.

On another occasion, leading a workshop at a rustic retreat, I had a strong sense of a presence in the cabin where I was sleeping alone. Scanning, I picked up the image of Veronica, a woman in the workshop. Though I liked her well enough, I was initially a little testy; I don't encourage uninvited visitors. She reminded me telepathically that I had promised the group that we would experiment with shared dreaming; it seemed she wanted to make an early start. She demonstrated her ability to shape-shift, assuming the form of a long-beaked bird.

I lifted out of my body and flew with Veronica through a light, very high up, that opened like a portal.

We discussed various experiments we might try. I was interested in the visions of the departed that Veronica had shared with the group that morning. We agreed to travel to the prime locale in her death dreams. We came to a body of water, dark and choppy. There was no light on the far side. I felt we must hide our light to make the crossing. We agreed that we should not do this now.

We came together in our bodies of light. The experience was far beyond physical sex. The confluence of our energy fields produced sensations of tingling all over, and also of auditory toning, of rippling patterns of sound.

I sought information from Veronica that I could use to confirm our encounter. She showed me personal objects she had inherited from her grandmother: an antique pin and a cameo. In the morning, when I quizzed Veronica about her astral visit, she confirmed that her grandmother had left her these two pieces of jewelry, which she especially valued.

Astral sex, like physical sex, is a game for consenting adults. There are abusers in the dreamworld, just as there are in waking life, and you do not want to tolerate them or (worse yet) become one of them. Remember the guidance offered in the first chapter about protecting your psychic space, especially as you venture deeper into the dreaming of the shamans.

CHAPTER 4

≋

Wings of the Shaman

I was in many shapes before I was released.

Taliesin

Healing the Wound Between Earth and Sky

The Aborigines of southeast Australia say that our ancestors were able to journey to the spirit worlds in their physical bodies. They climbed the Dreaming Tree to visit the Sky World. But there was a falling-out within the family. A young man loaned his dogs to his brothers so they could hunt in the Sky World. He was enraged when he discovered that they had killed and eaten one of his dogs on a day when they were unsuccessful in the hunt. So he drilled a hole in the taproot of the tree and inserted a glowing coal that burned its way through. The next day, as the brothers started descending the tree, with a great crack the tree fell. This cosmic catastrophe is etched in the sky and in the earth. The Koori of Victoria say the canopy of the great Tree of Dreaming is a black patch in the Milky Way. The brothers who could not return to earth are a cluster of stars; travertine lumps in the Wimmera district of Victoria are the seed cones of the tree; a depression by the Richardson River is the place where the trunk came down; Lake Buninjon marks the great hole where the roots were burned.[1]

This story, so deeply embodied in the contours of the most primal continent, resonates through the world's mythologies in countless variations. Released from the specifics of culture and landscape, the story runs like this:

In a primal paradise, humans could walk and talk with the divine. We were at one with everything around us. We could speak the language of the birds. We could communicate by thought. Earth and Sky were joined.

Then came the fatal separation. In the Bible version, man fell, pushed by woman. In the Iroquois version, woman fell, neglected by man. In other versions, the beneficent Creator went away, disgusted by the conduct of the two-legged creatures he (or she) had made. In the Aboriginal version, the loss of the Cosmic Tree, the bridge between the worlds, was simply the result of the confusion and darkness of men.

The outcome is the same: there is a rift between Earth and Sky. Now people can no longer walk with God, and we have lost the language of the birds. In our diminished state, we no longer know who we are. East of Eden, we use each other, and other species, worse than any animal would do.

After the separation, after the Fall, can we hope to bridge this aching divide, short of physical death?

Shamans and dreamers know the answer.

It is suggested in a beautiful teaching story from the Makiritare, a native people of Venezuela. This story is used in the education of apprentice shamans. It gives rich insight into the shaman's way of dreaming.

The First Dreamer

Not long after the creation of this world, the Creator became disgusted with the behavior of the people he had made. He went back to the Sky World, leaving humans to the darkness and confusion they had chosen to inhabit.

In their benighted condition, no longer able to talk with God or walk in the spirit realms, people forgot who they were. They mated with peccaries and anacondas and lived as they did, and before long they thought they were wild pigs and water snakes and acted accordingly. They forgot they had human souls, and counterparts in higher orders of being.

Then a man called Medatia began to dream. He dreamed sitting on a bench in his thatched hut. He dreamed so strongly that a hole opened up in the roof of his house. He went whirling upward, through the hole, through an opening in the sky. When Medatia passed through the clouds and entered the first of the upper worlds, he was unable to understand anything that was going on around him. He encountered beings in various forms—animal and human, godlike and beyond naming— but could not comprehend who they were or what they were saying, until they changed his sight and his hearing.

With new eyes and new ears, he was able to enter a succession of higher realms. He was cleansed and made new in a lake of blue fire. In each of the upper worlds he encountered powerful beings who were intimately related to him. They taught him their songs.

When he returned to earth, Medatia was not the same. He had become the first shaman, the first of the great dreamers of his people.

He was saddened to see how low his people had fallen. He made it his mission to open their eyes, to awaken them to the knowledge of what it is to be human.

Night after night, while people were sleeping, Medatia called their dream-souls out of their bodies and instructed them, one by one. When the dream-souls returned to the sleepers, they reminded them that they were not meant to live their lives like pigs or snakes. One by one, awakened by their dream selves, Medatia's people returned to their villages and began to live again as human beings.[2]

The message of the story is simple and profound: we dream to awaken to who we are. And it is the strong dreamers—the shamans—who can heal the wound between Earth and Sky.

Young children know this and may tell you about it in surprising ways if you are willing to listen.

When she was just four, my daughter Sophie told me the following story, which had sprung from one of her dreams, and solemnly enjoined me to write it down and "get it right":

When the Sky Went Away

Once the sky was very close to the earth. But people kept climbing up to the sky. They were eating the sky and dropping the pieces left over on the ground.

Thunder and lightning came.

The sky said, "If you don't stop, I'll go away and you won't be able to visit me anymore."

So people changed.

Then a rich man in a big black car came along. He started eating the sky and throwing pieces on the ground.

Thunder and lightning came.

Then the sky went away and didn't come back.

Now the only person who can visit the sky is a man who dreams.

If you can't find a shaman to consult, talk to a child. All kids are dreamers. And because we were once children, we may reclaim the power to journey to the Sky World.

At Home with the Spirits

On a visit to Sydney more than two decades after I had left my native Australia, I wandered rapt among the painted worlds of the Aboriginal artists gathered at *The Eye of the Storm,* an extraordinary exhibition in the Museum of Contemporary Art.[3] The Rainbow Serpent coiled and stretched, shape-shifting into the prizefighter's bulk of a bull kangaroo, sprouting the horns of a water buffalo. Yes, I remember you. My mind went whirling back to a boyhood dream—a dream more real and more terrifying than anything in my waking life—in which something immense, with the horns of a bull, had ripped me apart, scattering the pieces of my dismembered body to the four quarters. I was told:

You were born for this.

I put stakes through your body.

You did not die. You did not even cry out.

In the face of the horned dragon, these thoughts that had come to me from a source intelligence beyond my normal mind returned to me.

I moved on around the gallery, skirting the coils of a serpent laid out on the floor in ridges of white sand. I froze in front of a series of ghostly figures. I seemed to know them, too. I looked at the personal statement by the artist, who lived in Arnhem Land. He stated that he had depicted the lives of the *mimi* spirits because when he got sick, he went to live with them in the spirit world, and when he got well, he came back to his home in the surface world. I felt slightly giddy. I was hurled back again into the serial medical emergencies and temporary deaths of my boyhood. I remembered diving down into the earth, plunging into a world of ghostly pale spirits, with whom I lived and knew the love of women and grew to manhood—from whom I returned when I recovered from illness, swimming up from the deeps of the underworld into the greenfire of the living, growing world.

Shamans are at home in the spirit world. They have second homes—even multiple homes—in the spirit realms. This can make it rather hard for shamanic types to keep their feet on the ground and helps to explain why shamanism is such a resolutely earth-centered tradition. Frequent fliers and "feathered sages" (as the Taoists call their birdmen)[4] need reminding that home is *here* as well as *there*.

Even if you are uncomfortable with the word *spirits*—even if you have convinced yourself, in your everyday mind, that there are no such things as "spirits"—you will have to contend with two kinds of spirits in life. The first are the spirits of the land where you live: of previous generations who struggled and loved and died here, of the First Peoples, of other species that share life on this soil, spirits of the earth itself. The second are the spirits of your ancestors, going back all the way through the bloodlines to an ancestral Eve in Africa (or wherever else you may find her).

These are not theoretical matters. You can dress up the discussion, if you choose, by borrowing Jungian references to "archetypes of the collective unconscious." But if Jung were still with us, I suspect that—as the shaman he was—he would be talking about spirits, too, given the way our society has opened up and made it easier to mention what was hitherto held to be unmentionable. *Spirits* is simpler and more accurate. You may benefit or suffer from their influence while remaining oblivious to their presence, as so many do in our society—including the drunk at the bar who is drinking for half a dozen dead alcoholics as well as himself, or the woman who is gaining weight and losing energy because she has her dead mother on her back. You can go to a psychic to receive spirit communications or open yourself to similar messages by becoming a channeler. Or you can learn the skills of Active Dreaming and shamanic soul-flight and journey to meet the spirits in their own realms.

The Way of the Shape-Shifter

On the walls of the Paleolithic cave of Les Trois Frères, the shaman dances, wearing the antlers of a stag, yet seems caught between a plurality of forms; his penis is slung like a lion's, his eyes are whirlpools of raw energy. Ho-Chunk (Winnebago) images depict winged beings with the heads of birds and the bodies of humans. Stand or sit on one of the scores of bird-effigy mounds in Ho-Chunk territory—as I have done in Wisconsin—and you will *feel* the power of flight and transformation these images evoke. From the ancient Aegean come statuettes of women who are both goddess and serpent, draped with snakes, half-metamorphosed into snake form, trancing into the deep trackways of the earth. Olmec figurines embody creatures that are both man *and* jaguar. A recently deciphered Mayan pictograph captures a shaman-priest in the midst of his shape-shifting; part of his body belongs to a jaguar and wears the spotted pelt. There is a Mayan name for this glyph, which translates as "the Way." The Way is that of the shape-shifter who embarks on dream travels in the company of animal allies and borrows their forms.[5]

> I was a bridge that stretched over sixty estuaries;
> I was a path, I was an eagle, I was a coracle in seas

sings the Celtic seer in the *Cad Goddeu,* the "Battle of the Trees," extending our sense of the possible scope of shape-shifting while underscoring its importance as a path.[6]

One of the defining characteristics of the shaman is a close relationship with animal and bird companions that includes the ability to borrow their forms. These relationships are part of a broader connectedness with all of nature—with the spirits of trees and plants, of stones and mountains—that flows from the awareness that everything is alive, everything is ensouled, everything is related.

If you are born in an indigenous culture, your relationship with the animal powers may be totemic or part of your personal dreaming. A traditional Mohawk is born a member of the Wolf Clan, the Bear Clan, or the Turtle Clan. If you are born into the Bear Clan, a part of you comes from its group soul; the Bear lives in you. But you will find other animal companions, or they will find you. A shaman may have many such allies and be able to call on their help in different areas, such as tracking or healing. He or she may dress in their skins or feathers and mimic their movements and cries in community rituals. In dreaming, the shaman flies on their wings or runs with their limbs. Shape-shifting is the shaman's shortcut into conscious dreaming. Especially powerful (though not necessarily spiritually evolved) shamans and sorcerers are believed to have the power of *physical* transformation into the forms of their animal or bird familiars. The Navajo tell tales of their skinwalkers; the Dyaks of their were-tigers, sorcerers who assume the forms of clouded leopards. Similar stories were told against alleged witches in the European witch trials, and Scotswomen (redheads, of course) confessed to trooping together at night in the forms of cats.[7]

The quest for animal guardians is serious business among indigenous peoples, sometimes involving fasting, sleep deprivation, prolonged isolation in the wild, and extremes of physical hardship. In traditional Ojibwa culture, boys were separated from the community and led into the deep woods to fast and pray for a *big* dream. Sometimes a boy would be instructed to keep vigil in a "nest"—a rough platform set high in the branches of a tree. For days and nights, an elder might drum for him. The dream guide might initially show himself in human guise. In one encounter, the *pawagan* (vision guide) eventually told the boy, "Grandchild, I think you are now strong enough to go with me." Then the dream visitor began to dance. As he danced, he turned into a golden eagle. Glancing down at his own body, the boy observed it was also covered with feathers. The great eagle spread his wings and flew off toward the south—and the boy flew after him. He was led to a place of training and initiation, a place to which he was able to return in successive dream journeys.[8]

In hunter-gatherer societies, there are vocational reasons of the most practical nature for courting animal allies. A shaman who shares the Deer dreaming may journey to the spirits of the deer to ask for *permission* as well as guidance for the hunt. A Jesuit missionary preserved the story of a dream hunt on the early frontier: an Algonquin warrior dreamed of a moose that said, "Come to me," and showed him an unusual stone that was lodged in its body. When the warrior later tracked and killed the moose, in the corner of the forest he had been shown in his dream, he found an identical stone in the animal's gallbladder.[9]

In modern society, many of us have little contact with wild animals outside zoos and wildlife parks, and those of us who are not vegetarians tend to buy our meat in shrink-wrapped packages in supermarkets. Yet the animal powers stalk us in our dreams. The messages are manifold. Our animal dreams may be totemic, in the sense that they urge us to connect with our basic energy. If your dream animal is sick or sluggish or malnourished or cruelly confined, that is often a signal to get out of your head and into your body and feed your "animal spirits" what they hunger for. In chapter 9, we will see how spontaneous healing can flow rapidly and dramatically from reconnecting with the energy of the "wilding powers." Sometimes our animal dreams, like dreams of changing clothes or speaking a different language, encourage us to apply the arts of shape-shifting to different challenges in ordinary life—to play the fox in one situation, the wolf in another. Or to spread our wings and get above the clutter, to rise to a larger perspective, as in Gloria's dream:

I Become a Black Swan

I become a black swan, swimming serenely across a lake. White swans flock to me, snuggling and frolicking. A friendly owl lands on my back and holds on to my long neck. "Look how beautiful you are," she tells me. "This is how you will be perceived as long as you hold your head high." I am at peace. I feel strong and admired. I can now accept that I am different. The others will flock to me if I hold my head high.

Dreams of wild animals—*especially* the scary ones—may be an invitation to recognize and work with a transpersonal ally. The following dream adventures, shared by people leading mainstream, urban lives, have the elements of shamanic callings:

THE TIGER'S GIFT

Jim, a computer programmer in New York, was terrified by a series of nightmares in which a tiger came after him. There was nothing cute and Tigger-ish about Jim's tiger; he was certain it was a man-eater, out to get him.

It took some persuading to get him to agree to stay with the dream and confront his adversary or simply go with the flow if the tiger appeared again.

When the tiger came back, Jim fled from it, as before, but stayed with the dream, with fascinating results.

In the dream, the Bengal tiger drove Jim along a jungle trail. He did not like the jungle; he had the impression of huge serpents coiling and slithering among the shadows. But the tiger kept goading him on, snapping and ripping at his clothes and his flesh until he was torn and bleeding.

Aching with pain and fatigue, Jim finally staggered out into a clearing. Now that he had reached his destination, the tiger licked his wounds and they immediately vanished.

Jim looked around, trying to figure out where he was and why the tiger had been driving him here.

To his surprise, he realized that he had been brought to a flying school: a place where jet-fighter pilots were trained. The next section of his dream seemed to compress months of linear time. Jim was pushed through a rapid but rigorous training course until he earned his wings as a jet-fighter pilot.

He now knew the soaring joy of performing aerial acrobatics.

On one of his solo missions, he ran into another fighter plane. Suspecting it was an enemy, he was tempted to shoot it down. But he realized he must also learn to gentle his strength and clearly distinguish friend from foe. Instead of opening fire, he forced the other plane down and interrogated the pilot, who proved to be friendly after they sorted through their initial misunderstandings.

Jim was quite elated when he woke from this dream. He decided to honor it by signing up for one of my advanced programs, which involved training in psychic defense. He told me he remembered that at a previous workshop, I had placed a tiger rattle-staff, carved for me by an artist in Colorado because of a dream, at the center of our circle.

SNAKE DREAMING

Suzie was a working mother, quite satisfied with her life—except that her dreams were infested with snakes.

For more than ten years, she was terrified by a recurring dream of being enveloped by snakes:

> *I am sitting on the floor, with my back to a wall in a big room that is empty except for the snakes that are crawling all around me. Snakes are creeping up each of my legs, coiling around them like a spiral staircase. The tail of a large snake is wrapped around my midsection. The rest of his body is wrapped around my shoulders and chest, pinning down my arms. His head is right next to my face on my right side, and I am totally terrified.*

At night, Suzie fled from this dream, leaving it as an unresolved nightmare. It pursued her by day when she tried to meditate or take a nap, and she would find herself shaking with fear as she shook herself out of her daydreams.

> *I could actually feel the snakes moving on me, hear the hissing. My skin would literally crawl with fear. I don't know what type of snakes the small ones were, but I think the big one was a cobra, because he had a hood that stood out around his head. His tongue would dart out at me as if he was getting ready to strike.*

Finally, as the snake images rose again when Suzie was trying to meditate, she determined to confront her fears.

> *The snakes were around my legs, and the big one was around my chest and shoulders, with his head swaying from side to side*

on the right side of my face, coming close and then moving back.
As I resolved to go with the flow, I found I wasn't scared any-
more. I just followed his movements. Suddenly his head jerked
forward. I expected him to bite me. Instead, he licked or kissed
my cheek! At that moment I felt the most wonderful feelings of
love and peace, and he held me in his embrace. I now know he
is one of my guardians and he is always there to protect me and
offer me courage, support, and guidance. I can feel his shadow
behind me (and see it occasionally) when I need his protection—
or just a big hug.

The snake came to Suzie again and again, in his new role as an
ally. In a conscious dream, she found him waiting for her in a tunnel
between the worlds. He asked her where she wanted to go. She had
been suffering heavy-duty stress, and she told the snake she would
love to go somewhere she could relax. She found herself floating on a
peaceful, sunny pond. She watched droplets of water making countless ripples on the surface. Her snake crawled up on her belly, coiled
up, and sunned himself with her. Then he asked, "Would you like to
see the water world?" When she said yes, he pulled her underwater.
As they swam together, Suzie realized she did not need air. She
enjoyed exploring a world filled with brightly colored fish, waving
plants, and different landscapes.

Suzie returned to this setting many times, whenever she needed a
"stress buster." Some of these return visits became the occasion for
further lessons and explorations. She asked her snake about past-life
experiences and how she could learn the truth about such things for
herself. He grasped her with his tail and they began to fly. As her hair
streamed back, she realized she was traveling through time rather
than through the air. She witnessed dramatic scenes of a family
tragedy in the 1700s and felt this contained important lessons for her
present life. When she was ready to leave, she took the snake's tail.
This time, he brought her to a circle of stones within high rock walls,
open to the night sky. He told her to drink from a cauldron that was
simmering above a large fire. The contents were unappetizing; Suzie
had the impression of body parts bobbing about in the broth. Gin-
gerly, she sipped from the dipper. The potion was bitter, yet she felt
stronger and sensed the beginnings of deep healing.

Suzie returned to the rock circle in further conscious dreams. From above, it looked like the mouth of a volcano. Inside, it was like a circular room with high stone walls and no ceiling. When she came here the next time, she was escorted by another animal guardian, who met her when she swam behind a waterfall at the edge of her special pond. He took her down into the depths of the earth before leading her back to the rock circle. Suzie was again instructed to drink from the cauldron. This time, flowers were floating inside it and the contents tasted sweet and good. As Suzie drank, bright lights appeared inside the cauldron. The largest told her, "We are the druids and the real people of Faerie. We come to welcome back one of our own who was lost and now found."

The third time Suzie journeyed to the rock circle, the fire was unlit. A guide told her to ignite the fire with the power of her mind. When she stretched out her right hand, a great fire flared up. Now an ancient woman appeared as her instructor. The crone told her to drink again from the cauldron. This would help her to dream and to learn while her animal guardians watched over her. This time the drink was sweet with a slightly bitter aftertaste. The crone led Suzie to a sleeping place among the rocks.

I slept for four days and four nights, feeling warm and safe. During the days the sun warmed my body, and at night the moon bathed me in a warm silver glow.

She woke elated and happy, from her dreams within dreams, certain she had completed an extensive training course. She found her teachers gathered around her. She told them she wanted to apply what she had learned. She spoke of a young man who was desperately in need of healing, and they encouraged her to go to him inside the Dreaming. She found a gaping hole at the level of his heart with a piece of wood sticking out. She removed the stick and focused on filling the hole, calling in light and warmth. Afterward, her dream teachers told her that her training would continue, to prepare her to help and heal others in ordinary reality: "You will know whom to treat, when, and how."

Suzie's rich and thrilling experiences offer a teaching on many levels. When she confronts her nightmare adversaries, they show themselves as allies. The snake knows the passages into the earth and the underworld. It leads her to realms of primal healing and into ancestral territory. She discovers places in the Dreaming to which she can go again and again, in intentional journeys, for adventure, instruction—or simply to relax. At each turning, her courage and fundamental purpose is tested. As new visionary landscapes open to her, she encounters new guides and an ancient connection with the collective wisdom of her European ancestors. The mythic time is *now,* as she is invited to drink from a mixing vessel that may be both the cauldron of Annwn, the cauldron of death and rebirth, and the cauldron of Cerridwen, the cauldron of transformation, the source of magic powers.

The Journey for Animal Guardians

Confirming your connection with the animal powers and working with them intentionally is part of becoming a shamanic dreamer. If you are truly called to this path, your spirit helpers have already been stalking you in your dreams. Going back inside the dream and dreaming it onward—as Suzie did with her insistent snake dreams—is the best way to embark on this journey. But you may choose another gateway. If you are a happy camper (or even if you are not), you may wish to sleep or keep vigil at a place in nature and ask to meet an animal guardian associated with this landscape. You may use the Tree Gate meditation in *Conscious Dreaming* and journey to your special tree with the intention of meeting your animal ally. Or you may simply call up the image of a place in nature that is special to you and use this as your launch point:

PREPARATORY EXERCISE:
FINDING YOUR PLACE OF POWER

1.   Lie or sit down in a quiet, protected space. Close your eyes and follow the flow of your breathing until you are fully relaxed.

2.   Call up the memory of a place in nature that you love.

3.   Be there with all of your senses.

Look around you in all directions. What do you see?

When you are fully present in this special place, what do you hear?

Feel the play of wind or water against your skin. Is it cool or warm, moist or dry?

What do you smell?

Is there a taste that comes to you, in your special place?

4.   Enjoy! Let your worries dissolve as you float in the water or laze in the grass, as the sun warms you or the wind cools you. This is a place you can probably use again and again to get rid of stress and recharge your batteries.

5.   Now that you are feeling lighter and more playful, look around again. Is there a way you can see yourself going down into the earth? Maybe you see an opening—a crevice or hole in the ground, an animal burrow, the mouth of a cave. Perhaps your passage leads down through water. Maybe your special place includes a tree you know well, a tree connected to you. Perhaps you can feel yourself journeying down into the earth through the roots of your tree.

6.   Once you are fully at home in your special place, with all of your inner senses, you may use this as the starting point for your journey for an animal guardian, and for other shamanic journeys.

EXERCISE: THE JOURNEY FOR ANIMAL GUARDIANS

1.   In a quiet, protected space, call up the image you will use as your entry point: your special place or special tree, or a scene from a previous dream journey.

2.   Focus on your intention: you are going to meet a spiritual ally who will appear to you in animal form. You may find yourself confirming a relationship with an old ally, or encountering a new one. (Power animals come and go in our lives, depending on how we feed them, both literally and metaphorically.) You should carry with you the questions on which you most urgently need guidance in your life right now. You should aim to bring back gifts.

3.   Be open to the unexpected: You may encounter a series of animals before you meet your strongest ally. You may be required to "brave up" in order to forge a relationship with a powerful guardian.

Your power animal may lead you to another guide or teacher, in a different form. Your journey may take you in any direction.

4. When you have read through all the instructions, put on a drumming tape or (better still) use live, monotonous heartbeat drumming to fuel your journey. Be sure there is a clear recall signal at the end of the drumming session.

5. Begin your journey by entering the scene you have chosen. Your animal guardian may be waiting for you at your special place. If so, you will let it guide you on the rest of your journey.

6. If your animal guardian is not already present, you should be ready to journey downward, into the earth (or water). Look for an opening into the earth and go down it. You will probably find yourself moving through a tunnel at increasing speed. When you come out the end of the tunnel, you will find yourself in a different landscape. It may be brightly lit, in no way "subterranean." You will find your animal guardian in this new setting.

7. You will test each other, travel with each other, and explore the questions you have brought. You may be escorted to new landscapes and new guides.

8. Before you part company, establish your future mode of communications. How can you summon your helper? What does your helper require of you?

9. When you return from your journey, ground yourself by moving about briskly. You may want to walk, run, or dance in the mode of your animal helper. Notice whether your perception of your size and body shape changes as you do this.

10. If you have found a new helper, research its habits in books and in nature and see how these may relate to your own energy and your need to honor your new relationship. If you have hooked up with a night hunter, you may find yourself modifying your sleep-work patterns. If you have found the Deer, you may find yourself grazing on snacks and salads.

11. Do something each day to bring the power of shape-shifting into your daily life. Run with the wolf, stalk with the tiger, forage with the crow. See how your field perception, your energy flow, and the way you carry yourself shift in everyday situations.

12. Play shape-shifting games with a sexual partner. (But remember to velvet your claws, gentle your bill-pecks, and avoid breaking

the bedsprings with your stomping.) If you are sensitive to such things, you may notice changes in the shapes of each other's energy body. Improvise. These are games for conscious, consenting adults; I don't recommend jumping on a partner in your animal form unless he or she has been prepared!

As you become more practiced, you will notice that shape-shifting has some interesting applications. They include tracking and reclaiming lost energy.

Tracking

Shape-shifters tend to be quite good at scouting forward or backward through time and across large distances in space. The Pentagon's "remote viewing" experiments, to judge by the published accounts[10] are far from catching up with the Paleolithic tracker's ability to examine a situation remote from himself in time or space. The Celtic bards, with those sonorous lists of transformations, affirm not only the shaman-seer's ability to change his shape, but to range across time and space and gain firsthand access to any area of knowledge. Nikolai Tolstoy suggests that "the purpose of this out-of-body exploration was to answer questions brought to the bard by earnest enquirers."[11]

Some of these questions survive in Welsh verse in the Y Cymmrodor:

Why is a stone so heavy? Why is a thorn so sharp? . . . Who is better off in his death, the young or the gray-haired? Dost thou know what thou art when thou art sleeping, whether body or soul, or a bright angel? Skilled minstrel, why dost thou not tell me? . . . What supports the structure of the earth? . . .
The soul . . . who has seen it, who knows it?[12]

Answering some of these questions, of course, would require journeying to the Upper or the Lower Worlds. We'll be traveling there soon. But I will keep the focus for now on the shaman's Middle World journey: tracking across time and space while remaining quite close to physical reality.

At one of my workshops, I asked participants to journey for a partner, with the aid of their animal helpers, on a question of importance to them. I specified that the question should be such that the information brought back by the tracker could be verified afterward in ordinary reality. This experiment produced many interesting travel reports, some of which were confirmed by later developments or subsequent research. The most fascinating to me was the following experience of shamanic time travel assisted by a splendid animal helper.

TIME TRAVEL WITH SCOTTIE

Kathleen and Diane met for the first time at the workshop. With understandable emotion, Kathleen gave her partner a hugely challenging assignment. She wanted Diane to find out whether her murdered sister was aware beforehand that her husband was going to kill her. Kathleen described the external appearance of the building where the murder had taken place—a residential hotel on Cape Cod—but said nothing about the interior of the apartment.

During the journey for animal guardians, Diane had connected with a black Scottish terrier. I had reassured her—and several other people who had teamed up with dogs or cats—that "domestic" animals are not disallowed as shamanic allies! And a terrier, bred to burrow all the way to China to get at its quarry and to hold on to it for dear life, seemed an excellent helper for a tracker.*

Diane's Scottie led her directly to the hotel at the Cape. She realized that she was looking at the building as it was *now*. She felt herself "dialing back" through time, for about four years, to the evening of the murder. Scottie now led her up the stairs to the murdered woman's apartment. They proceeded to go over the "physical" evidence with the care of a forensic investigator. Diane brought back a minutely detailed description of the kitchen, down to the pattern of

---

*I know very few cats of any size that consider themselves pets; dogs are often household protectors; and there is a reason why psychopomp figures in many mythologies go escorted by a black dog. Over the past decade, my own household has included two black dogs.

the linoleum, the grocery bags that were scattered, half-unpacked, over the counter and the table, the jar of Jiffy peanut butter lying on its side.

She described the dead woman's body—the bloodstains, the way she had curled up in fetal position before she was shot, the stare of frozen horror—with equal detail.

She reported that her attention wavered because she sensed a second body was in the apartment—a dead boy in the bedroom.

Scottie nudged her to keep her focus on the question. Though she felt slightly queasy, Diane peered into the dead woman's eyes, trying to read an answer there. It came to her clearly that the woman's expression of horror was not caused by her husband's attack on her but by something that had happened shortly before, in the bedroom. Had someone else—a boy—also been murdered?

Diane's report brought gasps of recognition from Kathleen. She had not told Diane that there had been *two* murder victims; the second was her young nephew. Diane's impressions suggested that the boy had been murdered first.

Diane could have produced this information by telepathy with Kathleen. But other details in her description of the murder scene— such as the jar of peanut butter—went far beyond Kathleen's knowledge. Kathleen was later able to confirm some of these details.

This is not a "one-off" story. It is one example, plucked from the hundreds I have collected in my teaching and practice, of how shamanic tracking with the guidance of animal helpers produces valid, helpful, and verifiable information for ourselves and others. Try it for yourself, once you are confident of your connection with an animal ally, by journeying with a partner's question.

Timefolding

After attending several of my workshops, a successful Wall Street attorney reported a conscious dream in which he felt he was in two time periods simultaneously. He found himself in a large institutional building he guessed might be a Victorian-era mental asylum—"a place where nobody gets cured." Realizing he was dreaming, Bob set out to explore his surroundings. He found a blacksmith making horseshoes and carriage parts out back. In one room, he found two women in flowing lace gowns and a man in a formal, dark English suit. The women seemed to be seriously ill but were not going to get better here. Bob wanted to help but was unsure whether he could get through to them. Nobody in the dream seemed to have noticed him.

When he spoke to the three people in the room, they looked at him for the first time. He asked them to go outside with him, and they all left the building. The women fell into the background as Bob conversed with the formally dressed man, who said that his name was Robert. They walked on cobbled streets under damp, cloudy skies. Bob felt he was in London in the 1850s.

But when they stopped at the curb, reality flickered. Bob saw modern cars rushing by; the traffic was heavy.

"Do you see the cars?" Bob asked his Victorian companion as they crossed the street.

"The what?"

"The cars. C-A-R-S."

"I am quite familiar with the English language," Robert said testily. "But what on earth are you talking about?"

"Cars are like carriages without horses. Did you see them?"

"No."

"Then why did you wait to cross the street?"

"When the woman frowned"—he pointed to her—"I stopped. When she stopped frowning, I crossed the road."

Reality flickered again. Bob realized he could still see modern cars in the street. One was moving slowly. He took the Victorian gent's hand and placed it on the side of the car. "Can you feel that?"

"I feel *something*." The Victorian gent was perplexed. "It must be some new kind of building." He still could not see the car.

The driver got out of the car and demanded, "What do you think you're doing?"

The Victorian gent did not see or hear him.

"I have something important to tell you," Bob told Robert. "It is going to sound quite unbelievable. But first let's find a place to sit down." The scene flickered again. Now Bob found himself with the Victorian gent among red-rock formations characteristic of the Sedona area in the American Southwest. They sat on the rocks and Bob told his dream companion, "I have traveled from another time, more than a hundred years in the future."

Robert did not believe him. But when Bob asked if he would like to give it a try, he agreed to experiment:

> We talk some more and decide to do it. There is a cylinder-shaped object nearby. We get inside the cylinder, which has controls and levers that are quite unfamiliar to me. It occurs to me that maybe I don't need the cylinder.

In his dream—which was the Victorian gent's reality, at least in the London scenes—Bob was conscious he could operate in two time periods simultaneously.

His experience is quite similar to that of shamanic dreamers who develop the conscious discipline of folding time, journeying into the past or the future to find answers to questions. When I moved to upstate New York, I found myself in an active dialogue with Iroquois dreamers of long ago. I had the sense that the warrior-shaman who had walked in on me from three centuries ago was tracking forward through time, trying to gather information that might be helpful for his people in a time when their survival was threatened by white men's diseases to which they had never previously been exposed.

As you become an Active Dreamer, you will discover that time does not flow only one way. In chapter 6, you will learn how to step in and out of the River of Time, quite literally. But first we must talk some more about soul, which is what all of this is about.

≋

CHAPTER 5

Paleopsych 101

Dreams are wishes of the soul.

Iroquois saying

Dreamwork Is Soulcraft

Alicia, a woman in her late thirties, dreamed she was on top of an immensely tall school building. A young girl in a smart red coat beckoned to her from the edge of the roof. Frightened the child would fall, Alicia rushed to pull her back. Instead, the child tugged at Alicia with surprising strength, dragging her over the edge. Alicia was terrified she would fall to her death until the child showed her they were flying.

When she went back into the dream, Alicia recognized the young flier as her five-year-old self, a part of herself that "went away" because of childhood pain and trauma. When they embraced, their bodies fused together in a blaze of light. Alicia told me, "I know I got back a part of my soul that went missing, the part of me that knows how to fly." Alicia has become an active dreamer, journeying far and wide. And she carries the sparkling energy of the five-year-old who came back.

Notice how Alicia multiplies in this simple telling of her story. There is an Alicia who is lying in her bed, and later on the rug in our workshop space. There is an adult Alicia who is traveling and eventually flying in a separate reality. There is a child Alicia who finally merges with her.

The story presents at least three aspects of Alicia, three facets of soul: the dormant body, sustained by its energy field; the dreambody, the vehicle of her traveling consciousness; and a part of her soul energy that was lost in childhood.

Vital healing is taking place here, but we hardly know how to describe it in modern language, which is short on the vocabulary of soul. Until the day before yesterday, many people in mainstream Western society were as prudish about "soul" as the Victorians were about sex. Now the word *soul* is back in favor. Best-selling books explore the realm of soul as a shifting horizon: as a sacred depth in our lives, as the vital energy that sustains and animates our physical vehicles, as the source of a personal destiny we may have chosen before we entered this life experience. Archetypal psychologist James Hillman writes beautifully of the soul's *code,* a pattern more fundamental than DNA that contains the shape of our lives as the acorn contains the oak.[1]

All these usages are valid, yet the concept of soul is slippery and amorphous in our hands, compared with vital, living experiences of soul travel and soul recovery such as Alicia's. We need to come out of the fog and develop an anatomy and vocabulary of soul that are adequate to our needs and our possibilities. They must be based on firsthand experience and observation, especially that of active dreamers, mystics, intuitives, and the original doctors of soul, the shamans. Iroquois traditionalists recognize and respect the separate nature and destinations of three aspects of the soul. They say that after death, the vital energy of the body becomes one with the earth. Another part of the soul stays close to the earth—which is why, in the *ohki-wes,* or feasts of the dead, all the spirits of the people from the earliest ancestors to the newly buried are honored and fed spirit food. The higher spirit returns to the Sky World that existed before the creation of this earth.[2]

This threefold distinction is echoed in many indigenous cultures and spiritual traditions. In practice, many further distinctions are made. Shamans regard the soul energy or "vital soul" that sustains physical life as something divisible, visible, and tangible. Pieces of soul may be lost or stolen; this is viewed as one of the principal causes of human illness and misfortune. Journeying for a client, the shaman may perceive that missing soul-part as a younger version of the sufferer, stuck somewhere in nonordinary reality. In our own dreams, we may encounter the pieces of soul we have lost along the way when we see a younger self as a separate being. When shamanic practitioners bring back lost soul, they blow it into the client's body. Soul travels on the breath. In other words, it has substance, though it is woven from a much finer stuff than the physical body.

As in Alicia's story, all of this is immediately accessible to us through dreaming. As we become active dreamers, we facilitate spontaneous soul recovery for ourselves and can help to bring it to others. We come to grasp what may have been missing, not only from our intellectual models, but from ourselves. Heraclitus reminds us that we will never find the boundaries of soul, however far we journey.[3] But as active dreamers, we can share in the *experiential* insights of the past and future masters of this field, the paleolithic psychologists.

The Challenge of Paleopsychology

At a benefit dinner, the wife of a bank president asked, "What exactly is it that you do?"

I told her, "I'm a paleolithic psychologist."

She nodded respectfully, possibly associating me with the clinical psychiatrist seated above the salt.

I had stolen the phrase from Frederic Myers, the great Victorian psychic researcher. Myers coined the term *paleolithic psychology* as an erudite joke, to describe "the habits of thought of the savage who believes that you can travel in dreams."[4] He apologized to his respectable readers for "the apparent levity of a return to conceptions so enormously out of date"—while sowing the seed of doubt that "modern science" had actually surpassed the "primitive" understanding of the soul. Myers chose the path of true science, which is always ready to revise the reigning hypotheses in the light of fresh evidence. "My own ignorance . . . I recognise to be such that my notions of the probable or improbable in the universe are not of weight enough to lead me to set aside any facts which seem to me well-attested." He arrived at a "root-conception" of "the dissociability of the self, of the possibility that different fractions of the personality can act so far independently of each other that the one is not conscious of the other's actions," and that "segments of the personality can operate in apparent separation from the organism."[5] Myers observed such phenomena in "true apparitions" of the departed, but also in "traveling clairvoyance" by living persons, which sometimes produce "phantasms of the living" that are visible to people in other places.

Myers's contemporary Edward Tylor, who held the first chair of anthropology at Oxford, beautifully summarized the challenge to modern science that is posed by shamans and frequent fliers who are at home with the spirits and often journey in their realms:

> The issue raised by the comparison of savage, barbaric and civilised spiritualism is this: do the red Indian medicine man, the Tatar necromancer, the Highland ghost-seer and the Boston medium share the possession of a belief and knowledge of the highest truth and import which, nevertheless, the great intellectual movement of the last two centuries has simply thrown aside as worthless? Is what we are habitually boasting of and calling new enlightenment, then, in fact a decay of knowledge? If so, this is a truly remarkable case of degeneration and the savages on whom some ethnographers look as degenerate from a higher civilisation may turn on their accusers and charge them with having fallen from the high level of savage knowledge.[6]

Basics of Paleopsychology

The basic insights of paleopsychology, all of which may be tested by the methods explained in this book, are as follows:

1. Spirits are real.
2. We are not alone: we live in a multidimensional universe peopled with beings—spirits of nature, gods and daimons, angels and ancestors—who take a close interest in our affairs and influence our lives for good or ill.
3. We are more than our bodies and brains, which are only vehicles for soul.
4. The soul survives the death of the body.
5. Soul journeying is the key to the spiritual worlds and the knowledge of ultimate reality. The soul makes excursions outside the body in dreams and visions. The heart of spiritual practice is to learn

to shift consciousness at will and travel beyond time and space. Through soul-flight, we return to worlds beyond the physical plane in which our lives have their source and are able to explore many dimensions of the Otherworld.

6.   Souls are corporeal, though composed of much finer substance than the physical body.

7.   People have more than one soul. In addition to the vital soul that sustains physical life—closely associated with the breath—there is a "free soul," associated with the dreambody, which can travel outside the body and separates from it at physical death, as well as an enduring spirit whose home is on the higher planes.

8.   Souls—or pieces of soul—can be lost or stolen. This is the principal cause of disease and misfortune.

9.   Some people have more souls than others and have the ability to make excursions to different places at the same time.

10.   At death, different vehicles of soul go to different lots. Through conscious dreaming, it is possible to explore the conditions of the afterlife to prepare for one's death and to assist souls of the dying or departed.

11.   We are born with counterparts in nature. For example, we are born with a totem animal and a relationship with natural forces (wind or water or lightning) that are part of our basic identity and help to pattern the natural flow of our energy.

12.   We are born with counterparts in other places and times, and in other dimensions of reality. When we encounter them through interdimensional travel, they become allies and sometimes teachers.

The Anatomy of Soul

We need to start by recognizing the threefold distinction: body, soul, spirit. Somewhere in the evolution of Western society, we lost the clear understanding that humans are threefold beings.

The moment of confusion can be dated quite precisely, to the year 869, when a Church council ruled that humans are divided into only two parts—body and spirit—suppressing the distinct category of *soul*. In the process, the Churchmen drove an iron wedge between God and man, by denying (perhaps without realizing what they were doing) that the Trinity is reflected in the human constitution. Inside our churches, as well as outside them, the terms *soul* and *spirit* are now used as fuzzy synonyms. The founders of Christianity and the mystics of the Church knew better. The founders of the Church recognized that, in addition to a physical body, we have a subtle body that can travel outside the physical vehicle and survives physical death but is not to be confused with the immortal, enduring spirit.[7]

The realm of body, properly understood, includes both the physical vehicle with all its complex instrumentation, including the brain, and the energy field that surrounds and maintains it. The brain is not the seat of the mind but a transceiver that picks up only a tiny trickle of thoughts and impressions from the continuum of consciousness that operates at higher levels. The brain has been aptly described as a "reducing valve" for mind, as an instrument that does not *produce* thought but *reduces* thought so that it can be translated into nerve impulses and everyday awareness.

The realm of soul encompasses a subtler anatomy. The care of soul, in practical terms, involves working with at least three subtle vehicles, which I shall call the energy body, the dreambody, and the shining body. Just as the physical universe corresponds to our physical bodies, subtler orders of reality correspond to the subtle bodies. We enter different levels of nonordinary reality in embodied form. Both the energy body and the finer vehicles of consciousness survive the death of the physical body, for greater or lesser periods. They have different fates; different vehicles go to different lots, or wrecking yards.

Cross-culturally, two favorite metaphors are used to describe the bodies of man, both gross and subtle. First, they are called *garments* or robes of spirit. As we come into incarnation, we put on a physical body as we might slip into a suit of clothes. In dream travel, and at physical death, we slip out of the body and may discard a succession of finer garments, progressing to higher worlds through a kind of sacred striptease.[8]

In the Book of Genesis, God gives Adam and Eve "garments of skins," which may refer to their entering into physical bodies. The Greek shaman-philosopher Empedocles called the body *sarkon chiton,* the tunic of flesh. In the Bhagavad Gita, the physical garment can be cast off and changed: "As a man, casting off worn-out garments, takes new ones, so the dweller in the body, casting off worn-out bodies, enters into others that are new." The Upanishads describe five sheaths or "coverings" of the spirit.[9]

Second, the subtle bodies are also called *vehicles,* the literal translation of the Greek term *ochemata,* favored by Porphyry and the Neoplatonists. Your Ka is also your car.[10]

These twin metaphors come alive in our dreams. Our dreams of changing clothes are not always about the state of our wardrobes. Our dreams of taking the car to the train to the plane are not always about conventional travel.

THE ENERGY BODY

The human energy field is enmeshed with the body and is basically inseparable from it. The energy field, perceived by sensitives and psychic healers as a pattern of colored lights, is evoked by the halo or nimbus in religious art and has been reproduced by Kirlian photography, a process developed in that spiritual mecca, the old-time Soviet Union. The energy field acts as a template that shapes and maintains our entire physical system, "like a jelly-mould" according to Harold Saxton Burr.[11]

We can receive and transmit healing through the energy body, by methods such as reiki and therapeutic touch. If we are excessively open or constantly exposed to negative people and environments, "energy thieves" can drain our energy body. I asked a woman who complained that she felt that her batteries had been drained to go to the place where she felt most vulnerable and bring up an image. She told me she felt that someone was sucking energy from her abdomen, as if through a straw. When I asked her to find the person at the end of the straw, she identified a grasping, needy relative who was stealing her energy without returning it. We proceeded to cut that unhealthy link; our health depends on a fair exchange of energy.

The energy body is often called a double (the "etheric double" in Theosophical literature) because it is virtually a duplicate of the physical body.[12] If it is completely detached from the physical body, the result is the loss of vital bodily signs and physical death, either temporary (as in near-death experiences) or permanent. Anesthetics, drug overdoses, and alcoholic blackouts cause substantial separation of the energy body from the physical body.

Part of an individual's energy field, or etheric substance, may be projected outside the body, intentionally or unintentionally. This is how genuine mediums produce table rappings and ectoplasm shows at séances. Such procedures usually leave the practitioner—and others in the room who have contributed their energy, often without realizing it—exhausted and depleted, and I can think of no sensible reason for performing them. However, powerful healers and shamans can develop the ability to project one or more energy doubles that can operate at a distance from the practitioner, enabling them to work in more than one place at the same time. The ancient Egyptians, who were no slouches at operations of this kind, believed that great magicians might have many doubles, or Kas.[13]

During sleep, an energy double may hover just above the physical body. As already noted, conscious dreamers sometimes use this as the launchpad for journeys beyond the body.

When the lights are down, sensitive people can often perceive the energy fields of those around them, even when they do not know how to account for what they are seeing.

For example, Dinah thought her boyfriend, Joel, was getting weird. As they lay together in bed, he told her he could see something "strange" that seemed to be covering her body. He described it as a "substance," silvery and opaque. As he moved his hands over the surface of Dinah's skin, he reported that he could see and feel himself molding it and moving it around. On several more occasions over the next few months, Joel claimed he could see this "silvery substance" coating Dinah's body. One night, as Dinah dozed, Joel thought he saw the same "substance" on the ceiling above the bed.

Dinah wondered whether her boyfriend was seeing her aura. She did not see auras herself and had never heard of them having this kind of plasticity, or drifting up to the ceiling. She did not know what to make of her boyfriend's sightings until, one night, she saw for herself. She was in bed, on the cusp of sleep, when she picked up an odd impression—of something that resembled a human, floating up toward the ceiling. When she opened her eyes, the form was clearly there. But as she tried to focus on it, the form became indistinct, like a vanishing mist. Dinah looked at her hand and found it was covered with a silvery substance. When she spread her fingers, they appeared to be webbed. The "substance" had a pattern she could reshape by poking and stroking it with her finger. She was absorbed in this game for an hour or more. "I was totally mesmerized," she told me. "This stuff surrounded me. It made me think of a protective cocoon."

Dinah was learning that the energy body is composed of a very fine material substance that can be reshaped and partially extruded from the immediate periphery of the physical body.

As a survival principle, it is rather important to keep track of this energy; your health and vitality depend on it.

Jean Houston tells a wonderful story of how she became aware of the energy body. She was six years old, vacationing with an uncle who had lost a leg in combat in World War II. One day her uncle pointed at the empty space in front of him and asked her to scratch his toe. She protested, "You don't have any toe." "I know that," he told her, "but it still itches, so scratch it anyway." When she poked at the air where his toe might have been, he gave a great sigh of relief.[14]

EXERCISE: EXPERIENCING THE ENERGY BODY

Shake your hands as if you are shaking off water. Now bring them toward each other, palms facing, until you feel a subtle *something*—a change in temperature or in your perception of the density of the air.

In Egyptian inscriptions, the symbol of the Ka is a pair of identical hands joined by a square bracket. The image evokes the way the energy body and the physical body mirror each other's form. Through simple movement, you can develop a stronger sense of your energy double. Jean Houston suggests an excellent series of exercises in *The Possible Human,* from which I have borrowed some of the following suggestions:

1.   Stretch your arms, out and up, several times. Then let your arms drop to your sides. Now see and feel yourself continuing to stretch with the arms of your energy body.

2.   Whirl your physical arms around you. Then let them drop to your sides and feel yourself continuing the motion with the arms of your energy body.

3.   Jump forward as high and far as you can. Jump back. Repeat this a few times, then stop and feel your energy body jumping forward and back. After you have done this a few more times, leave

your energy double standing in front of you, at the end of its jump. Then leap back into it with your physical body.

4.   Experiment with a partner. Reach out and touch her with your physical arm, then with the arm of your energy body.

Kinesthetic projection along these lines has proven value in sports and in many other areas. Jean Houston says she uses it to remove the possibility of writer's block by sensing and seeing herself seated at the keyboard in her energy body. When she feels that her energy body has slipped into a writing mode, she joins it with her physical body. I have tried this myself and find that it works like a charm; it also reminds me that writing is a highly tactile and physical activity.

THE DREAMBODY

Dreaming, you generally find yourself traveling in a dreambody. This is often called the astral body, though the Greeks, who invented that term, meant something else by it. The dreambody often resembles the physical body but is constructed of finer stuff and is quite malleable. Because it is strongly driven by our emotions, appetites, and desires, it is sometimes called the emotional body. Synonyms for the dreambody, in different cultures, include the *linga sarira* or *kamarupa* (India), the *fravashi* (Persia), and the *soma pneumatikon* (Greece).[15]

For the Theosophists, the astral body or dreambody is "a vehicle, to clairvoyant sight not unlike the physical body, surrounded by an aura of flashing colors, composed of an order of fineness higher than that of physical matter, in which feelings, passions, desires and emotions are expressed and which acts as a bridge between the physical brain and the mind, the latter operating in the still higher vehicle— the mind-body."[16] Everyone has a dreambody, though conventional Western religion, psychology, and medicine tend to ignore its existence.

THE SHINING BODY

In conscious dreams and shamanic journeys, you may find yourself leaving the dreambody behind to enter higher realms in a different form: as fire or lightning, as a point or curl of light. You are now at one with your shining body, or Body of Light.

The Gnostics called it the garment of light. The Neoplatonists called it the *augoeides,* or "light-formed" body. In many of the Mystery traditions, this is not something that is yours by entitlement; it is something that is acquired through spiritual initiation or divine grace. In the Jewish Revelation of Enoch (which dates from about 160 B.C.) we read that an angel will clothe the righteous with "the garments of life and wrap them in a cloak of life that they may live in them an eternal life."[17]

It seems that as consciousness moves through higher dimensions, it travels in corresponding vehicles. Perhaps this is the inner teaching of the shaman's story from the Makiritare of Venezuela, in which the great *dreamer* Medatia travels through nine worlds beyond this one and discovers that he has a counterpart in each.

The Lost Tradition

There is a Western, as well as an Eastern, tradition concerning the "subtle bodies" that offers both intellectual clarity and experiential depth. Its seminal texts are in Greek and date from the first centuries of the common era, a time of interplay between several great world-religious movements. Its principal teachers were mystics and Mystery initiates as well as scholars and philosophers. They were no strangers to shamanic soul-flight. Unfortunately, through literal "Vandal-ism" and early Church censorship, some of their works survive only as fragments or have been lost altogether. Key dates in the burial of this metaphysical tradition were the closure of the Academy of Plato in 529 by an edict of Justinian and the torching of the great library at Alexandria in 640. The books that survived were largely in the care of the Church, which lost no opportunity to suppress works that were judged heretical. A few survived in Arabic translations and were translated back into Latin. Curiously, some of the surviving texts have not been translated into English or are not available in accessible editions. For the most part, the academic establishment has neglected the great Neoplatonists: Proclus, Plotinus, Porphyry.

The Neoplatonists distinguished a "spirit body" *(pneuma)* associated with the breath, and a "celestial body," often described as light-formed *(augoeides)* or starry *(astroeides)*. Our grasp of this vocabulary is complicated by the fact that Paul elevated *pneuma* into a description of the *higher* vehicle, while *astral body* has been used in modern times as a synonym for the dreambody.

The breath-soul or spirit body pervades the physical organism. It survives death but does not accompany the higher aspect of the departed on his upward journey. As a shade *(skia)* or mirror image (eidolon) it goes to Hades, a realm of the dead that is often depicted as subterranean but also includes the whole region between Earth and the moon.[18] More evolved beings leave this shell behind and journey to celestial regions in the shining body.

In the early Church, there were many who shared similar conceptions. The early Christian Olympiodorus spoke of a subtle body that survived physical death and had the shape of an egg.[19]

The whole of the New Testament resonates to the notion of a vital soul energy that travels on the breath. In the Gospels, the Holy Spirit is a fluid substance that is breathed into people. It is a concrete force that Simon Magus tried to purchase (Acts 8:18).

On Mount Tabor, the disciples see Moses and Elijah as well as Jesus, and Jesus "was transfigured before them, and his face shone like the sun, and his garments became white as light" (Matt. 17:2; cf. Mark 9:2–4, Luke 9:29). In the New Testament Greek, the word used for Jesus' transformation is *metemorphothe*—which literally means that he shape-shifts. The disciples see Jesus and two departed prophets, Moses and Elijah, in their celestial or shining bodies.

A careful reading of a famous passage in I Corinthians suggests that Paul had experience of the subtle bodies and believed that humans are threefold beings, composed of body, soul, and spirit. The Revised Standard Version reads, "If there is a physical body, there is also a spiritual body." The earlier Authorized Version reads, "There is a natural body and there is a spiritual body."[20]

Unfortunately, the Church—in its fear that direct experience of the sacred might undermine its authority—went on to proscribe even the discussion of subtle bodies. In 1311, the Council of Vienna condemned the views of theologians like Peter Olivi (1248–98), who had taught that there are several vehicles of spirit beyond the physical body.[21] As Dr. J. J. Poortman observes, "Extremely little has been heard in Roman Catholic Christianity since that time of bodies of fine matter either of the souls of men or of the angels."[22] A Catholic author who dared to write about the "psychical body," or dreambody, was rewarded by having his works placed on the Index of forbidden books in 1952.

Yet while Church dogmatists labored to bury the wisdom of the soul journeyers, the Christian mystics spread their wings. Hildegard of Bingen saw the soul taking possession of the fetus inside the womb, descending into flesh "like a fiery globe." She saw how soul energy travels with the breath. John of the Cross spoke of "the garment of the soul in three colors." Jakob Böhme (1575–1624) wrote about "subtle flesh" and a "force-body" so subtle it could pass through stones. He also described an "inner, holy body." Struggling for words to contain direct visionary perception, he suggested that this might be called the "spiritual tincture-body."[23]

Bilocation and the Dream Double

I was attending a conference in the Boston area when I was approached by a pleasant-looking couple who might have been in their early forties. The husband, David, introduced himself as a medical equipment salesman from Connecticut; his wife was a registered nurse. They seemed intelligent, articulate, and well-grounded; they had brought a cooler full of provisions they offered to share over lunch. The only oddity was that they seemed unusually deferential to someone who was simply another conference attendee.

"We want to thank you for that workshop we attended last fall," David said. "You changed our lives."

"Which workshop do you mean?"

"The weekend workshop in upstate New York."

"What was I teaching?"

David looked puzzled as he told me how my workshop had brought shamanism and dreamwork together. "You showed us how to journey through the images from our sleep dreams."

I was flabbergasted. I had been *thinking* about going public with the approach I now call Active Dreaming. I had *dreamed* on several nights of leading workshops in shamanic dreaming. But I had not yet held one in physical reality—at least, not in *my* physical reality.

I told David, "You must have confused me with someone else."

David looked at his wife, who knitted her eyebrows.

"That's impossible," she protested. "Your voice, your white hair, your whole way of being—"

"You're a pretty hard guy to mistake for someone else."

"And we spent the *whole weekend* with you," his wife came back. "I'll never forget it."

"That's very interesting," I told them. "I've *dreamed* of holding a workshop like the one you describe. But I haven't done it yet, not in *this* reality."

"You're kidding."

I shook my head. David looked at his wife, who made a face and tugged at his arm. As they walked away, she scowled back at me, obviously convinced that I was toying with them. Later in the day, when David passed me on the way to the cooler, he gave me a conspiratorial wink and said in a stage whisper, "Shamans are tricky characters."

What was going on here? Did my dream reality somehow become waking reality for that earnest couple from Connecticut? Dreaming, could I have projected a double who seemed solid enough—*un hombre de carne y hueso*—to students at a holistic center? Were we caught up in some kind of time loop, so that in *their* reality the Connecticut couple went to a workshop that I gave two years later in *my* physical reality (in which they were not present—at least, not yet). Or were the three of us somehow caught up in a collective, confusing hallucination?

If I had been quicker off the mark, I suppose I might have asked the Connecticut couple if they had a receipt for the workshop they attended. Maybe the center where it was held owes me money!

There are doubles and doubles. St. Augustine left us the intriguing story of a philosopher who urgently wanted to consult a colleague living several hundred miles away. To his great delight, his friend called on him that night, and they had a long conversation in which the philosopher was able to clarify his thinking in areas critical to his work. He wrote to his colleague afterward to thank him for his providential visit—and was astonished to receive a letter back in which his friend told him that he had never left his hometown, but remembered conversing with the philosopher in a dream.[24]

The Capuchin monk Padre Pio rarely left his cloister but reportedly turned up on scores of occasions at other locations in a second body to preach sermons or counsel those in need. He attributed these feats to what he called a "prolongation of the personality."[25]

St. Anthony of Padua was credited with similar gifts. As he lay on his deathbed, he appeared to a friend hundreds of miles away, in seemingly corporeal form, and informed him that he had left his "donkey"—his physical body—in Padua.[26]

In her remarkable book, *Dancing in the Shadows of the Moon*, Machaelle Small Wright describes her experience of a "split molecular process" resulting in bilocation in two separate orders of reality. "My soul operates out of two separate, but related physical bodies." One is her own; the other belongs to a servicewoman who was killed in World War II and now lives with a group headed by "Eisenhower" in an (astral?) locale called the Cottage. Machaelle says the Cottage is situated in the "England equivalent" of "a planet that exists in a sister dimension of reality . . . within a band of form identical to our own." She travels there by picturing the locale and willing herself to go. She insists that this is something distinct from a dream or an "out-of-body" experience, because "real" time elapses, she eats "real" food, and she is subject to "real" pleasure and pain.[27]

While the sight of one's energy double, or doppelgänger, arouses fear in many cultures—especially the fear of impending death—the double may be something more. In Charles Williams's novel, *Descent into Hell,* Pauline goes in fear of her "double" all her life—so terrified she avoids walking alone—only to discover it is no horror, but her spiritual self, her "unfallen self" as originally conceived in heaven. When the two come together, she can begin to live her true destiny, which includes helping to release earthbound souls.[28]

A Brief History of Soul-Flight

The science of dream travel is ancient: in the evolution of our species, it probably predates speech and may have helped to generate language. Dream travel has a fascinating pedigree.

In many human cultures the most profound insights into the nature of the divine and the fate of the soul after physical death have been attributed to ecstatic journeys beyond the body in waking dream or vision. In most human cultures, the existence of parallel worlds inhabited by gods, daimons, and spirits of the departed has been accepted as simple fact, a fact of extraordinary importance. Visiting these other worlds was a top priority for our ancestors, as it still is wherever there is *living* spirituality. From the travel reports of the boldest and most successful journeyers between the worlds, mythologies and religions are born. Soul journeying was understood to be the key to orders of reality, hidden from the five physical senses, that are no less "real" than ordinary reality and may be *more* so. For the Jivaro people of South America, everyday life is regarded as "false." "It is firmly believed the truth about causality is to be found by entering the supernatural world, or what the Jivaro view as the 'real' world, for they feel that the events which take place within it are the basis for many of the surface manifestations and mysteries of daily life."[29] Among dreaming peoples, the reality of the soul journey and the objective, factual nature of the travelogues brought back are not in doubt. The travel reports will be compared with those of previous explorers.

Shamans ride their drums to the Upper and Lower Worlds to gain access to sources of insight and healing, to commune with the spirits and rescue lost souls. Aboriginal spirit men journey to the Sky World, climbing a magic cord projected from their own energy bodies, at the solar plexus or the tip of the penis.[30]

Before compass and sextant, before charts, the great open-sea navigators guided their shipmates across the oceans by fine attunement to the patterns of waves and wind and stars and by the ability to scout ahead and consult a spiritual pilot through dream travel. Traditional navigators in the Indian Ocean reputedly had the power to travel ahead of their vessels in the form of seabirds or flying fish to set a safe course. The shipmakers and sea captains of the Bugis of Sulawesi—who once had a fearsome reputation as pirates—still journey to the spirits for guidance on the right trees and natural materials to use in the construction of their *prahus* as well as on their ocean crossings.[31]

The ancient Taoist masters were known as the feathered sages because of their reputed power of flight, which sometimes involved shape-shifting into the form of cranes.[32]

In ancient Greece, shaman-philosophers were renowned for their ability to travel outside the body, appear in two or more locations at the same time, and commune with their colleagues across time and space. Aristeas of Proconessus was said to journey outside his body in the form of a raven. He reputedly dropped down "dead" in a fuller's shop in his hometown on the Sea of Marmara. At the same time, he was seen alive and well in Cyzicus, four hours' sail away on the mainland. When the report reached his village, people were sent to examine his body, which had been laid out for burial; his body had mysteriously disappeared.[33] The Pythagoreans taught and practiced soul travel and believed that spiritual masters born centuries apart could communicate by this means. The philosopher Proclus, who believed he was the reincarnation of an earlier Pythagorean, communed in this way with the spirit of Plutarch, the great historian and adept of the Mysteries.[34]

The ability to project consciousness beyond the physical body, to fold space-time, influence events at a distance, and project a double are all recognized *siddhis*—or special powers—of advanced spiritual practitioners in Eastern traditions.[35] When Paramhansa Yogananda shifted awareness beyond his physical body, he was able to achieve 360-degree vision, the vision of a being at home in a higher dimension.[36]

Vedic literature from India is full of vivid accounts of soul-flight by humans and beings-other-than-human. In the Mahabharata, the dream-soul, or *suksma atman,* is described as journeying outside the body while its owner sleeps. It knows pleasure and pain, just as in waking life. It travels on "fine roads" through zones that correspond to the senses, the wind, the ether, toward the higher realms of spirit.[37]

Shankaracharya, the ascetic exponent of Advaita Vedanta, practiced soul-flight and the projection of consciousness to another body. Challenged to a debate on sex—a subject of which he was woefully ignorant at the time—he is said to have left his body in a cave under the guard of his followers while he borrowed the body of a dying king, whose courtesans schooled him in all the arts of the Kama Sutra.[38]

Soul travel was well understood in the Sacred Earth traditions of Europe, from the earliest times until the murderous repression associated with the witch craze. One of the most fascinating accounts— less reliant than most on confessions extracted under torture—is

Carlo Ginzburg's monograph on the Benandanti, or "good-farers" of the Friuli region, who journeyed to defend the health of the community and the crops.[39]

Soul journeying is also central to Christian spirituality. In II Corinthians, Paul refers to his own soul journey when he speaks of "a man who was caught up into the third heaven, whether in the body or out of the body I know not." St. Columba, the founder of the great monastery at Iona, regularly traveled outside his body to scout developments at a distance. His talents seem to have been inherited by later clerics in the Border country. In 1068, a monk from Lindisfarne terrified the fierce Earl of Northumbria with his account of a dream journey in which he had encountered the spirit of St. Cuthbert and learned the truth about the theft of church property. A century later, Godric, a Saxon monk in Cumberland, witnessed in a conscious dream journey the murder of Thomas à Becket three hundred miles away.[40]

St. Anthony of Padua was renowned for his ability to travel outside the body and appear in two places at once. There are reports of him preaching in two churches at the same time. In Jewish tradition, the story of Elijah's chariot of fire is the model for visionary ascent to higher realms.

Among the Kabbalists, soul-flight to the higher planes was held to be the reward for long years of study and solitary meditation. A key element in Kabbalist meditation (hitboded) was the chanting and correct vibration of sacred texts. Rabbi Isaac Luria (1534–72) recited phrases from the Zohar over and over, as Eastern meditators use their mantras. He entered an altered state in which he received visitations from spiritual teachers—notably Elijah—and could travel freely outside the body. "He was also worthy for his soul to ascend every night, and troops of angels would greet him to safeguard his way, bringing him to the heavenly academies. These angels would ask him which academy he chose to visit." Sometimes he chose to visit the school of a great Kabbalist who had lived on earth before Luria's time; sometimes he went to school with the ancient prophets.[41]

Abraham ben Hananiah Yagel, a Renaissance Jew in Mantua, wrote a fascinating account of a series of soul journeys that deserves to be much better known. Yagel was an educated businessman whose deceased father appeared to him when he had been thrown into jail after a falling-out with his partner. His father not only offered him counsel and support but took him on a thrilling adventure: a heavenly journey in which he learned from other souls about the purpose of life and the transition after death. Yagel described himself taking flight from his physical body in "a garment of translucent pure air," noting, "I went out from my body as a man exiting a narrow place. A wind swept me and we went roaming to and fro together as flying birds."[42]

As Yagel's story suggests, soul-flight is not an art reserved for yogis, mystics, and shamans. The projection of consciousness by "remote viewing" or "traveling clairvoyance" has been central to the history of warfare. Go back through the old battle sagas and you will find tales of warrior shamans who shape-shifted to spy out enemy positions. The druid MacRoth, in the Irish epic the *Tain,* performs this service for his royal patron, flying over the enemy ranks in the shape of a black warbird. Native American sorcerers were employed by both the French and the English to carry out similar scouts during the French and Indian War. Celebrated military commanders have been credited with highly developed abilities to travel beyond the body. Alexander the Great is said to have gone beyond his body to achieve a god's-eye view of three of his battles. Napoleon reputedly watched the battle of Austerlitz from *behind* a hill that screened it from physical sight.

One of the most famous soul journeyers in European history was the Swedish scientist Emanuel Swedenborg (1688–1772), the son of a Lutheran bishop. He was in his fifties when powerful visitations by the spirits transformed his life; he then embarked on repeated journeys into their realms. He encountered angels who escorted him on guided tours of many kinds of heavens and hells. These experiences enabled him to construct a personal geography of the afterlife that rivals the Tibetan Book of the Dead; we will examine it in chapter 10.

It is not surprising that the dream explorer who coined the term *lucid dreaming* was another soul journeyer. Dr. Frederik van Eeden (1860–1932) was a Dutch writer, physician, and member of the British Society for Psychical Research (SPR). In 1913, he gave a lecture to the SPR in which he reported "lucid dreams" in which the dreamer retains the memory of his waking life, remained conscious, and could carry out "different acts of free volition." He observed that the phenomenon of multiple consciousness and "double memory"—of both waking and dream events—"leads almost unavoidably to the conception of a *dream-body.*" He later wrote a novel, *The Bride of the Night,* about dream travel outside the body.[43]

Frequent flier Robert Monroe asserted with reason that "a controlled out-of-body experience is the most efficient means we know to gather Knowns to create a Different Overview"—a new definition of reality.[44]

PART II

Journeying Between the Worlds

Celtic seers say that Fairyland actually exists as an invisible world within which the visible world is immersed like an island in an unexplored ocean, and that it is peopled by more species of living beings than this world, because incomparably more vast and varied in its possibilities.

W. Y. Evans-Wentz, The Fairy-Faith in Celtic Countries

When you learn that there exists a world with dimension and extension other than the world of the senses . . . a world of innumerable cities, do not hastily cry "lie," because the pilgrims of the spirit succeed in contemplating this world and they find there every object of their desire.

Sohrawardi

Night is the university of the dervish.

Sufi saying

CHAPTER 6

The Otherworld
and the Imagination

The concern of the Primary Imagination, its only concern,
is with sacred beings and events. . . . A sacred being cannot be
anticipated; it must be encountered. . . . All imaginations do not
recognize the same sacred beings or events, but every imagination
responds to those it recognizes in the same way. . . . The response of
the imagination . . . is a passion of awe.

W. H. Auden

Keys to the Third Kingdom

The Otherworld begins at the limits of the familiar world. In part 2,
we will learn to identify and use many crossing points and explore
many paths and locales within the imaginal realm, including places
we can visit and revisit for training, initiation, adventure, and healing. We will discover that the inhabitants of the imaginal world—
gods and daimons, ancestors, nature spirits, angels and aliens—are
much more diverse than those of the physical world and are quite
real in their own orders of reality. We will learn how to contact master teachers on these planes and investigate how collective and personal environments—including heavens and hells—are generated by
thought and desire.

If we call something "imaginary," we usually mean it is "made
up," something other than *real*. Yet poets and mystics have always
known that the world of imagination is a real world—a third kingdom between the physical universe and the higher realms of spirit—
and that it is possible to travel there and bring back extraordinary

gifts. The medieval Persian philosophers called this world the Alam al-Mithal, or Imaginal Realm. Kabbalists called it the Olam Hademut, which means the same thing. In both conceptions, this realm is ontologically real. "Its reality is more irrefutable and more coherent than that of the empirical world, where *reality* is perceived by the senses."[1] The soul is released into this kingdom after physical death and may go there in visionary journeys.

The Persian mystic philosophers teach that there are three kingdoms of experience: the first is our physical universe, the realm of sensory experience and space-time. There is a realm of pure Spirit, presided over by higher intelligences. Between the physical and spiritual realms is the Third Kingdom: the immense realm of soul, where cities and temples, heavens and hells, are formed by the power of active imagination, which is the faculty of soul.

Henry Corbin, the great French scholar of Islam, described the imaginal realm as "a world as ontologically real as the world of the senses and the world of the intellect, a world that requires the faculty of perception belonging to it. . . . This faculty is the imaginative power, the one we must avoid confusing with the imagination that modern man identifies with 'fantasy' and that, according to him, produces only the 'imaginary.'"[2]

The Persian philosophers also call the Alam al-Mithal the Place Outside of Where—*Na-koja-Abad*. It is "a climate outside of climates, a place outside of place, outside of where."[3] In its eastern region, in the city of Jabalqa, is the realm of the archetypal images, "preexistent to and ordered before the sensory world." In its western region, in the city of Jabarsa, is the realm of the spirits who have moved beyond physical existence, and "the forms of all works accomplished, the forms of our thoughts and desires."[4]

Sohrawardi insisted both on the objective reality of the imaginal realm and on fact that the way to grasp it is the way of experience: "pilgrims of the spirit succeed in contemplating this world and they find there every object of their desire."[5]

Medieval Kabbalists also spoke of the Olam Hademut, the imaginal world, as a separate reality. In their cosmology, it is one of *five* worlds. "There are five worlds, which in descending order are: The World of Divinity, the World of the Intellect, the World of the Souls, the World of Images, and the World of the Senses."[6]

Moses is said to have received the gift of prophecy through his visits to the imaginal realm: "Regarding Moses, to whom God showed the entire land and all of the past and future up to the last day, this occurred through the agency of the secret of the enclothement of existence before him, before his eyes, within the Olam Hademut. He who understands will understand."[7]

For the Kabbalists, as for the Persian Sufis, the imaginal world occupies an intermediate position between the physical universe and the higher spiritual realms. The later Kabbalists approach it with ambivalence. It offers great gifts, such as prophecy, and is part of the road to knowledge of the divine. But it is also the home of illusions and temptations that can captivate you and prevent you from rising to higher planes. Its gatekeeper is Sandalphon, the "master of images" and archangel of the planet Earth, who gives form to the body the soul enters at incarnation.[8]

The imaginal realm is, par excellence, the realm of soul. And it is here that true imagination, the faculty of soul, comes into its own. In this order of reality, imagination is not passing fancy, the fabricator of what is merely "made up." It is *maker* and creator. Blake understood that authentic imagination creates worlds, while reason only analyzes them. Coleridge wrote of "primary" imagination as "the living power and prime agent of all human perception" and "a repetition in the human mind of the eternal act of creation in the infinite I AM."[9] To which W. H. Auden added a provocative gloss: "The concern of the Primary Imagination, its only concern, is with sacred beings and events. . . . A sacred being cannot be anticipated; it must be encountered."[10]

To know the world of true imagination, you must go there yourself.

The House of Time

The imaginal world contains many environments created by human desire and imagination. In the following exercise, you will be introduced to a created locale in the imaginal realm that I call the House of Time. It has been built up by the active imagination of successive teachers and explorers. It has become increasingly solid and complex as more and more students and frequent fliers have visited it and probed deeper into its depths. You will find you can come here as often as you like, and that you can use this locale for a rendezvous with other dreamers.

I developed this particular visualization to offer workshop participants a variety of images they could use to embark on individual journeys to travel forward or backward in time or explore other life experiences that may be relevant to them now. I include the travel reports of members of the first group to experiment with this exercise. Most of the people who have worked with it have found it powerfully effective.

EXERCISE: JOURNEY TO THE HOUSE OF TIME

Preparation.   Relax. Follow the flow of your breathing. You will begin to see white light glowing around your body. You are robed in light. Release any negative stuff you are carrying—any fear or guilt, any stress or pain. You may see yourself dropping any negative thoughts or feelings into a deep well, or burying them in a hole in the ground.

Following the path.   You are ready to begin your journey. You are moving along a road. You are moving faster and faster. The landscape becomes a blur.

You are racing toward a tunnel. It is rather like a railroad tunnel, cut through a mountain. You speed into the tunnel. You follow its curve until you come out in another landscape.

You are now in a valley, among trees and flowers. Your path leads through a beautiful garden. You can slow down now and take in the view around you.

The River of Time.   Water is flowing beside the path. The current is strong, but the surface is smooth and clear. The surface of the water is mirror-bright.

You pause to look into it.

You see faces and scenes in the water. These are people and places from many times. They bob up, one after another. They flicker and change.

Maybe you feel drawn to one of these people, or one of these scenes.

You can return here, whenever you choose, to meet that person or enter that scene. To accomplish this, all you need to do is to step forward, into the River of Time.

When you step into the River of Time, you will find you have entered another time, perhaps another civilization or even another world.

The clocktower.   You are ready to explore further. You now walk forward along the path.

You can now see a fascinating building ahead of you. It may be a whole complex of buildings, constructed in many architectural styles. Part of the structure is Victorian red-brick; part is ultramodern.

The entrance is a doorway in a clocktower with a pointed roof.

As you approach the clocktower, a gatekeeper comes to meet you. He is the Timekeeper.

He may test your right to enter by asking you a question. The way you answer will determine whether you understand the conditions of this place.

He asks you, "What is the correct time?"

Weigh your answer carefully. There may be many acceptable answers, depending on circumstances. But there is one that is right under *all* circumstances: "The time is now."

(At different gateways, you may face different tests, and you will need to meet these alone—or by invoking the help of your personal guides.)

The Timekeeper will show you that the hands of his clock can turn backward as well as forward, at any speed you select.

The gallery of time.   The door to the House of Time is now open to you.

You walk up the steps and into a long gallery. It is filled with pictures and sculptures, masks and artifacts and icons from many cultures. Some of these objects are familiar to you. Some seem to belong to unknown civilizations, or to other worlds.

Walk through the gallery slowly. The pictures and objects you see around you offer a vast menu of possibilities for traveling through time, into the cultures and eras from which they come.

Let yourself be drawn toward an image or artifact that speaks to you strongly. Examine it closely.

You will be able to use this as a portal for a journey through time. You can walk into a picture or into the scene from which an artifact has come.

When you are ready, proceed to the end of the gallery and enter the lobby area on the far side.

The lobby. You will notice that many halls and corridors radiate from this lobby space. There are countless doors, some of them marked with dates or the names of different cultures, or with symbols. There is a library, and a video theater, and an arcade that seems to be filled with virtual-reality games.

On another visit to the House of Time, you may be able to open some of these doors or do genealogical research or play a movie about a chosen character or period in the video room. To do these things, you will need to have a clear grasp of your objective. You may find there is a price of admission. Some of the rooms that lie deeper inside the House of Time are reserved for members only. To enter them, you will need to satisfy the conditions for membership, which may involve extended education and testing.

You now realize that the House of Time is vast, possibly limitless. All periods of earth time are accessible from here, as well as dimensions that are totally removed from human conceptions of linear time.

The elevator of time. For now, it is sufficient for you to inspect the elevator you will find just ahead of you, in the center of the lobby area.

Step inside the doors.

You will notice that the control panel is different from that of a typical elevator. By turning the knobs, you can travel backward or forward through time. You may dial in a specific day, month, and year.

When you use the elevator to travel through time, you may have the sense of moving up or down. But it is just as likely you will feel you are moving sideways—or that the elevator remains motionless while the world outside you changes.

When you arrive at your chosen date, you will simply step out of the elevator and enter the scene in which you find yourself.

The return.   You are now ready to return, along the path that brought you.

As you walk back through the Gallery of Time, check to see whether you overlooked something important or need to memorize something in greater detail.

Remember to thank the gatekeeper. You may wish to ask him for advice on future travel plans.

Come back along the garden path, beside the mirror-waters.

See the white light glowing around you.

Think of your physical body and gently return to your ordinary surroundings.

Comment.   This visualization has steered you to four portals you can use to journey through time. You can return to them whenever you are ready. You may enter a scene that you glimpse in the River of Time. You may ask the Timekeeper to act as your travel agent and set the hands of his clock to the time you agree on. You may choose a picture or artifact in the gallery of time as your visual focus for a journey to another period or civilization. Or you can step into the elevator inside the House of Time and let it serve as your time machine.

Examples.   Here are some adventures reported by participants at one of my workshops when they journeyed through the portals they had chosen—after completing the preliminary visualization—with the help of shamanic drumming:

• Vicki took the elevator. She focused on entering a period where she was completely at home. She found herself swinging from the trees in a primal forest. She felt she was in animal form. Someone encouraged her to come down from the trees and act like a human. She tried it, but soon went back to swinging from the branches. She felt happier and freer as an animal.

• Rachel entered a scene she glimpsed in the river. The scene reminded her of Venice, a city that had always fascinated her, in an earlier time. She found herself in the upper level of a house on a canal. She noticed her dress was parti-colored—one side white, the other black. She saw theatrical costumes and accoutrements scattered over sofas in a grand, deserted room. She realized that other people were downstairs, at a costume party. When she joined them, a masked man in a Pulcinello-type outfit—large nose, jester's motley—approached her. She told him she did not feel this was the "real" Venice.

"This is a counterpart Venice," he informed her.

She told him she wanted the *real* Venice. She was instantly transported to it; all her senses came alive. She could smell the stink of the filth of the canals. She decided she liked the counterpart Venice better. Her escort immediately brought her back to it.

He indicated he would be available to her as a travel guide on other occasions. All she needed to do was to think of his image.

• Lonnie entered a picture in the gallery—a portrait of Joseph Brant. She found herself as a young white woman at the scene of a massacre during the American Revolution. Though she disliked Joseph Brant, he saved her from harm while other white captives were slaughtered by members of a Tory-Indian raiding party. John Johnson was there. Lonnie was consumed with hatred for him. She came back trembling with rage and fear, with many additional details (that could be checked with records of the Cherry Valley massacres).

• Rose used the elevator. She was impressed by the big round knobs, which she turned. She had the sensation of moving sideways. When the door opened, she was in the midst of a highly realistic Victorian scene. She was amused by the Timekeeper. She saw him as a frisky little old man in white stretch pants (ill-suited to his withered calves).

• Hilary found herself journeying—through the River—to a possible far future, to a time when the boundaries of sea and land on the planet have changed radically. She communicated with the fish. They showed her new lands that had once been part of the seabed. They tutored her in the vital importance of minerals beneath the sea to human and planetary survival and issued a sharp warning about human pollution and waste.

. . .

In visits by successive groups and in return trips by seasoned travelers, we have noticed an interesting phenomenon: this created locale has taken on increasing depth and solidity.

Gregg, an architect, started drawing floor plans and designs for stairwells, architraves, and vaulted ceilings after several repeat visits. The impressions of newcomers sometimes include striking alterations of scale or perspective. To Maureen, the doors at the end of the gallery were "three stories high." When Jim first entered this locale in a later workshop, he found himself struggling to get up even one of the gigantic steps. He reported feeling "like a small furry animal in danger of slipping into a crack in the stone." After a while, the proportions changed and he could move in a more familiar fashion. In the same class, Gail also had the vivid experience of shrinking and expanding in violation of physical laws. She initially held back from entering the House of Time, startled by "a flight of things like dragonflies, but each about fifteen feet long."

A radical change in perception of scale often signals the shift to another order of reality, especially for new voyagers. In the *Voyage of Malduin,* one of the great Celtic tales of the Otherworld journey, we—and the heroes—become aware that they are no longer sailing on familiar seas when they come to an island where the ants are the size of calves.

As we go on exploring the House of Time, travelers run into each other in interesting recesses that are not described or remotely suggested in the instructions. The exercise has become an interesting object lesson in how stable locales in the dreamworld are constructed by thought and imagination.

The Teaching Orders

Our ability to ascend to higher levels of knowledge is contingent on our relationship with higher intelligences. Beings of undoubtedly high evolution and intelligence occasionally communicate through passive trance channelers, as Seth communicated through Jane Roberts (who was in other modes a highly *active* and original thinker whose "aspect psychology" deserves an even larger audience). However, spiritual masters do not dwell in the lower astral planes and do not communicate in the mode of dear departed Aunty Emily, who is still worried about her dahlias. Communication with master teachers normally requires rising on the planes: ascending to a level of consciousness where active dialogue and instruction can take place. The ascent to the masters may take place in meditation, in shamanic journeying, or in conscious dreaming. It may take you to one of the "invisible schools" or "inner temples" in the imaginal realm, or to a level beyond human forms. Once you have forged a solid connection with teachers on this level—and passed the tests they will set for you—the flow of communication should become relatively smooth. It becomes a matter of slipping into a state of relaxed attention, raising your vibrations, and opening to dialogue. And of changing your life, because the side effect is transformation.

You do not open this door by banging on it or trying to force the lock. When Dante reaches the gate of purgatory, on his upward slog from the many cycles of hell, he finds that he must knock on his own breast, at the level of the heart.[11] Tap your own heart. If you are ready, you will find the door is already open, and your teacher is there.

In many traditions, it is believed that spiritually evolved people are reborn within the same orders or lineages. We may be privileged to share in the wisdom of many different traditions, and to find we have soul connections in many cultures. As we become a world society, it is highly desirable to identify and honor these connections. From early in my life, I felt a soul connection with Africa, long before I had ever set foot on that continent or even met a person of African descent. The very first time I made a shamanic journey with the drum, I walked through fire and was met by a maned lion who escorted me to a teacher who appeared as an ancient African, his skin the color of powdered ash. He reopened a path of instruction that included training in African methods of divination and spiritual healing.

If we are spiritually alive, we will also discover our links to the spirits of our ancestors and of the land we inhabit. Since I have been following a shamanic path, some of my Scottish ancestors have appeared again and again, in dreams and twilight states, eager to tutor me in "the way *we* did it"—meaning, specifically, the way of the *taibhsear,* or Scottish seer. They have called me to locations in the Hebrides and the Western Borders that I later set out to explore in physical reality. I have also been strongly influenced by dream teachers connected to the First Peoples of Australia, the land where I was born, and Northeast America, the land to which I have transplanted myself. In *Conscious Dreaming*, I described how after I moved to a farm in upstate New York, I started dreaming in a language I did not know, which proved to be an archaic form of the Mohawk language. I studied Mohawk to decipher my dream messages from a powerful woman healer and a warrior-shaman who had lived three centuries earlier, and I wrote a cycle of novels to honor these experiences. I learned (to quote an Iroquois elder) that the "great ones" of an indigenous people may stay close to the earth, to watch over it.

Yet the deepest connection, for someone who is strongly called to a spiritual path, may be to a teaching order or lineage that transcends time and place, though it may bear the stamp of a distinctive mindset. From early childhood, I have felt a strong affinity for a Mystery tradition that flourished in the Greco-Roman world. In *Conscious Dreaming*, I gave some account of my boyhood relationship with a vision guide who called himself Philemon (but did not resemble Jung's Philemon), who spoke to me in the difficult but precise vocabulary of the Neoplatonists and whose life dramas were played out in the second century of the common era in what is now Syria. Another of my dream visitors, in boyhood and in later years, was William Butler Yeats. While I was preparing this book, Yeats—that is to say, a being who *appeared* to me as Yeats—turned up, both in sleep dreams and twilight states, eager to instruct me in the methods of visualization he had developed as one of the founding members of the Hermetic Order of the Golden Dawn. He showed me a set of luminous balls that were multiplied to form points on a sphere, then blown up to the size of moons. In later research, I discovered that members of Yeats's circle—notably the actress Florence Farr—practiced a group visualization to double the middle sephiroth on the Tree of Life and project the whole image as a sphere over a selected locale, to call in spiritual energy and to serve as a psychic shield.[12] During the Second World War, British magicians such as Dion Fortune used similar techniques for psychic defense against the Nazis.[13]

That period, and that circle, have always seemed entirely familiar to me. Perhaps this is connected to my recurring dreams—which again began in early childhood—of a Royal Air Force pilot who belonged to an esoteric order before he was shot over Holland and killed by Nazi collaborators in 1941. I have always seemed to know "his" stuff, though my schoolboy Latin is not good enough to catch all of the material that sometimes comes through—in twilight states—from sources connected with the Order to which he belonged (for which I am sometimes reproached). If I had a straightforward view of reincarnation, I might grasp at an explanation that would seem either obvious or absurd to you, depending on your notions of such things. But I do not have a straightforward view of reincarnation. If you can go beyond linear time (as you go beyond it in dreaming), you may reach the conclusion that if you are connected to other life experiences, they are all happening *now*: that is to say, in a larger, more spacious present. From this perspective, time's arrow points both ways; what you do or leave undone in this life experience may impact someone in the past, as well as someone in the future, not to mention your possible counterparts in parallel worlds.

We will stay with the main theme, which is that *you* may be born with a connection with a teaching order or spiritual lineage whose adepts are accessible on higher planes—*and* may also have the ability to fold space-time and communicate across the centuries, from the past or the future.

The doors to these schools are carefully guarded. The role of the gatekeepers is not only to shut out those who come with unclean or evil motives, but to guard the unready against themselves. Signs and recognition codes may be required. There may be prescribed entry points. For example, in some Western esoteric schools, "pathworkings" based on the ascription of tarot symbols to the kabbalistic Tree of Life are used to establish entry paths to different levels of experience and contact with the inhabitants of the imaginal realm.[14] In one of my own experiments, I journeyed up to Tiphareth—the sun center and seat of the cosmic Christ—and decided to "shoot for Kether," by traveling up the long and challenging path of the High Priestess. To my astonishment and delight, I found an undoubted Priestess waiting for me in a kind of observatory at the end of my journey. I recognized her as the leader of an important Mystery school who had died half a century before. Through the curved window of the observatory, she showed me scenes of mermen—or people wearing diving suits that looked like the bodies of fish—that gave me firsthand insight into the myth of Atlantis.

Some of these "clublands" are sheathed in invisibility. When I was rereading the Tibetan Book of the Dead, I decided to investigate whether this approach actually works for someone who is not a Tibetan Buddhist. My dream journey took me to an imposing Eastern Gate, sealed by intricate locks. I did not have keys to these locks, and there was no gatekeeper in sight. What puzzled me was that beyond the gate, I saw only an empty, somewhat desolate plain. Curious, I prowled the perimeter of the area. I noticed a change in pressure, as if I had run up against an invisible barrier. It felt like pushing up against the surface of an immense rubber beach ball. I sought to adjust my sight. After a time, I was able to inspect the stupas and palaces of an immense Eastern city, inside a huge bubble that not only kept out intruders but prevented outsiders from seeing it at all.

Travels with G2

The easiest way to take you deeper into this subject is to share a more detailed report of some personal experiences. In these areas, knowledge cannot be acquired like a piece of property; it must be lived. The following excerpts from my journals cover a period of just four days in December 1995. They describe my dialogues and travels with a guide I regard as both a transpersonal being and yet as in no way alien. I think of him as an emissary from both a Western teaching order and my own Higher Self. In the later excerpts you will find me calling him G2. He declined to be identified by any personal name, which is the way of teachers connected with the Higher Self. I adopted G2 as shorthand for a couple of reasons. It suggests *intelligence* (we can skip the jokes about *military* intelligence). The G might stand for "guide." The digit might imply a second self. In the first installment, you will learn how G2 introduced himself in a way that was guaranteed to get my fullest intention. In subsequent episodes, you will read about some of the journeys on which he escorted me. These travels greatly expanded my understanding of the geography of nonordinary reality—including afterlife locales—and inspired much of my subsequent research and teaching work.

G2 INTRODUCES HIMSELF
(DECEMBER 10, 1995, 12:00–12:30 A.M.)

When I lay down, I resolved simply to open myself to higher guidance. I was stunned by what came through. Instantly, I began to receive a flow of instruction and counsel from an intelligence that seemed both entirely familiar and transpersonal. The opening of these communications is indelible in my mind.

"YHVH."

In my mind, the syllables of the "unpronounceable" Hebrew name of God were reverberated. Yod. Heh. Vau. Heh. Then a higher intelligence began to speak to my mind:

"It is time for you to understand the Tetragrammaton. Through correct toning, this name of power—held unspeakable by Orthodox Jews for reasons the Kabbalists understand—can call many things into manifestation. It is the most powerful formula of evocation for bringing sacred energies into manifestation on the physical plane that we have in the Western tradition."

I was given the keys for toning the Tetragrammaton, including the unwritten vowels, and enjoined to guard this knowledge—and to use it.

"Do not forget, in all your wanderings, that you come from an Order of the Western way and that its methods, tested and proven by adepts across the centuries, are your inheritance."

I was given signs, including the image of an ibis-headed Thoth wearing a curious lunar headdress. Some of these were symbols that had been shown to me in dreams and visions in early childhood. I was told, "Remember Abydos."

I felt completely at home with the intelligence that was communicating with me. Yet though it was familiar, I did not associate it with a personal name, and I had no visual image of the source. I asked for a name, a personal image. This was declined. I was told, "You may think of me as Adeptus Exemptus. But I have long declined the semblance of human form, and my thought processes are not confined to those of the human mind. However, I retain nostalgia and warm affection for human seekers, which is why I was chosen to communicate with you."

My guide told me that he had come, with the full endorsement of the Order, to help me with *Dreamgates*. I was urged to include practical guidance on psychopomp work: "The book should include tutorials and travel maps that can be used by lost or earthbound souls who are able to tune in to the thoughts and words of the living."

I was promised help with my fieldwork: "We will arrange a guided tour for you of the circles of the astral, in the sublunary sphere and beyond. We will show you portals you have not consciously explored, although you have used them in 'dreamless' sleep and in other life experiences. You will be able to describe the access to other life systems and the challenges of interpreting communications from entities whose thought processes move according to entirely different processes than the human. You had some experience in this area in your journey to Kamartet—which is *not* its name."

I had been conducting some new experiments in out-of-body travel. My guide insisted on clarifying the limitations of this approach:

"The *technique* of astral projection is entirely secondary. *Mind is never confined to the physical*. The brain is its instrument for attuning to the physical environment, as are the outer senses, and the transceiver through which you will either succeed or fail in capturing messages from other dimensions. But Mind itself is not contained by the brain and body; rather, the brain and body are contained by Mind, by consciousness. The experience of leaving the body in a quasi-physical way is a dramatic reminder of this reality. But exercises that focus on the transition to an out-of-body state can divert energy and attention from the primary purpose: access to higher levels of consciousness."

A number of visualization and mind-expansion exercises were then suggested that I have included in this book, after trying them out in my workshops. I interrupted my dialogue to go downstairs and type up my notes before I found them completely illegible. There was no sign-off. I felt that the connection remained open. This was confirmed by my dreams—which included a tour of the Oseirion at Abydos, or its astral counterpart—and by the renewed encounter with G2 the following night.

VISIT TO AN INVISIBLE SCHOOL
(DECEMBER 10–11, 1995)

Communication was renewed as soon as I lay down around 11:30 P.M.

"Prepare yourself for takeoff."

I let my consciousness travel through a tunnel that opened before me. I found myself moving smoothly and rapidly through a deep mist that opened to show a kind of island city with soaring spires. A mountain island, with an enormous church or temple.

What ensued was a tour of an "invisible school" and an encounter with a possible Albrecht Dürer that is fully described in chapter 8.

After a few hours' sleep, shortly before dawn, I had renewed contact with G2.

"Step through the portal."

A kind of trapdoor opened in inner space. I perceived myself flowing smoothly into a subtler dimension.

"Now we can proceed with the charging of the energy body."

I raised my arms above my head, in my second body. I was now holding a cup. An immense stream of light energy poured into it and through it, through the crown of my head. It streamed through my second body. A little disturbed by all the power I saw flooding into my second self, I returned to my physical body and soon drifted off to sleep. I woke two hours later feeling vastly restored, my sinuses clear after a week of blockage.

CLEANSING (DECEMBER 11–12, 1995)

I went to bed before midnight and rolled onto my left side. G2 immediately made his presence known by instructing me to lie on my back.

When I did so, I saw a trapdoor open to my inner sight. I stepped through it and was aware of the massive, *physical* presence of furniture. I realized I had stepped into my own bedroom, moving toward the dresser between the windows. I took this as a message to apply my attention to physical reality—starting with my renewed symptoms of cold and fever.

I realized I needed to break the fever I had felt rising since taking a shower a couple of hours before. I called up images of extreme heat and felt my body temperature rise until I was radiating hot, dry air. I wanted this to break in a sweat and called up memories of when I had sweated profusely—especially when sweating had been part of recovery from illness—of a steamy summer walk from the zoo to the French Quarter in New Orleans; of sweating under an inhalation blanket during childhood illness; of stepping off a plane in Bangkok; of suffering in prickly woolen trousers and turtleneck in front of a fierce woodstove in a farmhouse.

My wife groaned and woke. She told me she felt she was being "boiled in a stockpot." She thought I had turned the radiators up to full blast.

With more visualizations and "fire-breathing," I finally produced a light sweat. When Marcia returned upstairs, I asked her to pile blankets and covers on top of me. As the flow of sweat increased, I moved from thoughts of native sweat lodges and Nordic saunas to powerful imagery of an Iroquois "secondary burial."

Second Burial, Second Birth

I am a corpse, folded in the blanket of Mother Earth. My body is deliquescing, turning to jelly and liquid. I am sloughing off everything perishable. I am releasing all of the poisons I have ingested. When this process is complete, my bones will be picked from the earth and rinsed clean. They will be sowed in a new place, to give birth to new life.

These images are compounded with a strong sense of a powerful life force rising and renewing itself, an enormous serpent shedding its skin.

The fever was gone. I felt purged and renewed. I found myself traveling to a cavern. Among the shadows, I saw the faces of old adversaries, people who had caused me great pain. Part of me wanted to attack them.

"State your intention," G2 instructed.

"I wish to be servant and teacher for the Light," I responded. I opened my heart and saw light stream from it, and from the palms of my hands. I shared this light with my adversaries, forgiving them and asking their forgiveness.

I realized I was now standing within an immense pillar of light, a white flame that rose above the roof of the cavern. And that many people who belonged to the Light or were drawn to it had rallied to this place, to stand with me.

I was filled with images of the Man in the Tree, the sacrificed god. Of Osiris, dismembered and reassembled by the Great Goddess, in a primal act of soul retrieval. Of the grace and love of Jesus Christ, and the necessity of centering all my endeavors—human and spiritual—on the realization of the Christ consciousness.

I sensed G2 drawing nearer. I saw him as a point of light. "So now you are ready to sign into the collective belief systems?" he asked with wry amusement.

He encouraged me to "aim for Tiphareth"—the cosmic Christ center on the Tree of Life—and to meditate and work with the symbol of the Hanged Man.

I said the Lord's Prayer. I felt deeply cleansed.

TO THE HEBRIDES (DECEMBER 12–13, 1995)

I was in vastly improved spirits the next day, not at all tired, despite getting only an hour or so's sleep, and feeling much fitter physically.

I watched the TV-movie version of *Saved by the Light,* the account of the near-death experience of Dannion Brinkley, who is depicted as an unpleasant bully and philanderer before he was struck by lightning and his twenty-eight minutes without vital signs gave him an insight into how all of us are born to realize ourselves as "powerful spiritual beings" and to act out of love. The bequest of his NDE included considerable psychic gifts. The main interest of the movie for me was its portrayal of the trials of reentry. First, he has to explain his experience to himself and those around him. Second, he wants to make amends for the wrongs he's done—but his community isn't willing to forgive and let him change. Even his wife has difficulty allowing him to change. He becomes cynical and defeatist. He applies his newfound psychic gifts to making a packet of money at the track and in gambling halls, goes back to hard drinking and rough company. It's only when he gets out of his community—on the lecture circuit with Raymond Moody—and discovers that there are people who have shared his experiences all over and *people who need him* that he begins to conquer his despair.

I empathized greatly with Brinkley. I, too, had been through the experience of a tough reentry: with the problems associated with trying to mend the past; with backsliding and self-defeat and despair; with the tremendous need most of us have to be reassured—by those who have been there—that our nonordinary experiences are real and valid and that physical death is a homecoming.

I felt a deepening urgency in my work: in the effort to remind people that the reality of other worlds can be confirmed and explored right now, through the visionary doorway, and that this does not require the physical extremity of an NDE.

As soon as I lay down that night, G2 was back, to help me understand another aspect of this work.

G2: There is another to whom I would like to introduce you.

ROBERT: Fine.

G2: Her name is Morag. She comes from the isle of Skye. She also lived in Lewis. She has information of a specific kind about scrying in the spirit vision among the Scots.

ROBERT: I would like to meet her.

G2: I shall let Morag speak for herself. You may wish to shift out of your present physical focus to maximize the clarity of this encounter.

I shifted focus and found myself gliding into dense, light gray fog. It cleared and I was sailing over a high valley set among rocky hills, near the sea. Colors began to emerge from the prevailing gray—violets and purples. I could see the heather.

"Hello, Robert," a woman's voice greeted me.

"Where are you?" I could not see her at first.

"Look to your south."

My attention shifted to a cliff and the rocky beach below it. A standing stone, leaning at a steep angle, rose above the waves. Near it was a second standing stone. It had a hole in the middle, large enough for a person to crawl—or fly—through. With this vision came the impression of a woman with streaming reddish hair whose kinks and curls reminded me of seaweed. She was swooping back and forth through the hole in the stone.

She said something about the Stone Man and the Holy Man. I received the image of a stone with a hole that was actually shaped like a man and the impression of a man's name, something like Connor.

I received clearer images of the woman. I was struck by the strength of her connection with the sea. Her jewelry consisted of shells and ropes of seaweed or sea grass.

She told me, "My father was a sailor and a fisherman."

"I am told you wish to speak to me of scrying."

"Look there. Into the opening of the Holy Man. What do you see?"

I looked through the hole in the stone. Images flashed before my eyes of a whole historical pageant: the rise and fall of lords and kings of Scotland. Gentlemen in ruffs. Slaughter and betrayal.

Morag was pleased with my description of these images.

She told me, "You share the gift of my kind."

She issued a warning: "Never believe that the powers of darkness are mere fictions. They hunt such as you—such as have the gift—to win them or to wound them.

"For this reason, it would be harmful to anyone such as yourself to release the knowledge of the spirit sight before you are clear in your purpose. I believe you are now prepared.

"Take a moment to adjust your focus."

The scene shifted. I was now looking at a low stone cottage with a thatched roof and a stone barn or stable attached.

Morag showed me two methods of scrying that she practiced.

The first was divination by fire.

The second was to examine the patterns of dried herbs or seeds scattered in a pot or cauldron of water that she retrieved from a shelf built into stones behind the fireplace, which was open on three sides. The circle of water was mentally divided into sections to assist the reading. Thus the left half represented everything female; the right side, everything male.

. . .

My visit with the woman of the sea led me down fascinating avenues of research that deepened my sense of connection with my Scottish ancestors. I was intrigued to discover that Skye and Lewis—Morag's islands—figure prominently in early accounts of Scottish seership, notably Martin Martin's *Description of the Western Islands of Scotland,* published in 1703.

The most famous of the island seers was Kenneth Mackenzie, whose Gaelic name is Coinneach, pronounced "Connor." Kenneth's powers as a *taibhsear* (taisher)—a person able to see true visions, including visions of spirits and doubles, or "fetches"—was attributed to his possession of an extraordinary stone. In some accounts, his vision stone had a hole through the middle, through which he would peer to look into the future and the spirit worlds. There are rival stories about how he came across the stone. In one, he found it lying on his chest after falling asleep on a "fairy hill." In another, it was his mother, out on the hills after midnight—watching the cattle—who was told where to find the stone by the spirit of a dead woman.[15]

G2 has introduced me to other personalities, in different times and in different dimensions. He accompanied me in my exploration of an ancient Mystery initiation at the Cave of Trophonius, as described in the next chapter.

CHAPTER 7

Journeys of Initiation

I know that I hung on the windswept tree for nine full
nights . . . offering myself to myself.

Odin, in the Elder Edda

Personal Rites of Passage

In dreams and twilight states, we are called to a deeper life. Training
and initiation, as well as direct experience of the sacred, lie beyond
the dreamgates.

True initiation involves both ordeal and ecstasy. "The majority of
initiatory ordeals more or less clearly imply a ritual death followed
by resurrection or a new birth," commented the great religious historian Mircea Eliade. "The novice emerges from his ordeal endowed
with a totally different being from that which he possessed before his
initiation; he has become *another*."[1] The initiate is a *made* man or
woman.

The hunger for transcendence, through a primal, direct encounter
with the sacred, leads people down strange and dangerous byways:
into experiments with hallucinogenic drugs, into dubious cults and
ersatz Nativism. Yet the *authentic* call to initiation continues to res-
onate in our dreams. And through the dreamgates, it can be followed
to a genuine consummation. Arguably, it can hardly be pursued in
any other way since—whatever the externals of ceremony and culture—true spiritual initiation and apprenticeship always take place
on the inner planes, in a deeper order of reality.

Even in societies where Mystery initiation was regarded as central
to human fulfillment, and its gates and secrets were closely guarded,

the validity of an individual dream calling and initiation was honored. There is a fascinating story about this from the Hellenistic world, preserved by Sopatros, a teacher of rhetoric. A man dreamed he had attended the *epopteia,* the crowning revelation of the Eleusinian Mysteries. He recounted the secret rituals of the Telesterion in vivid and accurate detail to an initiate of the Greater Mysteries. But in ordinary reality, the dreamer was not a "made man." The initiate to whom he told his dream was shocked that he was speaking openly about things he had no right to know and denounced him for sacrilege. He was dragged into court, where his accusers demanded the death penalty. However, the defense argued successfully that the gods themselves had played the part of the hierophant in his dream. His dream of initiation was recognized as true initiation; the dreamer would now be respected as an *epoptes*—one who had "seen" and gone through the sacred fire.[2]

Contemporary dreamers who have never heard of Eleusis have dreams of the same quality.

At the winter solstice, just after her twelfth birthday, Rebecca had a powerful dream that carried her deep into the Otherworld. In her dream, she was invited to enter an immense hall. It was filled with robed figures she described as "wizards." They came from many races and traditions; she recognized a "Merlin" character among a Celtic contingent. A woman robed in white sat enthroned above the throng. She beckoned to Rebecca to approach her. The male wizards ignored Rebecca except for a forbidding figure who moved to block her path. He challenged her to pass a test. Only when she had passed the test was she allowed to ascend the steps to the throne. "The High Priestess was slim and dark-haired. She seemed to be in her late twenties. She spoke to me by thought rather than words. She appeared outwardly solemn as she held court over all the male wizards, but kept cracking mental jokes that only the adepts caught."

The High Priestess wore a striking pendant, which I asked Rebecca to draw for me. Her drawing shows an equal-armed cross, set within a circle. Crossed staves behind it make the pattern of a diagonal cross within a much larger circle, bordered by a two-headed serpent. The body of the serpent is engraved with writing in Greek characters. There are more inscriptions on scrolls that flank the central cross, which has four crystals in its setting. The wizard who challenged Rebecca wore a simpler version of the same pendant.

For a girl approaching puberty, this dream might carry many levels of meaning. But we spent no time in dream analysis. We celebrated the sense of strength and magic and possibility that Rebecca had drawn from it. She reveled in her special dream relationship with the High Priestess seated above all those powerful men. When I asked Rebecca to sum up the feeling of the dream, she said with little hesitation, "I am coming into my power."

Nearly three years later, in another spontaneous sleep dream, Rebecca reentered the great hall where she had encountered the High Priestess:

This time everything is different. Instead of everyone ignoring me, all the high priests from all the worlds bow down to me and hold out their arms to me.

The High Priestess stands and holds out her arms. She says, "Come, let me show you my mind." Only she does not exactly say it; she suggests it.

She takes my hand. From her forehead a bright light emerges, and in the bright light I see a gate. I walk toward this gate. When I pass through it, I encounter three beings. The first is a bird-headed man who has given me guidance before. He shows me what happens to people who sell out their values in life. The second is a woman I know to be an immortal. She wears a crowned helmet and carries a shield and spear. She tells me, "We are one and the same." The third is a man I do not know. I have the feeling this man will be important in my future life.

When I finish observing this man, I see another gate to walk through. I travel in this way until the bright light dims and all I can see are the eyes of the High Priestess, shining against a dark rectangle that may be a mask.

These dream experiences accompanied Rebecca's passage from girlhood into womanhood. In her outer life, no sacred ritual was conducted to mark this passage. But she was called through the dreamgates, into a larger life.

The Cave Initiation

Initiation often involves an underworld journey, a descent into the realms of Earth and Death and the ancestors.[3] But the itinerary is not confined to subterranean locales.

The sacred stories of both East and West contain fascinating, seemingly contradictory accounts of "cave heavens." You go down through an opening in the earth, and somehow you come out among stars and planets. Vedic literature describes a parallel reality called the Bila-svarga, or "subterranean heaven." It contains seven worlds, the counterparts of planets in the solar system, some of extraordinary beauty. The journey into this realm begins with descent into a cave where it is possible to cross rapidly into another dimension.[4]

Plutarch (who knew what he was talking about) describes a Mystery initiation at the Cave of Trophonius in ancient Boeotia in which the candidate, after lowering himself through a hole in the ground into total darkness, experienced a stunning shift in consciousness that released his soul from his body and set him sailing among the stars. Freed from the body, his soul expands and flows like a sail, among the "islands" of stars in the ocean of ether—each one presided over by a god except for the moon, which is inhabited by "Epichthonian daimons." He stays in the underworld two nights and a day. He receives much information from an invisible spirit about the afterworld and the beings who inhabit it. He is instructed on the relationship between higher and lower self—on how gross appetites pull people down, and how those few who listen carefully to their eudaimon ("good daimon") may become daimons themselves, playing the role of guardian angels to others.[5]

Though the Cave of Trophonius is named after a dead hero—renowned both as an architect and a thief[6]—the site is clearly in the realm of the Goddess. The cave is located beside a river named Herkyna, after a companion of Persephone's. The girl was said to be playing beside the waters when a goose fell from her hands and flew into a cave where it hid under a stone. Persephone brought it back, and water burst from the place under the stone from which she retrieved it. The temple of Herkyna by the river has a statue of a maiden with a goose in her hands. In the cave where the river has its source are statues with serpents coiled around their scepters.

The *kathodos,* or underworld descent, to the Cave of Trophonius was a true initiation ritual, requiring a *literal* experience of death and rebirth. The candidate goes into the earth dressed like a sacrificial victim, after eating the flesh and blood of sacrificed animals. He must drink from the waters of Lethe and of Memory, as souls do on the way to the afterlife or a new incarnation. He is going into the womb of the Mother—that this is *her* precinct is recalled by associations with Demeter and Persephone, and by the story that the oracle was discovered by a messenger who followed a swarm of bees. The place is one of the literal portals to the Otherworld: the sources of the river Herkyna are the waters of Lethe and Mnemosyne. The twenty-four-foot-long shaft the candidate descends (by a narrow ladder, like that of a Pueblo kiva) is man-made. However, the cavity is built in the shape of a pot-shaped bread oven, a clear image of the womb.

To enter the cave is to enter the womb of Earth, deep in the body of the Goddess. Here you are folded in a primal body-mind. Here intelligences that live beyond and before Time may speak to you.

You may come here in one of two ways:

By following the path of ritual and sacrifice prescribed by the priests.

Or by stealth, by cunning, by theft—the way of the philosopher Apollonius and of Trophonius himself, who is said to have burglarized a treasury he built for a king.

Under normal circumstances, it is hard to gain entry to this realm of direct experience. There is a long period of ritual preparation in the house of a mysterious "Good Genius" *(eudaimon)*—a time of cold baths, dreaming, and of gorging on animal flesh, the product of many no doubt expensive sacrifices to a panoply of gods and heroes. The priests are irrelevant to the direct encounter with the numinous in the womb of Earth, but they try—like most priesthoods—to control and profit. They have prescribed the succession of costly sacrifices. They claim to be able to read the will of the gods in the entrails of the slaughtered beasts. And the viscera will tell you, as likely as not, that it is going to cost you more.

When you have paid off the priests, you will be brought by night to the river, ritually bathed, and anointed with oil.

The priests will then conduct you to the sources of the river. You must drink first from the waters of Lethe (Forgetfulness), so you will forget your former self and all the things that have been holding you back. Now you will drink from the waters of Mnemosyne (Memory) so you will remember everything you see in your descent.

You are now ready to look at a secret statue of Trophonius, allegedly made by Daedalus. You may be shocked to find that the hero looks less like a man than like a snake—*and* a god.

You are now robed like a sacrificial victim and conducted to the top of the mound. The entrance is surrounded by a circular stone wall, with doors set between bronze pillars, and a set of iron spikes. No steps lead down into the tunnel. You will be given a narrow, light ladder several times your own height. The darkness is waiting for you.

Despite the priests, what lies ahead is a firsthand encounter with the sacred. You must now brave up to your fears. How long is the drop? Are there snakes down there? How do I get out anyway? The knowledge imparted inside the cave extends to the soul's journey between lives and the nature of reality itself. While the body lies entombed in the earth, the soul is released, as the dead person's soul is released. The masters of this Mystery tradition want to see the soul take flight from the crown of the head, through the fontanel, rather than from one of the lower centers.

What is the source of the wisdom that it is imparted? In different versions, the "invisible voice" heard inside the cave is that of a demigod such as Asklepios or Trophonius himself, who is said to have been a son of Apollo as well as the builder of Apollo's celebrated shrine at Delphi. The guide who will reveal himself in the depths of the cave and serve as escort on journeys to other realms is a daimon, a "genius" or spiritual mentor whose style and intelligence are likely to be closely related to those of the candidate. Plutarch (whose brother was a priest of Trophonius) says that the home of these beings is the moon. They are no saints. Some of them seem to be rather like Al, the stogie-chomping guide in *Quantum Leap*. For some, advising humans is part of their retraining or probation. If they screw up, they are punished—they can be pulled down into Hades or pushed back to earth to live out another life.[7]

After many hours—perhaps as long as two or three days—you will return to the surface world. You will probably be shaky and disoriented. You will need time to readjust to the daylight world. Now the priests of the shrine will seat you on the Throne of memory, near the sanctuary. They will question you closely about everything you have seen and experienced. They will encourage you to record your impressions on a wooden tablet to be kept in the library of the sanctuary. You will then be escorted to the temple of the good daimon to recover.

This is the conventional path—through sacrifice, purification and discipline—to initiation. But the Trickster is always at play when authentic shamans appear, and at the Cave of Trophonius shamanic types flout the rules. Philostratus preserves the story of a visit to the sanctuary by Apollonius of Tyana, a celebrated shaman-philosopher who rivaled Jesus in popularity a century after the birth of Christ. Apollonius told the priests, "I wish to descend into the cave in the interests of philosophy." The priests refused to let him in, telling the people they would not allow a "wizard" to enter the sanctuary. Apollonius went despite the priests. Under cover of dark, he and his companions pulled down part of the security wall. He went down the shaft in his regular clothes—his "philosopher's mantle"—instead of the prescribed shroud. He vanished for seven days, then reappeared miles away, at Aulis, with a book in which he had recorded the daimon's responses to his questions. This book distilled the teachings of the "golden chain" of the Pythagorean shaman-philosophers.[8]

The catch is that, one way or another, you will only prosper in this underworld journey if you come *prepared*—through ritual and sacrifice, or through a whole life's commitment to the path of soul. You should come here only when you have a sufficiently powerful *purpose*. The cave was first discovered—and Trophonius first spoke to the living—when the community faced a shared disaster: two years of ruinous drought. Apollonius came for confirmation of the nature of multidimensional reality.

The Cave of Trophonius may no longer be accessible in physical reality. But you can go there in dreaming, which is how I first learned about what may have happened there. A swarm of bees first guided me, in a visionary journey, to a site of Mystery initiation in ancient Greece. My dream steered my subsequent digging in Plutarch and Pausanias for confirmation of what I had *seen*.

Similar dreams may be plucking at you. A woman with no classical education dreamed she was at a banquet that reminded her of the

Last Supper, except that the feasters at the table were wearing curious masks. One of them had the face of a raven, another wore a veil, yet another a Roman helmet. Her own head was covered by a lion mask fashioned from a canvaslike material, possibly oiled paper. As I listened to her, I realized she was describing, *as if from the inside,* a communion rite of the Mithraic mysteries, whose initiates donned masks and headgear of this type according to their grades.[9]

The people of Hybla Geleatis, on the slopes of Mount Etna, in ancient Sicily, believed that the mouth of the volcano was not only a door to the underworld, but the gateway of dreams. On the southern flank of Etna, they operated a popular dream oracle. In their Mystery initiations, candidates lowered their bodies into bubbling pools of mud and water on the edge of the volcano, releasing their souls for the fearful descent to the realms of the dead. They were required to go through the dark fire at the earth's core and to confront all the terrors of the netherworld. Those who completed this dangerous passage earned the right of rebirth. Newborn, in a body of light, the initiate saw himself (or herself) shooting up into the heavens on the lightninglike flames of the volcano, said by the poets to "lick the stars." The shaman-philosopher Empedocles was reputed to have taken his leave of the earth in this way, diving into the crater of Etna before flying up to the celestial realms in a fireburst of lights.[10]

The way up is the way down, the way in is the way out. Shamans draw two-dimensional maps, hinting at a multidimensional reality. In shamanic workshops, you will be encouraged to journey to the Lower, the Middle, or the Upper World. You may find your experiences as an active dreamer cannot always be ascribed to such simple categories. To explain this is like trying to make you *see* a corner of your room in which five, six, seven, or more planes are set at right angles to each other. The stories of the "cave heavens," like Vedic tales of worlds contained within a rock, a pearl, or a pebble, are meant to help you slip into an understanding of hyperspace from which the linear mind flees in horror. When the Vedic writers describe Earth and the planetary spheres above and below it as flat disks, they should not be confused with "flat-earthers." As anyone who has used mandalas in meditation will know, it is easier to enter hyperspace through a 2-D image than a 3-D model.

Having said that, I want to share a personal account of an Upper World journey in search of a spiritual teacher. I made this journey with the support of a drumming circle, on top of a mountain in the Berkshires. We began by creating a sacred space and calling on spiritual allies. My visual gateway was the image of a place of ascent: my special tree. My intention was to contact a spiritual guide on the highest plane that was open to me at that time.

A PERSONAL JOURNEY: ASCENT TO THE MASTERS

The heartbeat of the drum helped me to shift consciousness quickly and smoothly. I was conscious of hovering above my physical body, then of moving into a different landscape, leaving the circle behind.

I journeyed to my Dreaming Oak. At the moment I reached it, a whirlwind of light appeared in the sky, inviting me up.

I traveled upward through a thin layer of cloud that stretched and opened like a membrane between this and the next level. I had strongly tactile sensations, of billowing sheets in the wind. I observed no life on this or the second level, perhaps because I was focused on my *intention:* to reach an authentic spiritual teacher.

On the third level, I was lost in fog until a white bird carried me up, turning and wheeling to find a way. We traveled a great distance, apparently toward the west, across an empty, drifting cloud-plane.

On the fourth level, I saw an immense tree with all kinds of fruit hanging from its branches. A welcome splash of green was around it, refreshing after the deserts of cloud and fog. I wondered if this was the Tree of Life. I did not linger because an inner voice kept urging, *Higher. Your path is higher.*

I encountered the lures and deceptions of roads and rivers that twisted and forked and turned downward. I had to get off several of these paths to find a way up. Sometimes the white bird helped me. Sometimes I had to swim against the stream or struggle up cliffs.

At a higher level—the fifth?—I encountered an ambiguous figure. He seemed more demonic than human, and his form seemed metallic. Bits and pieces flew off him, constantly changing shape. I went past him.

On the next level—the sixth?—shadow warriors barred my path. In profile, they looked rather like kachinas, with strange, elongated hats that jutted out at the sides, limbs whirling like scythes. I was afraid of them, but summoned my courage and rushed past. I saw a temple. A beautiful white goddess emerged from a crowd of acolytes. I asked if she was my teacher but received no response. I saw that she is terror as well as beauty. She is also Kali, with her whirling arms, her crone's face, her necklace of severed heads. I realized now that the warrior-guards were *her* shadows.

I journeyed on, confused by more false paths, zigzags, changes of direction—sustained by the inner voice that kept urging me higher.

Through the fog, I saw islands dotted in a cold sea. The Hebrides? The Islands of the Blessed? I was lost among them for a time.

The bird powers came to carry me higher. I now had the sensation that all birds were my helpers—even birds of ill omen, the vulture, the raven. I saw all the bird tribes, turning together. My closest ally among them was immense. I thought of him as Storm Bird.

To ascend to higher levels, I was obliged to change form. I became the lightning.

On the highest level I reached, I found a whole pantheon of superior beings. Some were familiar to me as gods and goddesses of various traditions. Above and beyond them was a being I could not see distinctly, let alone describe. To look at this being directly was like staring into the darkness at the heart of the sun. It ceaselessly whirled and projected god-forms from within itself.

Winged powers escorted me on a majestic flight across a green world as fresh and beautiful as the first dawn. I noticed I had acquired a new body, neither human nor bird yet recalling both these forms. I reveled in the joy and power of flight, in this excellent company.

There was a disturbance far away, far below me. I did not recognize it as the drummers sounding the recall. I did not wish to return to my body.

I noticed I had something in my hand. It was a skull, yet my hand enclosed it like a small pebble. I realized that in my new body, I must have grown to enormous size. I wondered if I could—if I dared—bring the skull back with me.

In another world, the drums were calling me back.

Now I saw the skull in the talons of Storm Bird. His wings shadowed mountains.

I saw a body in those mighty talons. A lifeless corpse. I recognized my own form. Was this my dreambody, my doppelgänger? The thing I left behind when I became the lightning?

I was a disembodied witness as the great bird carried my body down and down through the billowing sheets of cloud. He laid it gently at the foot of the tree.

My awareness reentered this vehicle. But I was still out of my physical body, and rather unwilling to return to it.

I was drawn to a passage to the underworld that I know in ordinary reality: it opens behind a waterfall in a limestone gorge in the Mohawk Valley. But I felt increasing pressure from the people around me in the shamanic circle. Reluctantly, I spread my wings and flew back to my physical body.

Meeting Your Spiritual Guides

Spiritual guides and teachers show themselves in the forms we are open to seeing. Dionysius the Areopagite, the Greek mystical philosopher whose description of the nine orders of angels is still the foundation of conventional angelology, observed that the visions we receive are "adapted to the nature of the seer." Dion Fortune put it even more bluntly in *The Cosmic Doctrine:* "The Masters as you picture them are all 'imagination.' Note well that I did not say that the Masters were imagination. I said, 'The Masters as you picture them.'"[11]

The masks are changeable. The energies behind them are real.

When we are moving toward a greater spiritual depth in our lives, at a time of spiritual emergence (which often involves an emergency; the words are related) we rediscover our genuine spiritual guides and protectors and the ways in which we are called to honor the unseen energies that support our lives. This is a profoundly transformative experience. It can take many forms. Perhaps you are ready for a dialogue with your own spiritual teachers. In all likelihood, they have already been speaking to you in dreams, whether or not you remember. Perhaps you would like to confirm contacts you have already made on the inner planes, or to explore further dimensions of possibility. I want to share some simple exercises I have found helpful in opening communication with spiritual guides on a higher level.

PREPARATION: CLEARING A SPACE

Light a candle. Sit comfortably and relax for a while, focusing your attention on the flame. You may also wish to burn incense—frankincense is best for invoking higher energies—and place a bowl of salt-water nearby. (Salted water is excellent for cleansing and will naturally absorb lower energies.)

Now go with your breathing. Release any negative thoughts or feelings—any stress or tension, guilt or anxiety—as you breathe out. See light energy flowing through you as you breathe in. Let it stream through your whole body. Let it flow out through the soles of your feet and rise up your back to the crown of your head. Let the light stream through you and around you, so you are filled with the light and shielded by the light.

You need to state your intention clearly.

You may want to use the following invocation, or rephrase it in your own words:

In the presence of earth and air, fire and water
In the presence of the unseen
I come in a sacred and loving way
To seek counsel from my true spiritual guides
To align myself with my Higher Self
To remember who I am and what I may become.

PATHWORKING: EXPLORING YOUR INNER TEMPLE

You may find it helpful to begin with a guided visualization, similar to the journey to the House of Time. This simple pathworking will help you build up a "place of your own" in the imaginal realm. It will also help you to recognize spiritual symbols that are relevant to you now, and to open paths for the journey that will follow.

1. Go to your special place, perhaps a tree or a place in nature you love. Be with it for a while. Then picture yourself moving at increasing speed, into a narrow valley between high mountain walls.

2. The valley opens out into gardens. The path is lined with reflecting pools. The sun and moon shine together in the sky.

3.   The path is leading you to a temple whose entrance is a simple arch, with twin pillars. A gatekeeper is waiting for you on the steps. He will permit you to enter; the time is right for you.

4.   You enter the outer court of the temple. Now you are moving through a long hallway. It is lined with statues and images from many religious traditions. Notice the images that seem to speak to you.

5.   Now you are entering the inner court of the temple. You walk up more steps into an immense circular room, suffused with golden light. The floor of this room is tiled in a checkerboard pattern of black and white. Pay close attention to anything you see in this room—symbols, furnishings, other people.

6.   Directly across the room from you is an alcove screened by a veil. Behind it a Lady waits for you. You may advance toward her. Perhaps she will allow you to look behind the veil. Be open to the unexpected! You may ask any questions you are carrying with you. Perhaps she will give you a gift. Perhaps she will ask you to undertake a task. Perhaps she will even tell you your spiritual name.

7.   When you are ready, bid farewell to the Lady with respect and look upward. A round opening is in the roof of the chamber, an oculus. Through it, you can see the sun, the moon, and the stars. Choose the path you would take if you were able to fly upward, into the sky. You can go up onto the roof to see better, if you choose. Maybe you feel your path leads another way, back down into the earth. Trust your feelings.

8.   Now you are ready to return. Don't forget to thank the gatekeeper, and ask him for a sign or a key you can use to come back to this place. Come back to your special place, your point of departure.

9.   Take a moment to ground yourself. Then note down your experiences.

JOURNEY EXERCISE: ASCENT TO YOUR GUIDE

You are now prepared for a *big* experience, one that will be fully your own. Shamans call this exercise an Upper World journey; in the Western Mystery schools, it is called rising on the planes. The use of shamanic drumming—a tape, if you are attempting this without a partner—will accelerate and deepen your experiences. However, as long as you are able to put yourself into a relaxed meditative state, you can perform this exercise without drumming.

1.   Choose your means of ascent. Visualize a place from which you can journey upward, through the sky. You may picture a mountaintop or the upper branches of a tree or a ladder. You may see yourself borne aloft by a bird or a whirlwind. You may even choose to put yourself inside an elevator (preferably glass-sided) that can carry you up to a space without walls.

2.   Go upward. Focus on your intention of meeting a higher spiritual guide. You may pass through many cloudlike layers, through dimensions that seem to be deserted or filled with beings that have nothing to communicate to you. If you are able to speak to the beings you encounter, ask if one of them is your guide.

3.   Keep climbing until you find a personality that responds. To pass beyond a certain level, you may find you have to change form. You may become fire or lightning.

4.   When you find your teacher, you should ask for some form of identification, which may be a symbol rather than a name. You may ask for counsel on any issues that you have. You should ask for a means by which you can resume communication.

5.   You are ready to return. If you are in a drumming circle, this will be signaled by sharp, peremptory fourfold beats on the drum. Come back to your point of departure.

6.   Take some time to ground yourself. Make notes of your experiences and a sketch-map of the territory you covered.

Caution: Especially if you are attempting this exercise in a drumming circle, you should make an explicit promise to come back when you hear the recall signal. People are sometimes caught up in such beautiful experiences that they are reluctant to return, which can result in unnecessary complications. You are needed *here,* and you have many more journeys ahead. The next will take you to the sources of creativity and healing.

CHAPTER 8

Creative Journeys

> To dream and altogether not to dream. This synthesis
> is the operation of genius, by which both activities
> are mutually reinforced.
>
> *Novalis*

Artists of the Twilight Zone

As you become an active dreamer, you will find yourself increasingly at home in the realms where creative discoveries are born. In this chapter, we will study the conditions for creative flow and several methods of creative incubation, including those of the ancient Celtic bards. You will learn specific techniques for embarking on conscious dream journeys to your creative source and hear from previous explorers who have traveled these paths.

The right place to begin (again) is the twilight zone. Twilight states of consciousness provide ideal conditions for the creative flash: the spontaneous birth and coupling of images, an at-onceness of perception, a mingling of ways of sensing and perceiving, an alliance with helpers from the imaginal realm.

Arthur Koestler maintains that "the ability to regress, more or less at will, to the games of the underground, without losing contact with the surface, seems to be the essence of the poetic, and of any other form of creativity."[1] This ability comes smoothly and fluently into play in the twilight zone. Who can guess how many creative breakthroughs have been achieved there, before sleep or after waking, or in one of those marvelous, gusting passages of hours— maybe a whole night—when you are riding the cusp, straddling the worlds?

Highly creative people have a gift for connecting supposedly unrelated elements and ideas. They cross borders without regard for customs posts or No Trespassing signs. They throw suspension bridges across immense distances. The mathematician Poincaré said that "among chosen combinations the most fertile will often be those formed of elements drawn from domains which are far apart."[2] These elegant and unexpected combinations flow together beautifully in the twilight zone, where metaphor and resemblance rule, in place of logic and classification.

Highly creative people also love to be surprised. They are open to the unexpected. They are ready to go with the flow. These attitudes are richly rewarded in the twilight zone, where images are constantly borning and transforming.

High creativity is almost always associated with high gifts of visualization, and receptiveness to visual images. Faraday *saw* electromagnetic lines of force; Kekulé *saw* the coils of the benzene ring. Einstein celebrated the *visual* component in his own process of scientific discovery and commented that "the psychical entities which seem to serve as elements in thought are certain signs and more or less clear images."[3]

In the twilight zone, many creative people work consciously with transpersonal helpers. Robert Louis Stevenson borrowed stories from his "brownies" in a state of reverie. William Blake took painting lessons in a similar in-between mode from an Otherworld teacher whose portrait he painted. Jung communed with his Philemon in a similar state.

Many creative people have expressed special gratitude for what comes through in the hypnopompic state, just after waking. Sir Walter Scott revealed that "it was always when I first opened my eyes that the desired ideas thronged upon me." Einstein declared that his theory of the relativity of time dawned on him as he wakened from sleep one morning.

For the dramatist Jean Cocteau, the gifts of the morning were (appropriately) still more dramatic. Waking from choppy sleep, Cocteau found himself watching a three-act play. "I woke with a start and witnessed, as from a seat in a theatre, three acts which brought to life an epoch and characters about which I had no documentary information and which I regarded moreover as forbidding."

This experience inspired him to write and produce the play he had witnessed. It was performed on a physical stage as *The Knights of the Round Table*.[4]

Nine Keys to Creative Flow

The springs of creation are mysterious. Goethe said that not only were the roots of his creative power veiled from him, but that he did not *want* to know the source of his tremendous gifts. But what can be said is that creative flow comes in a state of relaxed attention—or creative relaxation analogous to the condition you are in when you are playing in the twilight zone. Looking over my own experience as a writer and occasional artist, and at the lives of creative people in many other fields who have shared their experiences with me, I would suggest the following maxims as keys to opening to creative flow. Though I have written these with writers especially in mind, I think you will find that they apply in many other areas.

1. *Play first, work later.* Do you ever give more of yourself than when it's all for fun? On a book tour, I was once asked by a left-brain type, "What can you tell me about becoming a writer?" I told him, "Remember to play." As he solemnly recorded my advice in his notebook, I added, "I don't think you've gotten the message." It is not about *scheduling* an hour for play! It's about giving yourself to what you love, and letting the work flow from that unnoticed.

2. *Sidle toward your story.* Australian Aborigines say that the *big* stories—the stories worth telling and retelling, the ones in which you may find the meaning of your life—are forever stalking the right teller, sniffing and tracking like predators hunting their prey in the bush. Or like dreams. You don't want to startle them away. So, if you want to write, start by writing something other than what you are "supposed" to be writing—*anything* but your writing assignment. Letter writing and journaling are ideal; but even a grocery list will do.

3. *Every force develops a form.* Don't worry about structure! The structure will reveal itself organically when you follow the energy.

4. *Keep your hand moving.* Work at increasing speed. Let the flow of associations carry you along.

5.   *Release the consequences.* The best things you will ever create or perform are things you do for their own sake, the things you would do if you never got published and never received a check.

6.   *Don't ask for permission.* There is a time to check in with editors and producers—or simply to share with friends—but that time is *after* you have released what is trying to be born through you, not in the midst of conception and gestation. Never ask permission when you don't need it!

7.   *Your real story is hunting you.* Use peripheral vision. Be attentive to what is bobbing up on the margins of your awareness. Be canny as a traveler in the wood: don't turn abruptly to stare at these new creatures directly. They'll come closer if you let them. These might be the stories, or story elements, that will make your day/month/year. Remember that they may be hunting *you*. You made yourself easier to find by entering these thickets, by going down the writer's trail without following a route map.

8.   *It's as natural as breathing.* In the language of the Tewa Indians, the three-syllable term that is translated as "art" or "creativity" actually means "water-wind-breath." This is a beautiful evocation of the creative process. It's about catching the current, about breathing in and breathing out. In-spiration is literally breathing in spirit; exhalation is releasing it into the world.

9.   *Spread cornmeal for butterflies.* Many years ago, I had a dream in which a wise Native American woman told me, "It's okay to make money, but remember to spread cornmeal." The last phrase was a mystery to me until I learned, during a visit to the Southwest, that the Pueblo Indians spread cornmeal to feed the butterflies in some of their rituals. Cross-culturally, the butterfly is a symbol of the soul. Indeed, the Greek word *psyche* means both "soul" *and* "butterfly." It's all about feeding *soul*.

For me, the genesis of a creative work is both tactile and magical. It involves the urgent desire to touch and caress, and the sense of bringing something into manifestation from the imaginal plane where it already exists. We are about to explore locales in the imaginal world where you can go to review your own unwritten books, or future works, and receive personal guidance on how to bring them through into physical manifestation. But first I want to share the feelings, keen as the desire for a perfect lover, that helped to bring this book into your hands.

I FEEL LIKE READING MY OWN BOOK

The feeling comes in strong. I want to touch it, stroke it, leaf back and forth through the pages, linger over details of typesetting, the pleasure of rereading an especially felicitous passage. Stroking my previous books, reading over drafts, letters, journal entries, won't hack it. I want the real thing, the finished thing, bound and sewn.

I *know* it's there.

I've known for quite a time (well over a year) that my new book already exists. This is confirmed when I go through my journal and commonplace book. A paragraph here—and here, and here—a page or two there, are leaves from the finished product. Sure, I have recorded them out of sequence and need to figure out how to shuffle them to match the pagination in the actual book. There are big gaps where material has been left out in transmission. But these are not drafts, despite garbles, typos, and screwups by the filing clerk in my brain. They are the book—the actual, finished book—coming through. I think of a bronze by Ipousteguy in a sculpture garden in Washington, D.C., that shows a man moving through a solid door. An arm is coming through, up to the elbow. A leg is jutting through, up to the knee. A face bulges round as a moon, penetrating the membrane that only impersonates a solid barrier. My book has been coming through like that.

Now I want its whole body in my hands.

I could pause and give myself a lecture on the laws of manifestation, of bringing things into the surface world from the imaginal realm in which they are born. But I am not in the mood for a dissertation on Platonic forms or the Mundus Imaginalis of the Persian philosophers.

My need lives in my body—in my loins, in my gut, in my nerve endings. I want to cradle and caress, to touch and be touched.

Can I write from this?

I can do better. I can *deliver*.

My naysayer has nothing to say. My brakeman can't stop the

train. (The brakeman lives in the logical mind, as anyone knows who remembers his Greek; *phren,* "logic," is related to *phrenon,* which means "brakes"—and "damper.") Coming through!

You could call my condition relaxed attention, or attentive relaxation, as my fingers trip and skirl across the keyboard. I don't mind what you call it. As the screen fills and refills, as pages spill from the printer, I am simply bringing a book from my dream library into my physical space, to enjoy it with all of my physical senses.

Bardic Incubation

Up to the seventeenth century (and maybe later) Scottish poets in the Western Highlands practiced an interesting form of creative incubation. Master poets (who were treated with great respect; their Irish counterpart, the *ollave,* wore a cloak of rainbow colors and carried a silver branch) gave their students a theme for composition. Then the pupil retired into a "house of darkness." The apprentice bard lay in total darkness, without communication with the outside world—often with a large stone on his belly to ensure he did not fall asleep. In the dark, he tracks his verses through the forests of metaphor, down the pathways of cadence. And maybe the "good people" come to him with direct inspiration.[5]

It recently struck me that the writing patterns I have followed over many winters seem to parallel the cycle of training and incubation practiced by the traditional Celtic bard or *filidh:* turning night into day and dream into waking, living on the border of the Otherworld, in seclusion from the traffic and clutter of everyday things—but surfacing to share stories and jolly times with the community in an informal version of the *ceilidh* ("kay-lee"), the village storytime by the fire. Over many years, the bard in training (and the bard in practice) shut himself up in a windowless hut throughout the daylight hours for the entire winter, emerging only to take a walk after sunset. In this "house of darkness," he composed poetry according to complex rules of rhyme and meter; he practiced the art of memory, learning twenty oghams (lists) each season (these, as with the tree alphabet or the bird alphabet, are mnemonics to call back a vast corpus of oral and secret tradition); and he communed with the inhabitants of the Otherworld. Indeed, in these shut-up times, he belonged more to the Otherworld that surrounds and permeates our own world than to the physical realm.[6]

He lived in an in-between state, in the borderland between the worlds. If he was new to the game, he might have been instructed to lie with a heavy stone on his belly to prevent him from going to sleep.

There is another trick to be learned from the old Celtic bards: the practice of tuning in to the spirits of place, and writing from a soul connection with the land you inhabit.

When the Sons of Mil, the first human colonists to reach Ireland, land in Kenmare Bay, County Kerry, the first of the invaders to wade onshore is the druid-poet Amergin. As he sets his right foot on the ground, Amergin chants his famous poem:

> I am the wind which breathes upon the sea
> I am the wave upon the ocean
> I am the murmur of the billows
> I am a bull of seven fights
> I am an eagle upon a rock
> I am a ray of the sun . . .

He identifies himself with the spirits of earth, sea, and sky. Grounded on the earth, he claims that he is one with the spirits of the new land and has the right to call on their assistance.

What does this story out of the Celtic mist mean in the context of a modern life? It means going out into nature—into the neighborhood park, at a pinch—and connecting with the energies of earth and water. It means sitting with a tree. It means calling your whole sensorium into play, noticing the play of wind in your hair, the smell of lovemaking in the afternoon, the scamper of a squirrel across a maple branch.

Visiting Your Dream Library

You must have dreamed of a book-filled room, full of wonders to be unshelved. Ron dreamed repeatedly of a splendid room in his house—a room that did not exist in physical reality—that was both a library and a music room. Soon he found himself playing new compositions on the piano in his dreams, following music sheets that he found in this magical space. A keen musician, he soon applied himself to reproducing these scores in waking life.

When I am writing my books, I often find myself visiting dream libraries or bookstores and bringing back important research leads, and sometimes specific guidance on the process of publication. My decision to include a large section in this book on death and dying was influenced by a visit to a library in a sleep dream in which I studied a book that contained fascinating information on how the skills of conscious dreaming can be used to help ordinary people in our society to approach the last stage of life as a time of spiritual growth and adventure, and to embark on the afterlife journey with the confidence of seasoned travelers. In a conscious dream journey, I recently visited a favorite bookstore (the Quest bookshop in New York City) and examined the cover art, list of contents, typography—and public reception—of a book I had not yet published.

You can look up anything you like in your dream library. A woman in one of my workshops wanted guidance on planting gourds, and she returned with specific instructions, including a design for the garden. The possibilities are limited only by your interests and imagination. You can go to your dream library anytime, in a conscious dream journey.

EXERCISE: GOING TO YOUR DREAM LIBRARY

1.   Get relaxed in a safe space. Sit or lie down in a place where you will not be disturbed. Follow the flow of your breathing. You may want to flex and relax your muscles, working from your feet up to your scalp. Put on soft music if you find this helps.

2.   Visualize your dream library. Allow the image of a library to form on your inner screen. This library should be a special place. It may be a library you remember from childhood, where you spent happy, quiet times, made big discoveries, and began to explore the universe of ideas and imagination. It may be a library or bookshop you have visited in your dreams. Perhaps, like some dreamers, you have received an invitation to use a library that does not exist (or that you have not yet found) in ordinary reality. Maybe you have dreamed of a secret room in your own house, filled with books and

artworks and intriguing objects—a space waiting for you to occupy it. This is your chance to move in and use that space.

Perhaps the image that comes to you is of a space you are currently using: the neighborhood library, a favorite bookstore, a book-filled room in your own house. This image will work equally well, providing you remember you are not confined to your literal memories of this space.

3. Formulate your intention. You may be working on a creative project or a story idea for which you would like guidance. You may be seeking research leads or fresh angles on any subject that interests you—from boatbuilding to microbiology. Since you are going to a library, it may be helpful for you to look up a book on your subject. The book you consult may prove to be *your own book*—a book as yet unwritten and unpublished in ordinary reality. Remember that a book in a dream library may have magical qualities: you might be able to step through its pages, into other situations or other worlds. Remember, too, that the guidance of a master teacher in your field may be available to you in your dream library.

Keeping this range of options in mind, your statement of intention might contain the following elements:

- I am going to visit my dream library.
- I am seeking guidance or inspiration for . . .
- I will find a book that contains the information I need (perhaps my own future book).
- I will seek guidance from a master in my field if one is available to speak with me.

4. Journey to your dream library. You may wish to put on a drumming tape to deepen and accelerate your journey. Alternatively (since libraries are quiet places) you may prefer to use soft music or simply to visualize yourself stepping into the image you have brought up on your mental screen. As you travel deeper into the scene, let it become fully alive to you. Note the colors and furnishings of the room. Where are the books you need to consult? Is there a catalog or database you might wish to use? Are there other people in the library? Is one of them the teacher or favorite author you are seeking?

5. Bring back gifts. Immediately write down what you have seen and experienced. As with dreams, some of the material—especially

the verbal information—can be fleeting if you do not record it straightaway.

6.   Honor your vision. Read (or write!) that book, check out that name or research lead, play with that symbol, follow that guidance.

EXAMPLES

Here are some experiences reported by members of one of my creative writing programs who embarked on journeys to their personal dream libraries.

The Glass Apple

Susan recalled the library of the one-room schoolhouse in rural New York that she had attended as a child, many decades before. It was a dusty, magical place, with all sorts of treasures to be found if you delved deep enough through the yellowing piles of books and magazines.

In the writing workshop, Susan had been working on retelling an old folktale in a contemporary setting. She had selected the moving story of the Little Match Girl, who has only three matches left to sell. Hungry and cold, she strikes her matches in hopes of a little warmth. When she strikes the last one, her departed grandmother appears and carries her away from the pains of the world.

Susan decided that she would use her library visit to seek more insight into the meaning of this story and how to recast it for contemporary readers.

As soon as the drumming began, Susan found herself transported inside the schoolhouse library. The scene was vividly real to her; she saw the motes of dust swirling in a shaft of sunlight. She pulled a thick, heavy book with board covers from one of the piles. When she opened it, she saw a Linotype picture of Hans Christian Andersen. He looked quite handsome in his black coat and white, flowing cravat, with his hair tied back.

Susan heard the instruction, "Talk to the book."

She asked about the meaning of the story she had been exploring.

She found herself sitting next to the man from the picture—Hans Christian Andersen—at a big library table that instantly appeared. A single candlestick was on the table. Hans Christian moved it so his face now appeared to Susan in shadow.

He told her, "You have to remember it's about *all these lives*."

He handed her two gifts. The first was a glass apple. As Susan took it, it filled with yellow light from the candle.

The second gift was a little book, filled with stories of people in different times. The stories of "all these lives."

Susan proceeded to write a stunning contemporary version of the story of the Little Match Girl, in which the protagonist is a seven-year-old girl in a wretchedly dysfunctional family, left to watch TV all day. She discovers a set of video games in a forbidden place (her father's study). When she plays the last one, her beloved grandmother appears on the screen. The screen expands until it is bigger than the room. Grammy offers the child a glass apple. The child touches the cool glass convexity—then steps into the picture . . .

The Storykeepers

Carol journeyed to a room she had first discovered in a sleep dream and then revisited through dream reentry. She called it the Map Room, because it contained maps of many territories, in both ordinary and nonordinary reality, some spread out in sheets, some rolled up in tubes. She had discovered that she could "shoot through" one of these tubes and enter different landscapes. In Carol's dream travels, the map sometimes *was* the territory.

As she reentered her Map Room, Carol was intrigued to find a statue she had not seen here before: a carved figure of a Navajo woman, similar to one she had once admired in Albuquerque.

Native American characters had played an important role in some of Carol's recent dreams. That same morning, in the twilight time when she was just stirring from sleep, she had had the impression of dream visitors: an elderly, benign couple. They let her know they were Inuit and told her, "We are here to help you."

As she moved through the Map Room, Carol hoped to find her Inuit visitors again and learn what they had to teach her. She was not disappointed. The Inuit couple beckoned her into a cafeteria space. They wanted her to eat fish with them. As they ate together, Carol's Inuit friends described themselves as "Storykeepers." They showed her that the world is encircled by Storykeepers, a guild of invisible beings of all races and traditions. Their task is to keep the great sacred teaching stories alive and to find the right tellers to renew these stories in the lives of successive generations. "We come to you in dreams."

When Carol and her friends walked back into the Map Room, an older woman with long black hair rose from behind a desk and said, "I've been waiting for you." She led Carol to a tall bookcase. On the top shelf was a book with Carol's name on the cover. When she pulled it down, she found it was a collection of stories, many of them based on Navajo and Inuit traditions.

Skimming the pages, Carol was thrilled but also anxious. How much of this would she be able to remember? How much could she bring to fruition in ordinary life?

The Inuit couple placed their hands on her heart. "You will write from here," they told her.

They motioned her toward one of the rolled-up maps. When she shot through the map, she found herself floating with the currents of a sparkling river. She rose from the water, energized and triumphant, and saw herself burst into a shower of myriad shining droplets, which streamed back into the river as a gentle rain.

"It is about flow," Carol concluded. "It is about flowing with the river and giving back to the river."

As she approached subsequent writing sessions, Carol found that by reentering this scene—by feeling and seeing herself moving with the river, and giving back to the river—she could shift quite smoothly into a flow state that bypassed all her previous writing blocks.

Reading My Published Works

Wanda chose a library she remembered from her student days in Cooperstown, New York, a beautiful space in a handsome Federal-style house. The house had once belonged to her favorite professor, a man who had died many years before.

Wanda's intention was to seek guidance on how to get her manuscript published. She had been working on her book for several years, but had not yet succeeded in finding an agent or publisher.

At the start of the drumming, she found herself at the door of the familiar house in Cooperstown. The season had changed from late spring to deep winter.

Wanda knocked on the door. She was startled, though not wholly surprised, when it was opened by the professor. He ushered her into the library, where Wanda admired the nineteenth-century, wavy glass in the tall, glass-fronted bookcases.

She was bent on finding her own book. She located it on a top shelf, in a published edition. It had the title she had chosen, and a publication date that was two years in the future. She felt reassured that her manuscript had a publishing future, though frustrated that she did not identify the publisher.

She moved into an airy, modern room that did not exist in the literal house in Cooperstown. She saw an immense bookcase, ultra-modern in style, that contained many unfamiliar titles. She was elated to discover that her name appeared as the author of two more published books. One was titled *A Southern Odyssey*. This brought shivers of recognition, because she had just started writing her reminiscences of growing up in the Deep South.

Finally, on a butcher-block table, she found a brochure and a letter with a man's name that was unfamiliar to her. She decided to look him up in a writers' directory in the hope that he might be an agent or editor—someone who could help her on the road to publication. Two weeks later, a man with the same name called her out of the blue. Though he was not directly involved in the publishing business, his call opened up new connections that were promising for Wanda's publishing ambitions.

Invisible Schools

I suspect that the deepest creative inspiration often flows from a continuity of consciousness between creative spirits that transcends time and space. The channel opens in dreams and other altered states, and in the blessed condition of creative *flow*, when we are able to tap directly into deeper pools than are recognized by the linear reasoning mind. Conscious dreamers do not need a modem to hook up to this multi-world-wide web.

In a conscious dream journey on December 10, 1995, I explored some of this terrain. As soon as I lay down, the tutelary intelligence I had taken to calling G2 instructed me to get ready for takeoff. The transfer of awareness beyond the physical plane was smooth and seamless. I found myself moving easily and rapidly through a deep mist that rolled back to reveal a kind of island city with soaring spires: a mountain rising from the sea, connected with the mainland at low tide. It was dominated by an immense temple or cathedral. It reminded me of Mont-Saint-Michel, which I had viewed only in photographs.

"Adjust your sight," G2 instructed. "This is a *counterpart* of Mont-Saint-Michel. On this plane, nothing has physical reality. Everything is constructed by thought, but it is the thought of those who remember physical forms. Look carefully and you will see the material—the substance of dreams—from which this location is built."

I craned for a closer look and found myself inside the cathedral complex. I saw men dressed like medieval monks, writing and studying in a library.

"This place is within the collective belief territories," G2 informed me. "It is a place of study and contemplation. The disciplines practiced here are those of silence, meditation on sacred writings, and the *via positiva:* the exploration of the richness of sacred imagery. The work of some of the artists here is extraordinary, both in the traditional arts of illumination and in other media. There is one who resembles someone familiar to you."

I examined a series of marvelous woodcuts that reminded me of Dürer's famous portrayal of the *Knight, Death, and the Devil,* but took the story much further.

G2 asked me if I would like to meet the artist.

"Surely."

The artist who appeared to me had a long, deeply lined face, deep-set eyes, and a fine, curly beard.

I asked him, "Are you Albrecht Dürer?"

I had some initial trouble translating his response. His mode of communication was very different from that of G2. What eventually came through was this: "I am the essence of Dürer's life and work as they are remembered in the human dimension."

I wondered why we were having this encounter. I asked if we were related in some way.

He replied, with some humor, "We are seeds from the same pod.

There is a drawing in Basel that represents this quite exactly." He chuckled and asked if I would like to examine the library.

I walked with this possible Dürer between silent monks engaged in their labors or devotions. I was no longer conscious of G2 except as a disembodied presence, *almost* visible as a point of light, near my back. Surprisingly few books were in the library. Most, if not all, were handwritten. I noticed that some were contemporary journals and manuscripts, beautifully bound and illustrated.

I picked up one of the volumes in the library and opened it at random. The words were blurry at first. Then one passage leaped into brilliant definition:

> The way to the formless Oneness of God is through the world of Forms from which physical reality is projected. It is not correct to dismiss the imaginal realm as a world of illusion. Though its forms are "creations of the created," they may recall those of higher reality as well as earth and may be models for what is brought into being on the physical plane. Who is to say which came first, the Mont-Saint-Michel in this dimension, or the physical achievement in France?

I was tremendously excited by this statement, which I resolved to commit to memory. It seemed to go to the very heart of things I had been struggling to understand and communicate clearly.

Dürer asked, "Do you have any questions?"

"What is the nature of your work here?"

"I perpetuate—while constantly improvising upon—the work of a master who still influences physicals and nonphysicals. I am a receiver and helper to those who come here for a period of study and contemplation."

I wanted to know how much of the environment that surrounded us was personal to this Dürer. "Are there things here you have created, in addition to your artworks?"

"I planted an apricot tree in the garden. I stocked a pool with perch and trout." He smiled as he added, "I set mayflies buzzing in the garden to capture the whisper of their wings in flight."

He laughed and engaged in a game of shape-shifting. I saw him turn into a rabbit, springing through the window with a push from his powerful hind legs. Outside, he became a mayfly. I flew after him, enjoying the sport, reveling in the superb, sharp-edged detail in which everything was defined: the mayfly's shimmering wings, the stamen of a flower, the slash of a blade of grass.

G2 intervened at this point. I saw my guide as a light-form, then as a radiant youth of androgynous beauty. I had a throng of questions. I wanted to know how much of what I was experiencing was the work of imagination. I had retained multiple consciousness throughout these adventures. Was I truly outside my body?

"I thought you had made more progress in your intellectual grasp of these things," G2 communicated, blending a note of mild reproach with the infinite patience of a gifted teacher. "Consciousness is never confined except by your own choice. You have expanded your mind to occupy several realities that share the same space—or lack of space. The Upper and Lower Worlds are with you in a single moment point. All of you, all of *them,* can be found in the space between a proton and an electron inside a single cell.

"The way in is the way out."

"Make that a motto for your book."

I think I could study art with *my* Dürer, just as I have studied the novel with "Balzac," psychology with "Jung," and high magic with "Yeats" in the corners of the imaginal realm where I have encountered them. Soon after my dream journey, I went to an exhibition of the work of master engravers that included several of Dürer's lesser-known works and was fascinated by the depth and keenness of observation he applied to depicting the natural world. For an artist who delighted in bringing each hair on a rabbit's back into quivering life, it seemed a natural extension of the work to enter fully into these forms as a shape-shifter.

But my thronging questions would not leave off, and in ordinary reality they had the full weight of my left-brain skeptic behind them. Just *who,* exactly, am I dealing with? *My* Dürer discouraged the notion that I was dealing with a simple ex-physical, i.e., the individual spirit of a deceased artist, operating on his chosen level of the imaginal realm. Was my Dürer more than a lively projection of myself?

From the artist's viewpoint, the answers may be of little consequence. If I can contact a part of myself that is *like* Dürer (or Chopin or Balzac) and work with that to create something fresh and vital and beautiful, that is more than sufficient. The results will be valued on their own merits. Their validity does not depend on whether we assess the source to be a discarnate spirit, a "personality essence" of a master teacher, or a projected aspect of the artist's own self. All such definitions fail, in any event, to convey the nature of multidimensional reality. My own experiences lead me to several *practical* observations:

1. There are schools, libraries, and academies on the imaginal planes that can be visited by conscious dreamers and are visited by other dreamers who do not remember their experiences but may be influenced by them in their waking lives. Access to these centers of training and instruction is conditioned by your ruling interests, your affinity for those who teach and practice there, and your ability to rise to their level.

2. Our feelings, experiences, and creative energies survive physical death and color a new phase of growth and experiment. All of this can be perceived by the living through dreams and inner communications and may be a vital source of guidance and inspiration.

3. The personality essence of a great teacher, or great creative mind, may communicate to vast numbers of people long after this individual has passed over and moved beyond levels where direct contact with the living (with the exception of a few highly evolved spirits) is possible. This personality essence may take the form of a kind of animated hologram, living and operating within an environment composed of the thought-forms of the person who generated it and those congenial to him. I believe I encountered something like this in my visit to "Dürer" in a "counterpart" Mont-Saint-Michel.

4. Through dream travel, we can visit studios, schools, and temples on the astral planes and receive instruction that we can apply directly to the creative challenges in our lives.

CHAPTER 9

≋

Healing Journeys

The real is what works.

C. G. Jung

Asklepian Dream Healing

The dreamgates open paths to spontaneous healing. This was the shared wisdom of the ancient world. It calls to us again, in our dreams, to move beyond our fixation with physical symptoms to the spiritual causes of wellness and illness. It invites us to draw on transpersonal energies to heal ourselves and others.

Pilgrims came from all over the Greek world to Epidaurus, to the precinct of Asklepios, the man-god who personified healing.

They came here to dream. Asklepios is, beyond all else, the Dream Healer. When you enter the precinct of Asklepios, if you are fortunate, you will have a dream experience that will be more than diagnosis or prognosis; the dream will *be* the healing.

You take in the plays and processions and sleep in a guesthouse for the first night, hoping for a preparatory dream—a dream that may qualify you for the *big* one. You are bathed in the sea and smudged with incense.

You make your offerings and are admitted to the temple of Asklepios, where you view the gold-and-ivory statue of the god. You ask him for the gift of a healing dream. If you have doubts about what is possible here, you may be reassured by the evidence of dream healings that have happened here before: votive stelae and tablets line the walls, thanking the god for the use of an eye, a leg, a kidney, a heart.

You look down and see the coiling shapes of the yellowish white snakes that are the mascots of Asklepios. You feed them with honey cakes. As Jean Houston writes beautifully, you are entering the "snake world, the world of the healing energies of earth."[1]

You are ready to dream. You dress in white, for holy sleep. You go to the *abaton*, the "forbidden dormitory," with other dreamers and are given the simplest bedding, a pallet on the stone floor.

The priest invokes the presence of the god. What, exactly, is he evoking? The word *Asklepios*, according to Robert Graves, means "unceasingly gentle." His birth is miraculous: the mating of god and human. He is the son of Apollo by the Crow-maiden, Coronis. He was exposed at birth and left for dead, but was suckled by a dog and a she-goat. He heals the sick, gives sight to the blind, and calls the dead back to life. His mentor in healing is Chiron, the centaur, the model of the wounded healer. He knows that poison is also medicine; he uses Gorgon's blood, the gift of Athena, to heal minds and bodies.

He heals in the manner of the shamans. Soul retrieval is one of his specialities. He is so successful in bringing back souls from the Land of the Dead that Hades complains about him to Zeus. Zeus hurls a thunderbolt at him and does not miss his target. In dying as a man, Asklepios becomes a god. Relenting, Zeus raises him to live with the immortals and sets his caduceus among the stars. He continues to exercise his healing influence among humans. And even among the stars, his strongest connection is still with the primal energies of Earth and sexuality. He is god and man, but he is also a snake.[2]

Asklepios is believed to reveal himself to those who seek his aid. One of the Christian Fathers, Origen, conceded that "a vast multitude have frequently seen, and still see, no mere phantom, but Asklepios himself, healing and doing good and foretelling the future."[3]

Now he has been called, you are instructed to remain silent and fear nothing that may transpire during the night.

"Dream now, and dream of the god of healing who will come to you in the night."

Who knows what will come? If you go by the accounts of previous dreamers at this shrine, a dog may come to lick you. A huge serpent may come, testing your courage as well as your willingness to accept the healing. Asklepios not only has snakes as mascots, he is known to shape-shift into snake-form himself. Maybe your dream visitor will be a beautiful young woman, one of the daughters of Asklepios; their names are Hygeia and Panacea. Or the god himself, in human or transhuman guise.

In *The Possible Human,* Jean Houston evolved a spirited modern adaptation of Asklepian dream incubation from which I have borrowed, both in this section and in some group experiments. At the start of some residential workshops, I have people come down to our gathering space dressed as they would normally dress for bed. I get them to lie down in a cartwheel formation, heads facing in toward the center. "Dream now . . ." I chant the words over and over to lead them into sacred sleep.

We can practice dream incubation at any time and place in our lives. But it is especially powerful when done with the drama and energy of a simple group ritual in a special place. Many societies have had—and indigenous peoples and spiritual lineages still have—their own version of Asklepian dream ceremony. In the Celtic world, in the first centuries of the common era, dreamseekers trooped to the shrine of the goddess Sequana, at the source of the river Seine, in the Dijon country of Burgundy. They came with modest offerings to be cleansed in the sacred spring and to seek permission to sleep under a rustic shelter and hope for a numinous encounter with the goddess or one of her messengers.[4]

However, the fundamental journey of healing is not the journey to a sacred site. It is the journey to the hidden orders of reality where dis-ease and healing have their source. The distance between you and that sacred source may be inconceivably vast or a fair hike or *no distance at all,* depending on your courage and imagination.

The Theater of Dream Healing

The records do not tell us whether the Greeks put on dream theater at the shrines of Asklepios, but my guess is that they did. Coming and going to the places of healing, you were surrounded by strolling players, jesters, capering satyrs complete with goat-foot dance rattles and huge make-believe penises long enough to flap in your face, by scenes of low comedy and deepest tragedy. The enactment of the *big* dreams of intercourse with the gods and the ribald, sexy, silly dreams that bring you back to earth would have been a wholly natural way to honor the Dream Healer, superbly well suited to the Greek taste for drama.

I have helped to facilitate spontaneous dream theater for many groups over many years, and I find I am still constantly awed and astonished by what it brings through. Dream theater is the pinnacle of improv, the source of endless creative play and rich entertainment. It validates the dreamer, builds caring and compassionate communities, and honors the dreaming and the powers that speak through dreams. It is also, in its own right, a powerful tool for healing that brings through tremendous energy.

SNAKEBITE

Emily, in midlife, looked far older than her years and seemed to be seriously lacking in energy when she arrived at the workshop. She dragged across the space, shrouded from neck to ankles in clothes the color of wet dead leaves. She spoke in a low, monotonous mumble and was almost inaudible when her turn came to share a dream.

In her dream, Emily was walking through a dead forest. Everything was moldering and decayed. She came to a fallen tree, hollow and rotten. Under the tree, she noticed a serpent. The snake was enormous, almost as thick as the tree that had pinned it to the ground and possibly longer, its tail lying coiled. Its colors were fading. It seemed close to dying.

In waking life, Emily was terrified of snakes. In her dream, without understanding her actions, she lifted the fallen tree off the snake. She was surprised, as she did so, to find that either the tree was extraordinarily light or her strength was greater than she had suspected. She then fed the snake, taking the food from a cone-shaped pile of grain.

When she had fed the snake, it reared up, gigantic and vigorously alive. Its eyes blazed, its colors streamed back. Emily was unable to move as the snake's jaws came down, and it sank its tooth into her hand.

Emily shook like a blown leaf as she finished recounting the dream.

"Its *tooth?*" someone echoed. We were all interested in Emily's description. "Don't you mean its fang?"

Tooth or fang, whatever had pierced Emily's dreambody was no ordinary item in reptile anatomy. She now told us that the "tooth" was shaped like a crescent moon and was composed of electric blue light. She felt no pain when the snake bit her.

I asked Emily if she had a question about her dream. She wanted to know why the snake would attack her after she had fed it.

"If it were my dream," I suggested, "I'm not sure I would feel that the snake was *attacking* me. I might feel it was giving me a gift."

Emily nodded, the light of recognition in her eyes. "But I'm so *afraid*," she stumbled.

"Of the serpent?"

"Of *life*."

I asked for Emily's permission to turn her dream into theater. I explained that she would be the producer, scriptwriter, and casting director; I would simply be a consultant in the wings. Emily became more and more excited and animated as she picked people in the workshop to play figures in the dream—the hollow tree, the many segments of the snake, the blue tooth, the dreamer herself.

Emily's eyes widened as she watched the scene being rehearsed and replayed: the drabness and lifelessness of the dead forest, the moment of resolve, the shock as the six players impersonating the serpent stirred and uncoiled and raised up, and the crescent tooth—portrayed by a nimble dancer—arced down.

At the end of the performance, all the players were invited to speak to Emily from the perspective of the characters or elements they had portrayed. The dead forest and the hollow tree spoke of things the dreamer knew well: of emotional blight and physical symptoms of disease and decay. The snake-people told Emily, "We are your vital energy. We are your Kundalini fire." Emily's dramatic double told her, "I am ready to move beyond fear and accept my blue fire."

I asked Emily if she wanted to add to the script.

She said, "I need to do that now in the theater of my life." She told us she saw clearly now that everything in her dream was the landscape of her psyche and her embodied life. "I need to release and feed my vital energy and accept its gifts."

Emily had dressed in colors of her dead forest for years and had no other clothes at our residential workshop. But the next morning, she delighted us by appearing draped in a bloodred scarf she had borrowed. And when we shared personal stories, songs, and rituals, this shy, life-fearing woman enthralled us by flinging her body into a sinuous snake-dance. The group theater had done more than bring through an intellectual analysis; it had brought through a powerful and palpable transfer of energy.

Deer Mountain

In Heather's story, dream theater is the portico to a journey that will take us deeper into the realms of shamanic healing, into the precinct of the wilding powers.

GETTING INTO THE SHOWER

I was leading a weekend workshop at a lodge atop a special mountain. The night before we began, I dreamed I threw a woman over a cliff to show her she could fly.

I recognized the woman from my dream as she banged into the lodge, shaking rain off her clothes, nearly two hours after we had started our Friday-evening orientation session. Heather arrived full of terror. One of the black sorcerers of Western allopathic medicine had just diagnosed her with a disease of the autoimmune system, told her she had just months to live, and described the way she was likely to die. This was a board-certified equivalent of the Aboriginal sorcerer pointing the bone.

Heather was starting to develop the prescribed symptoms. A friend had urged her to come to our gathering and simply be open to the possibility that there were other options. Heather had havered until the last moment. She had no experience of "inner work," she protested. She did not remember her dreams. She did not believe in miracles. She was here, nonetheless. But she had missed the relaxation exercises, the group bonding, and the Tree Gate meditation in which the circle had become a sacred grove, as each participant merged her awareness with her special tree. Heather looked about to throw up. I had no inkling of how to help Heather that first night, or whether we *could* help her. Hugs and late-night cookies by the fire weren't hacking it. We would have to dream on this.

In the morning, the friend who had pushed Heather into coming gave me something to work with. She told me that for the first time in ages, Heather had remembered a dream. Just a couple of scraps, which she was inclined to dismiss as an "anxiety" dream, but a dream all the same. In a gentle moment that Saturday afternoon, I asked Heather if she would share her dream with the group. She told us:

I'm Scared It's Too Late

I am walking in the woods with my friend. We're at a place where we often go, walking among the trees on a beautiful clear day. I know where I am and I'm safe.

Then I'm here at the lodge and I'm anxious I'm going to be late for the workshop. I have to shower and wash my hair and put on my makeup. I'm trying to get my stuff out of my bag.

We explored the contrast between Heather's "safe place"—the woods—and the workshop on the mountain. She had come from a place where she knew just what to expect to a place where anything could happen.

I asked Heather's permission to turn her dream fragments into theater. Suddenly Heather—completely new to dreamwork—was in command of the proceedings, as I appointed her producer and casting director.

Heather chose someone to play herself. This was an interesting choice, since the person Heather had chosen had been fizzing with excitement and energy since the start of the workshop and had reported a series of powerful initiatory experiences during the journeying. Heather had picked the most energized and "shamanic" person in the circle to play her dream double.

Heather chose other dream actors to play the other elements in the dream, including the bag and the trees in the woods. She picked the tallest, most handsome man in the room to be the shower she was trying to get under.

What followed was pure magic—the magic of spontaneous creativity, drawing on group energy. As scene one (the walk in the woods) unfolded, Heather's eyes widened as most of the workshop participants shape-shifted into the trees from her dream. She had missed the tree meditation the night before; now she was deep inside it.

In the rehearsal, the players could not confine themselves to scene two as it was scripted. Without discussion, without planning, they dreamed the dream onward, getting the dreamer under the shower. As the tall guy mimicked the hard spray, Heather's dream double reveled in washing her body and hair, bouncing and swirling. We were all laughing, including Heather, whose eyes were wide and shining. With her permission, we kept the shower scene—as scene three—in our "finished" production. In this joyful, organic resolution of the dream, we sensed the promise of something more.

After watching our sacred grove reemerge during the dream theater, I decided to lead another Tree Gate meditation. Heather was now ready for this. She spread her arms, as the limbs of her special tree spread high and wide, and let her awareness flow into the deep dream of the heartwood. After this, she found her inner screen was no longer blank. She was beginning to enter fully into the visualizations. She felt safe and at home.

FIRE CLEANSING

That night, we conducted a simple fire ritual for cleansing. I asked members of the group to make bundles representing whatever they needed to cast out of themselves. Some people made birchbark containers and filled them with twigs embellished with ribbons, rotten wood, drawings, even deer pellets. I drummed and asked them to approach the fire—one by one—when they felt ready, and announce what they were casting out. I instructed them to blow into the flames, releasing whatever needed to be released through their breath as well as through the transfer to the personal bundles. This became a powerful process. One of the women sounded as if she were retching as she gasped, "Get off me!" We could *see* the space each person was opening up, a space now ready to be filled by the brightness of spirit.

THE STAG OF THE MOUNTAIN

We now formed a healing circle. Powered by the drumming and chanting, we were seeking guidance on what needed to be accomplished *now*. I was drawn to try to help several people, including a woman who had a three-year-old version of herself (perceptible to my inner sight) dancing about in high excitement. But the strongest tug was toward Heather. I asked her permission to journey for her.

I lay at the center of the circle, a bandanna over my eyes, to journey for Heather. Almost at once, a magnificent stag leaped to meet me. He was enormous. His antlers were huge. He guided me in all the work for Heather that ensued. He led me to kneel behind her, probing into the area at the top of her spinal column and the base of her neck. At the top of my head was a cone of intense white light.

Now I felt myself searching with the stag's antlers, as if they were part of my own being. Laser beams of light moved between me and Heather, as if directed and focused by the prongs of the horns. I saw her head and upper back laid open, as if by complex surgery; layer upon layer of tissue was opened. I saw the laser beams of white light working to repair the damaged tissue and re-form the immune system so that her killer cells were no longer attacking what belonged to her. I knew that the stag is a great protector, one who can instantly recognize what belongs in the herd and what does not, one who is capable of defending his own. Without analyzing, without pushing my little everyday mind in the path of the process, I trusted completely in what was unfolding through an agency beyond myself.

Afterward, all of us were convinced that genuine healing had come through, though of course there was no way of knowing how this would affect the physical symptoms of Heather's disease.

Awed and grateful, I went out to a gallery overhanging the mountain and grazed on slices of peasant bread. A local woman followed me out. "I need to tell you the story of the stag of this mountain. Hunters have been talking about him for the last eight or nine years."

"Please go on."

"The hunters say a magnificent stag still lives up here, with an immense rack. Several hunters have encountered him. Each time, the same thing has happened. When they look into the stag's eyes, they lay down their guns and give up hunting for life."

I felt shivers of recognition. If I had tried to cook up a visualization that might be appropriate for a victim of an autoimmune disorder—which basically stems (as far as I can understand it) from the confusion of the self and the nonself, so that the hunter-killers of the immune system are attacking the body's own fabric—I could not have done as well as this. I was learning about a protector of the herd whose very gaze compels hunters who are in the wrong place to give up killing for good. The hunters' story was confirmation from the world. But it was far more. We realized, in that moment, that the spirits of the mountain were supporting our work. In the morning, I led the group up to the lookout to perform a ceremony of thanks to the mountain spirits.

And what about Heather? She fooled her doctors. Her symptoms went away. She declines to die according to a medical prognosis. The turning point, I believe, was the gift of laughter and the loving energy on that magical day when she watched her dream double get under the shower and the courage she derived from these.

The Wilding Powers

The energy of the stag stayed with me after the weekend on the mountain. At another healing circle, I felt drawn to perform soul retrieval for a woman who had suffered horrific sexual abuse in early childhood. The stag came to help me and showed me a young fawn. I ran with the deer for a time. They led me to a nine-year-old Charlie who had stayed out in the woods, apparently because of abuse. I asked her what she needed to come back, and I was charmed and amused when she told me I had to promise she would be allowed to wash her hair with shampoo. The deer led me to other Charlies, and to something I would have preferred not to deal with: the insistent image of huge spiders crawling in and out of a medicine cabinet. I associated these images with cancer, but I did not need the word; the images were stronger.

In addition to the soul retrieval, I felt called on to perform extraction healing, my least favorite aspect of this work and something I never touch unless a larger agency is working with me and through me. The agency is usually that of the wilding powers, the animal guardians. On this occasion, the stag guided me and worked with me again. He drew me to bend over Charlie's abdomen and suck out the spidery roots of her disease. I spat into a cup and saw a furry, dark thread come out. The experience was disgustingly real. Charlie told me later she had had a hysterectomy, and serious problems in the area I had identified. She felt that we had removed both the roots of the disease and the legacy of abuse.

Dream healing works with *soul*. When it relieves or expunges the physical manifestations of disease, it is by tackling their psychospiritual causes on a level that is closed to ordinary sight and ordinary medicine.

I will share a little more of what flowed from my reacquaintance with the Deer (an important ally at an earlier period in my life) to open up the question of what the wilding powers can do for—or through—*you*.

A week or two later, I dreamed I had changed my skin. I was admiring the silky threads of the thick matting of reddish brown hair that covered my whole body. My legs had grown long and fleet.

Then, during the drumming at another healing circle, the Deer came through in a different way. I had asked members of the circle to journey on two questions: How can I be healed and how can I help to heal others? The participants lay on the ground, feet toward the candle at the center, arranged like rays of a sunburst, apart from a man I had asked to drum with me. I was becoming frustrated. I wanted to move around the circle to work with individuals, some of whom were carrying urgent issues. But the other man's drumming seemed slightly "off." I realized I would have to stay in place, drumming and watching over the whole group. Yet I felt an urgent need to respond to several unspoken cries of help.

Wait for the Deer, an inner voice instructed.

What came this time was a man with antlers, a deer-man. He was holding a snaky staff, a kind of primal caduceus. I realized that he looked quite a lot like me. He was beyond my personality, but in no way alien. I felt some part of my energy move with him as he went around the circle, helping various individuals. I was fascinated by the clear perception of a second self doing this work while my focus personality watched him and the group.

A deeper shift in my perception began before the appearance of the deer-man. Instead of simply checking in on individuals in serial fashion, I felt my consciousness expand to encompass the whole group. It was as if the whole scene—and things beyond its immediate borders—were now enclosed in a dome or sphere. I could observe from every point around the perimeter of this sphere *simultaneously*. Somehow my mind had expanded to bring the whole circle within itself. I could see everything—and be everywhere—at once.

Several participants in the circle told me later they had seen the deer-man moving among them, doing his stuff.

The world of the animal powers is not the world of mainstream psychology and medicine. Yet we urgently need to build bridges between them. I was once at a conference where a well-regarded psychologist presented a case study in "dream healing" in which a woman who had felt menaced by wild animals in her dreams goes into the woods in a sleep dream and kills a bear. *Maybe* she was braving up to her fears. It seems more likely to me that she was killing her medicine. If the bear was about to dismember her, as she feared, maybe she *needed* to be dis-membered (in her dreambody) to re-member and reclaim her animal spirits and capacity for self-healing. In any event, if she had become a conscious dreamer, she could have *asked* the bear why he was on her case.

Getting in touch with your animal spirits and feeding them (both literally and metaphorically) will boost your vitality and put you back on the natural path of your energy. When a shamanic practitioner helps you to bring back your animal spirits, the operation is called a "power animal retrieval." Working with animal guardians is *not* about regressing to some earlier, "subhuman" stage of our evolution. It is about becoming whole, and reconnecting with the earth we share.

How do you know who your animal allies are? If you have worked your way through the exercises in this book, you should be quite familiar by now with at least one of your animal guardians. They stalk us in dreams, and sometimes in waking life.

A woman in the Southwest had a male friend who cared for young wildcats that he found injured or abandoned. One evening she went to his home for dinner and found that a young male cougar was sharing his house. When the friend went out to the kitchen, the cougar sprang up onto the woman's lap and clamped its jaws around her windpipe, shutting off the air. She started to asphyxiate. Terrified, feeling she was close to blacking out, she could not call for help and did not dare to struggle, with the cougar's teeth biting into her throat. Her friend came out of the kitchen and freed her before she lost consciousness.

Later, she asked me what I thought was going on here.

"Speaking for the Cat People," I told her, "one of two things could be happening. Either the cougar thought you were food. That isn't likely, because he did not break the skin. Or else he thought you were one of his kind. You've seen how young cats rehearse that way for the hunt. Maybe he didn't realize that you were a mere human who could be choked to death by simple play."

"What should I do about it?"

"You might find a way to bring that cougar energy into your life."

This led to a power animal retrieval in which the cougar energy was blown into her solar plexus. There were interesting consequences. The woman had her lens prescription changed because she found her eyesight had suddenly improved. She reported that she was now able to get around very well in the dark. And from time to time she found (as the Mohawk say) that something in her belly was biting her, demanding red meat.

Earthing the Lightning Force

Access to the wilding powers involves working with larger energies. Cross-culturally, one of the most common names for the shaman (almost as common as "one who dreams") means *one who has power*—i.e., an unusual access to the life force.

The access to raw energy brings the challenge of grounding.

KUNDALINI CRISIS

A pleasant, rather shy young man with dark blond Prince Valiant hair started shaking uncontrollably an hour into one of my weekend workshops. Jeremy gasped about the terrific effect of the drumming. His energy was wild, running amok. He was groaning and gasping and heaving. I thought of the beliefs of Tibetan Bon practitioners and others that uncontrolled shaking of this type is a sign of demonic possession. When I searched Jeremy's energy field, I found a big serpent snapping as its head reared above his left shoulder. However, I did not feel this energy was alien to him. I felt I was dealing with a Kundalini crisis—with his own raw "boiling" energy thrashing about without grounding or safe channels for expression.

During the break, I took Jeremy outside, to get his bare feet on the ground. I was suddenly inspired to lead him to a tree. I asked him to hug the tree and see if he felt he could release some of his excess energy into the tree with the intention of strengthening the tree and helping it to grow. He began to feel the transfer taking place at the level of his solar plexus—the right center. After a time, I asked him if he could now begin to bring in a cooling, centering, grounding energy from the tree. A little later, bowing his head so the crown touched the tree, he said he could feel something passing into him at the top of his head. I asked him to focus on letting the grounding influence of the tree move down through him from the crown of his head all the way down to the soles of his feet—while continuing to release his excess energy from his solar plexus. This effected a dramatic transformation. The shaking stopped. Jeremy returned to the group—after tea and half a platter of cookies—centered and was able to harness the energy in subsequent sessions, dancing up a benign storm during our healing circle the next day.

Dreams teach us about harnessing and grounding transpersonal energy, as well as about the need to monitor our personal energy and avoid allowing the energy thieves in our environment to drain our batteries.

GREEN FIRE

A young Australian woman had an initiation dream in which this problem was beautifully resolved—yet left her with the task of confronting her fears about this issue. She dreamed of green fire, hurtling down on shafts of lightning. It struck the earth and streamed toward her within the earth. She was terrified. Children were nearby, and she feared they would be electrocuted. But the children were not fearful at all. They placed the flats of their hands on the earth, showing her it was safe to receive the green fire, because it has been grounded in the earth.

Journeys to Recover Lost Soul

Shamans journey, riding their drums, to locate and bring back lost souls. *Soul-loss* is perhaps the most common shamanic diagnosis of the spiritual causes of disease and misfortune. Because of unbearable pain or trauma, because of sorcery or unhealthy relations with the dead, or simply because of bad habits and keeping bad company, some part of the client's soul has gone away. It may be lost in the void or stuck in the astral counterpart of a situation in earlier life. It may have strayed into the lands of the dead. It may be attached to a former partner or lover. So long as you are missing some part of your vital soul energy, you are not whole, and you are vulnerable to negative intrusions. You may try to fill the gap with addictions. You may become an unwitting carrier for lower entities that seek to use you as a vehicle, a state of affairs the Church used to call "obsession" that may extend to possession. With the best will in the world, doctors and therapists can provide only limited help if they are working with only a part of you.

A good therapist—who may be simply a good friend—may help to facilitate spontaneous soul recovery. You change your habits, you start to clean up your life, you kick your addictions (without making the mistake of continuing to identify yourself by them), you take some creative risks, and some part of your bright self returns to you. Often your dreams announce when you are ready to get a missing piece of your soul back. You find yourself back in your childhood home, and you see your five-year-old self, who cowered in the face of an alcoholic father rampaging like a bull elephant. Or your nervous, spotty, fifteen-year-old self who was terrified of the opposite sex. Dreams of this kind are frequently an invitation to welcome back your lost children, deal with the bad memories, and forgive yourself and others. Similar invitations come in waking life, when we return to scenes of our earlier life and encounter younger selves.

But some situations call for special help and intervention, the kind genuine shamans know how to give. I believe that soul retrieval is the most important and most urgently needed contribution that paleolithic psychology has to make to the practice of healing in our contemporary lives.

A soul retrieval is part of a life process. The intervention may be brief; the consequences may take years to integrate. The side effects of soul retrieval include transformation. This may be disruptive to the existing structures of your life. It may tear you away from old habits, from familiar people and patterns. It can blow up a relationship or bring it together on a deeper level. You are going to have to figure out how to care and feed your larger soul-family. And you will have to work this out for yourself, because our needs—and the natural paths of our energy—are different. After soul retrieval, some people take up jogging; others drop it. Some give up alcohol; others don't. You might become a vegetarian, or you might break a vegetarian regime that you've observed for a quarter century because you need to feed your carnivore, too. A soul retrieval may be accompanied by processes of spontaneous soul *recovery* that go deeper than the shamanic intervention in itself.

Soul-loss may date back to the circumstances of birth. I still feel the stab of pain in my chest that had me shaking uncontrollably when I journeyed to bring back a part of a young man that had left him in the labor room; he was born with a serious heart defect. In another soul retrieval, I found a part of a mature woman that looked like a baby. It was completely hairless, soft, and pale. It was living in a strange misty limbo on the borderlands between the living and the dead with a second being that looked like a replica of itself. My guides told me that I needed to separate these two baby souls. The first of these belonged to my client; the second, though closely connected to her, needed to be helped to move along a different path. My client later told me that she had a twin sister who had died at birth. She had often sensed that a part of herself had left with her twin, and that this might be connected to the ease with which she had always seemed to be able to leave the body and wander between the worlds— a powerful gift when used with intention, grounding, and psychic screening, but a source of dangerous vulnerability without them.

In the journey to bring back lost soul for another person, it is common to discover details that are initially meaningless to the client. Soul-loss often results in memory loss, even full-blown amnesia about the events of weeks, years, or decades. As the rescued soul-parts take up residence where they belong, memories come back. They may be deeply painful and embarrassing—another reason why it is important to establish that the client has a caring support network. In her "fun days" back in the 1970s, for example, Nina had overdosed, catapulting a large chunk of herself into another reality. When I found this younger Nina, she seemed to be floating above Tulsa, Oklahoma. When I asked her where she thought she was, she said, "Oh, I'm on cloud nine." Though she seemed a bit fuzzy, my guides urged me to bring her back. After I did, Nina suddenly recaptured *years* of life memories—good, bad, and indifferent—and powers of visual imagination that had gone missing with this part of her that had been so desperately hungry for transcendental experience.

I journeyed for a woman I'll call Karen. I knew that a younger Karen was ready to come back, because the woman had reported dreams of watching her five-year-old self, and because, as we talked, I perceived a five-year-old version of Karen hovering just above her, with the same big round face and carroty hair. I found this younger Karen quickly. But before she would agree to come back with me, she told me, "You have to make them promise they won't hurt me for breaking the dishes."

"Nobody will hurt you for breaking the dishes," I promised. I explained to this lost child that Karen had become an adult, independent woman, with a responsible job and kids of her own.

After the soul retrieval, I described this conversation to the grown-up Karen. At first, its content was meaningless to her. Then she gasped as memory came flooding back. She described how her father, in a drunken rage, had once beaten her elder sister for dropping a plate while drying the dishes. Karen's sister had rushed screaming into the night. The family had never seen her again. They were later informed by the police that the girl had been assaulted and murdered on the streets.

The journey to recover lost soul may take you to the Lower, the Upper, or the Middle Worlds. My journey for a musician once carried me to the celestial realm of the Gandharvas. But the soul retrieval journey may also lead to some dark places.

The Deep End

Inuit shamans believe that a major cause of soul-loss is abduction by spirits of the departed. This may happen because a dead person is afraid to walk the paths of the afterlife alone. The *angaqok*'s journey to retrieve a soul taken captive by the dead is particularly dangerous. He must be careful not to eat the food of the dead, or he may find himself a prisoner in their realm.[5]

There is a caution here, one that we must heed. The basic techniques of soul retrieval are simple and easily taught. But to know only those techniques is like learning to swim in the shallow end of the pool. You'll have to learn not to get spooked when you can't put your feet on the bottom, or when you can't see the bottom at all. . . . And *then* you'll discover that beyond the training pool is the ocean, where there are unpredictable riffs and "undertoads," and all manner of other species.

To come and go safely to the realms of the dead the Inuit warn about, you will need to learn when to conceal your light. I had to robe myself in darkness once to make the crossing to rescue a missing soul I perceived as an eleven-year-old boy, naked and quivering. He had left Tom, now a man in his early thirties, when he was an altar boy. Tom had been used as a sex toy by a pedophile priest. This spiritual and physical violation, it seemed, had not ended with the death of the priest. I found that he and some of his criminal kind were holding that part of Tom captive—as some kind of astral sex slave—in a very dark place. I had to bring that part back by force.

There are depths here, of both light and dark, that beggar description. But we can now see why the best-known stories of soul retrieval involve entry into the kingdom of Death. This is work for those who have died and returned and know the roads of the Upper and Lower Worlds because they have journeyed them.

One of the great teaching stories about soul retrieval comes from the Buryat, a shamanic people of Siberia (the land that gave us the word *shaman*). According to Buryat legend, a powerful shaman in a certain village had become so skilled in his craft that people had ceased to die. When someone in the village fell sick, the family sent for the shaman. He mounted his drum and rode it like a horse until he found the soul that had left the patient and might already be crossing into the land of the dead. He caught up with the wandering soul, flew back to the village with it, and blew it back into the heart and head of the patient. As a result, the Lord of Death was no longer getting his dues. The terrible Death Lord, Erlen Khan, went to the high God to complain. The high God decided to put the mighty shaman to the test. The high God leaned down from his high throne and plucked the soul of a perfectly healthy villager out of his body. He put the soul he had taken in a bottle and sat on his throne with his thumb over the neck of the bottle, waiting to see what the shaman would do. The family called in the shaman, who rode his drum through the Middle World and the Lower World and then up through many levels of the Upper World until he saw the high God sitting on his throne with the captive soul in the bottle. Did the shaman accept defeat? Not on your life! He shape-shifted into the form of a wasp. He flew at the high God and stung him in the middle of the forehead. In his rage and pain, the high God released his grip on the bottle. The shaman snatched up the missing soul and started flying back with it to the village. The high God hurled a thunderbolt after him, which split his drum in two. This (according to the Buryat) is the reason why shaman drums, once double-headed, have only a single head today.[6]

The shamanic journey to bring back a lost soul is the source of some of our most enduring myths and popular folktales, though the experiential content and the practical teaching of these stories is often forgotten. The best-known example is the Orpheus legend. In the versions told and retold today, Orpheus loses the wife or sister he has reclaimed from the underworld because he looks back too soon. But there are indications that in the original story, Orpheus succeeded in bringing the soul of Eurydice back to her body. This seems plausible in the light of the tremendous popularity of the Orphic mysteries in ancient Greece and Italy; it seems unlikely that all the people who vested their hopes for a fortunate afterlife in Orphic initiation were placing their trust in a *failed* shaman.[7]

In Polynesian versions of the Orpheus story, the hero succeeds. Sometimes this involves hiding himself from the powers of the underworld; sometimes it involves recruiting their help. The Maori hero Hutu goes down to rescue the soul of Pare, who committed suicide for his sake. Hutu encounters the Great Lady of Night and persuades her to help him; the Death-Goddess tells him the roads he should follow and gives him a basket of food so he will not be tempted to eat the food of the dead, which will be deadly for him. The Maori hero finds his woman among the shades and puts her soul back in her body.[8]

In a Hawaiian version, the princess Kawelu dies of grief after Hiku abandons her. Hiko climbs down to the Land of the Dead on a vine, captures Kawelu's soul, and brings it back in a coconut. He then forces it into the big toe of the left foot and massages the foot and calf until he makes it enter the heart. In his journey, Hiku hides his light, covering himself with rancid oil so he will smell like the dead.[9]

The Orpheus theme—as tragedy and as triumph—reverberates through Native American folklore. One of my favorite variants is the firsthand report of a Huron dreamer as recorded by a Jesuit missionary, Father Brébeuf, in 1636. A Huron man was grief-stricken over the death of his beloved sister. He fasts and keeps vigil until he establishes contact with her. She is now journeying along the road to the Village of the Dead. The Huron tracks his sister along the Path of Souls, overcomes a terrifying challenge at a perilous bridge, and finally catches up with her at a gathering of dead relations and ancestors. She flees when he tries to bring her back. But as they struggle, her soul shrinks until he is able to trap it inside a pumpkin. After further ordeals, he gets back to the village, where he finds his sister has been buried. He has her body exhumed. While he is chanting power songs, getting ready to put the soul back into the body, someone peeks inside the pumpkin—and the sister's soul escapes.[10] As in the conventional version of the Orpheus legend, the Huron shaman fails. But the story has not been prettied up and tamed—it has the raw authenticity of a traveler's tale, and there is a practical lesson in *why* the shaman failed, particularly relevant in a time when our hospitals are heavily invested in the artificial prolongation of physical life. The Huron was too late. His sister's soul had already crossed over, and she did not wish to return to a physical existence (and a decaying sack of meat and bones) she had simply outlived. The shaman's grief—and perhaps his egomania—blinded him to the natural balance of things, and to his client's own wishes.

Presumably Lazarus felt differently from the Huron woman. Maybe his soul had not traveled quite so far from his body. The raising of Lazarus was understood by many of Jesus' contemporaries to be a characteristic manifestation of the power of a *magos* to guide and relocate souls. According to Morton Smith, this is why Jesus was depicted, in one of the earliest images of him, holding a wand.[11]

One of India's best-loved folktales carries us into the same territory. Savitri loves her husband so much that when Yama, the death lord, pulls his soul out of his body with a noose, she pursues them along the road that leads south to Yama's realm. She pleads and nags and connives until at last the god of death agrees to release the soul of her husband.[12]

The travelers' tales are not enough. We must look at Death face-to-face.

≋

PART III

A Manual for the Psychopomp

We do not know where death awaits us, so let us
wait for it everywhere. To practice death is to practice
freedom. A man who has learned how to die has
unlearned how to be a slave.

Montaigne

Our deepest fears are like dragons
guarding our deepest treasure.

Rainer Maria Rilke

He who feeds on death that feeds on men
possesses life supereminently and excellently,
and meets best the secret demands of the universe.

William James

≋

CHAPTER 10

New Maps
of the Afterlife

The world of imagination is the world of eternity.
It is the divine bosom into which we shall all go
after the death of the vegetative body.

William Blake

Toward a Modern Art of Dying

In night dreams, we often encounter dying as a metaphor. People confronted with the prospect of their own death dream of going to a wedding, taking off in a mysterious plane, entering a foreign country, crossing a river or body of water. Quite often they dream of leaving their clothes or their luggage behind. The Tibetans call the physical body *lu*, which means "something you leave behind."

By working with dreams of this kind, for ourselves and for others, we can help to recover a vital practice that Western society almost lost: the art of dying.

In most human societies, preparation for death and the afterlife is a central part of life. The practice of the *ars moriendi* does not reflect some morbid preoccupation. It is actually life-affirming rather than life-denying. By coming to know Death as a friend, you release the energy you have invested in trying to bottle up your darkest fears. When you establish for yourself—through personal *experience*— that there is life after life, you will find you take a more relaxed and generous view of the vicissitudes of everyday life. When you examine your life from the standpoint of your death, you will surely find that there is no reason to perpetuate old quarrels and jealousies. You will wish to put things right between yourself and others, to give up petty agendas and live fully and creatively for the years allotted to you.

In postindustrial Western societies, the neglect of the art of dying has led to a vogue for spiritual practices drawn from other traditions, such as Tibetan Buddhism, which offers a detailed geography of the afterlife that may or may not be relevant to you if you are not a Tibetan Buddhist. Our general neglect is fed by both fear and denial. The denial thrives on our hurry sickness, our tendency to fill up our time with compulsive, external activities—interspersed with infusions of passive consumer entertainment, IV-fed through the TV tubes—leaving no space for the inner search. Filling our lives with a bustle of responsibilities that leaves us with "no time" to commune with soul is mockingly described by a Tibetan master as "housekeeping in a dream." Sögyal Rinpoche asks, "Would anyone in their right mind think of laboriously redecorating their hotel room every time they booked into one?"[1]

Our fear of death is bound up with our confusion about who we are. We fear losing all the props, connections, and résumés that we confuse with identity. We are terrified of being stripped of rank and title and credit cards and cell phones and being sent naked into the next world, as Inanna must descend naked into the underworld.

Your death is a rather important subject, not just the when and how, but the question of what follows, and what it all means. On a subject this vital and this intimate, you would be ill-advised to take answers on trust from other people. But how can we know before dying what lies on the other side, and know this as personal truth? In two ways: through a *visitation* by a resident of the Otherworld whose information can be verified; or by soul travel, by making a personal *journey* to the Other Side. My book *Conscious Dreaming* explores dream visitations by the departed. In what follows, I will offer a variety of techniques by which you can embark on conscious dream journeys to explore the conditions of the afterlife for yourself.

An art of dying adequate to our needs and yearnings today must address at least these five key areas:

1.   Practice in dream travel and journeying beyond the body. By practicing the projection of consciousness beyond the physical

plane, we settle any personal doubts about the soul's survival of physical death.

2. Developing a personal geography of the afterlife. Through conscious dream journeys, we can visit "ex-physicals"—and their teachers—in their own environments. We can explore a variety of transit areas and reception centers, adapted to the expectations and comfort levels of different types of people, where the recently departed are helped to adapt to their new circumstances. We can tour the "collective belief territories," some established centuries or millennia ago, where ex-physicals participate in shared activities and religious practices. We can examine processes of life review, reeducation, and judgment and follow the transition of spirits between different after-death states. We can also study the different fates of different vehicles of consciousness after physical death.

3. Helping the dying. The application of insights and techniques gained in these explorations to helping the dying through what some hospice nurses describe as the "*nearing* death experience."[2] In many of our hospitals (where most Westerners die) death is treated as a failure, or merely the loss of vital signs, followed by a pulled-out plug, a disconnected respirator, and the disposal of the remains. As we recover the art of dying, many of us in all walks of life—not only ministers and health care professionals and hospice volunteers—will be able to play the role of companion on the deathwalk, helping the dying to approach the next life with grace and courage and to make the last seasons of this life a period of personal growth. The skills required in this area include the ability to communicate on a soul level with patients who are in coma, are unable to speak or reason clearly, or have suffered severe memory loss. A vital aspect of this work is facilitating or mediating contact between the dying and helpers on the other side—especially departed loved ones—who can give assistance through the transition. Dreamwork and meditation are invaluable tools in helping the dying to prepare for the conditions of life beyond the body.

4. Helping the departed. We pray for our dead in our churches and temples, and no good intention is ever wasted. However, you may have a hard time finding a priest who is willing to take on the role of *psychopomp,* or guide of souls, and provide personal escort service to spirits of the departed who have lost their way and gotten

stuck between the worlds, causing pain and confusion to themselves and sometimes to their survivors. Yet the living have a crucial role to play in helping to release earthbound or troubled spirits. For one thing, some of these "ex-physicals" seem to trust people who have physical bodies more than entities that do not, because there is comfort in the familiar, because they did not believe in an afterlife before passing on—or quite simply because they do not know they are dead. An art of dying for our times must include the ability to dialogue with these spirits and help them to find their right path.

5.   Making Death your ally. Finally, we are challenged to reach into the place of our deepest fears and master them: to face our own death on its own ground and re-value our lives and our purpose from this perspective. When we "brave up" enough to confront our personal Death and receive its teaching, we forge an alliance that is a source of power and healing in every aspect of life.

Scientists of the Afterlife

Shamans are the original scientists of the afterlife, the once and future masters of this field. By definition, the shaman has died and come back. He has firsthand knowledge of what lies beyond the gates of death and can return *intentionally* through those gates to communicate with the spirits, to guide and relocate souls, and to further his understanding of the geography of nonordinary reality.

The lamas who bequeathed us the rich narrative of after-death transitions translated as the Tibetan Book of the Dead also knew by direct experience: the deliberate projection of consciousness into the bardo states beyond the physical plane.

Reliable maps of the afterlife are the gift of clear-sighted explorers. By the time they have been edited and canonized as mythology, scripture, and literature, they are already leached of some of their freshness and authenticity—though they may serve quite efficiently to shepherd people into collective belief territories after physical death.

At this stage in our evolution, we need something better than ancient travelers' tales, edited and bowdlerized by people who did not journey those trails for themselves during physical life. We need experiment and experience. Let's expand our sense of the possible by examining the practice and the travel reports of two Western explorers of the afterlife who brought *real* science to their observations, in the age of Newton and the age of quantum mechanics. Then we will be ready to go beyond the maps, on our own expeditions.

SWEDENBORG'S "WAKEFUL ECSTASIES"

Emanuel Swedenborg (1688–1772) was the son of a Lutheran bishop attached to the Swedish court. Living at the dawn of modern science, he mastered all the sciences of his day. He was driven by a passion for knowledge. He became fluent in nine languages. He made his own telescope and produced designs for a submarine and an airplane. He published a whole library of scientific treatises on subjects ranging from algebra to fossils, from hematology to the brain. In the words of one of his biographers, "he exhausted all the known sciences after founding several of them."[3]

Then he brought his towering intellect and his experiential approach to the study of the unseen. He was called to the new work by his dreams. In his fifties, he began keeping a dream journal in which he was wholly frank about erotic dreams as well as spiritual adventures. In twilight states, between sleep and waking, he found himself being drawn into experience of a deeper reality. Surfacing from sleep, he found himself entering "wakeful ecstasies."

> *I lay awake, but as if in a vision; I could open my eyes and be awake if I wanted to, but yet I was in the spirit—there was an inward and sensible joy through my whole body.*[4]

In the city of Delft, on the night of April 6, 1744, Swedenborg experienced the vision that transformed his life and work. Retiring early, he wrestled with an entity he described as the Tempter. After his struggles, he heard a noise under his head, which he interpreted as the departure of this dark being.

He started shivering uncontrollably.

He was at last able to snatch a few hours' sleep. Then:

> *I trembled violently from head to foot and there was a great sound as of many storms colliding, which shook me and threw*

*me on my face. In the moment I was thrown down I was fully
awake and saw how I was thrown down.*[5]

Terrified by this wholly vivid experience of being propelled outside his physical body, Swedenborg prayed for help. As he held up his
folded hands—the hands of his subtle body—"a hand came which
clasped mine hard." He found himself in the presence of a radiant
being he took to be Christ.

*I saw him face-to-face. . . . He spoke to me and asked if I had a
certificate of health. I answered, "Lord, thou knowest that better than I." He said, "Well, then act."*[6]

Afterward, Swedenborg found himself traveling far and deep into
nonordinary reality in a state that was "neither sleep nor wakefulness." He conversed and interacted with beings in the spirit world
"the same as with my familiars here on earth, and this almost contin-
uously."[7] He encountered and dialogued with dead people "of all
classes," including many people he had known during their physical
lives. They gave him information he was able to verify and put to use.
These encounters also gave him a firsthand understanding of the conditions of the afterlife. Previously, his religious faith had convinced
him that the spirit survives physical death. Now he could begin to
study *how* it survives.

He gained important insights from encounters with departed people
he had known before their deaths. He discovered that dead people
are frequently confused about their situation because they cannot
distinguish between the physical body and the subtle body. During
the funeral of Christopher Polhem, one of his former teachers, Polhem
"came through" to Swedenborg, "asking why he was buried when he
was still alive." The dead man was puzzled by the fact that, while the
priest sermonized about the resurrection of the dead at the Last Judgment, "he was still alive" and "sensible of being in a body."[8]

Swedenborg's observation of the condition of other spirits in the
afterlife led him to formulate the important observation that "when
a man dies, his soul does not divest itself of its peculiarities." He
observed the condition of the executed nobleman Eric Brahe and

reported that two days after his death "he began to return to his former state of life, which was to love worldly things, and after three days he became just as he was previously in the world."[9]

The departed follow the path of their desire and understanding. In his soul journeys, Swedenborg tracked them into many regions in the Otherworld. He encountered an angelic guide who told him that the "other members of his society" were appalled by the "crass ignorance" of the real conditions of the afterlife that prevailed among Westerners even after they took up residence in the spirit world. Swedenborg's mentor told him that "angels" of his rank are instructed to gather newly arrived spirits, find out their ideas about heavenly joy—and give them what they desire. "You know that everyone that has desired heaven . . . is introduced after death into those particular joys which he had imagined."

For example, there is a heaven for big talkers and another for big eaters. There is a paradise for those who believe the promise that they will rule with Christ forever; they see themselves enthroned as kings and princes. If you think of heaven as a beautiful garden, you get to smell the roses. But in all cases, according to Swedenborg's mentor, you will be bored to distraction within two days. Now that you are ready to move beyond your expectations, the guide assigned to you can begin to instruct you on further possibilities. By one means or another, you will learn that happiness requires "doing something that is useful to ourselves and others." Swedenborg's angel explains that heaven is not a fixed environment or program of events, but a state that *corresponds* to—or is actually created by— the spiritual condition of its inhabitants.[10]

The local clergy were not enthusiastic about Swedenborg's road maps, or the fact that his example might encourage others to go exploring for themselves. Inflamed by Swedenborg's observation that few priests ("that order of which very few are saved") seemed to prosper on the other side, a Swedish minister plotted to have him judged insane and committed to a lunatic asylum.[11]

Swedenborg's geography of the afterlife was the gift of experience, which invites us to go beyond his maps, just as he went beyond the maps of previous explorers. His basic travel techniques are already familiar to us. They included:

- Deep relaxation: He would close his eyes, focus his attention on a single theme or target, and slow his breath. He first practiced this approach, especially breath control, in childhood during morning and evening prayers. He spoke of the "passive potency" of his meditation practice. The heart of it was to "withdraw the mind from terms and ideas that are broken, limited and material."[12]
- Experiment in the twilight zone: The half-dream state on the cusp between sleep and waking was Swedenborg's favorite launchpad. He described this state as "the sweetest of all, for heaven then operates into [the] rational mind in the utmost tranquillity." He worked with both spontaneous and familiar photisms. For example, he writes of an "affirming flame" that would appear on his inner screen at the start of a journey or in the midst of a writing binge, reassuring him that conditions were favorable and that he was on the right track.

> Such a flame appeared to me so often and, indeed, in different sizes with a diversity of color and splendor, that during some months when I was writing a certain work, hardly a day passed in which a flame did not appear as vividly as the flame of a household hearth. It was a sign of approval.[13]

- Soul journeying: Swedenborg developed a fluid ability to shift consciousness and travel beyond the physical plane. "When I am alone my soul as it were out of the body and in the other world; in all respects I am in a visible manner there as I am here."[14]

Night and day, he lived and worked as an active dreamer. His banker friend Robsahm observed that Swedenborg "worked without much regard to the distinction of day and night."[15] Swedenborg himself noted, "When I am sleepy, I go to bed." He kept a fire going at all times, drank large quantities of coffee with a huge amount of sugar. His dress at home was a robe in summer, a reindeer coat in winter.

Across the centuries, his words echo as a clarion call to new generations of explorers to refuse to settle their accounts with possibility and just *do it*:

> I am well aware that many will say that no one can possibly speak with spirits and angels so long as he lives in the body; and many will say that it is all fancy, others that I relate such

things in order to gain credence, and others will make other objections. But by all this I am not deterred, for I have seen, I have heard, I have felt.[16]

MONROE'S "ULTIMATE JOURNEY"

Robert Monroe's wife, Nancy, was diagnosed with cancer while he was working on his last book, *The Ultimate Journey*. Monroe followed her on his own "far journey" not long after her passing. In his last years, with Death close to him, Monroe set himself to applying the techniques he had developed for journeying outside the body to exploring the condition of the departed and to developing a personal geography of the afterlife.

He had moved beyond the "bumps and grinds" of his early experiments in out-of-body travel. He found that he could embark on a journey by a "quick-switch method":

> The process was becoming so smooth that it was hard to define when I actually left the body. It was more the fading out of one state of being and into another, similar to falling asleep and staying conscious while doing so.[17]

Like previous explorers, Monroe found the nonphysical universe to be "thickly settled" (as they say on Massachusetts road signs). In keeping with his distaste for the old vocabulary of the Theosophists and the esoteric schools, he described a zone of "H Band Noise"— "the peak of uncontrolled thought that emanates from all living forms on earth, particularly humans"—enveloping physical reality. He inspected the fate after death of different types of people and concluded, like the true explorers before him, that "being physically dead doesn't change you much at first." He observed a "pile" of "ex-physicals" writhing and thrashing like adders in a snakepit in an endless attempt to have sex with each other.

As he became an increasingly frequent flier in these realms, Monroe noticed that he was often receiving appeals for help from departed people who were lost or scared. His task was sometimes to alert dead people to the fact that they were dead. He helped a dead woman in hospital who thought she was dying and wanted to die, because of her pain; she was still experiencing pain because she would not detach herself from her physical body.[18] He assisted a man who knew he was dead but could not see anything but darkness and "thought that was it." Monroe described how he would literally offer a helping hand:

> I take the hand of the person who has died—they still feel very physical to me because they are still attuned to being alive. Then I go towards what I call the belief system territories. The people soon find themselves moving along exit ramps towards their belief systems and then, all of a sudden, they just disappear. I am no longer holding their hand—they have spotted what they believe in. . . . They have moved into the non-physical reality system which is their belief system.[19]

Monroe found a higher intelligence beyond the H Band Noise who gave him guidance on how things work in the afterlife. He learned that "ex-physicals" keep the memory of human experience—and in most cases the perception of forms that resemble worldly life—after "graduation" from the physical body. You stay human, it appeared, as long as your reference point is human. Monroe was curious to see what realms of possibility lay beyond recognizable forms and was told by his guide, "Stretch your mind to there, what you know Home to be. Then release from here and you will be there." Monroe found himself joining in a dance of "energy curls" performing repetitive motions to the strains of celestial music. He soon became bored with this and decided that if he had his druthers, he would rather evolve into something like his guide. And who was Monroe's guide? With his penchant for Trekkie-era terminology, Monroe dubbed this intelligent light-form an INSPEC, i.e., Intelligent Species, Other-Than-Human. He eventually came to feel that his INSPEC was in no way alien to himself.

The Death Workshop: Part I

Of all the workshops I lead, my favorite is one I call "Making Death Your Ally." Over several days and nights, we embark on a series of journeys to contact guides and departed loved ones on the other side and to explore reception areas and transition zones in the afterlife. The climax is a face-to-face encounter with your personal Death. There is nothing morbid or funereal about this program. There is shock, and rank terror, but also raw, almost sexual vitality. Participants generally leave full of passion and courage, with the clarity that only Death can bring.

The twenty members of the first group expedition of this kind that I led were highly motivated. Some were keenly concerned about the spiritual condition of friends who were close to death or had recently crossed over. Two of the women in the group were nurses who regularly worked with the dying. Some participants had survived close encounters with death. The majority reported that they had felt called to this workshop by dreams of the departed. Pat had hedged about attending until she had this dream the night before the workshop:

The Train Station

I am at a train station where a lot of commuters—mostly men in business suits—are rushing to catch their trains. They are running and jostling, forcing their way into the compartments. There are two other groups. There are people who don't have regular bodies; they're shaped more like bubbles, with lights twinkling around them. And there's another bunch of passengers who seem drained and exhausted; they move like automatons, going through a routine they've been following for a long time. I don't know any of these people. I wake up to the fact that all of them are dead. I try to tell the people with hurry sickness they don't need to rush around anymore; they won't listen to me. The robot types don't even seem to hear me. I'm yelling to all of them, "All you people are dead!" I wonder what I'm doing here—am I dead, too?

What is a train station? A place of transition, of coming and going. A place where you wait until it is time for you to leave. A place where you choose between many lines. A place of *training*, and detraining (of which the frenzied commuters seemed greatly in need).

Pat felt, as I did, that she had visited a transit zone on the other side, where the newly departed are allowed time and space (or the semblance of time and space) to adapt to their new environment and accept new training. She also felt the dream was connected to the fact that several people who had been close to her had recently died.

EXERCISE 1: JOURNEY FOR A GUIDE

After initial discussion and relaxation exercises, I asked the members of the group to journey with the help of shamanic drumming to contact a teacher on the other side. I hoped that this encounter would produce a personal source of inner certainty and continuing guidance on issues of death, dying, and the afterlife for each member of the circle throughout the four days of the series. I suggested that this foundation exercise should be approached as an Upper World journey.

For this and subsequent journey exercises in the death workshop, I will give the instructions as if I am speaking to *you* directly, to make it easy for you to follow them if you wish to experiment for yourself. For the journey itself, you may use a drumming tape (see resources section) or meditation music, unless you are fortunate enough to have someone to drum for you. For some of the later exercises, you may wish to have the support of a partner.

Instructions for the Journey

1.   Guard your space and relax. Lie down or sit comfortably in a quiet, protected space. You are becoming very comfortable in your body. Totally relaxed, but not at all sleepy.

2.   Picture a place of ascent. Your place or means of ascent may be a mountain, the upper branches of a tree, a spiral staircase, an elevator that goes up and up, a whirlwind.

3.   Frame your intention clearly. I suggest something along the following lines: "I wish for guidance on the nature of life after life and on how to help others through the passages of death and dying." Carry your focused intention in your consciousness as you travel: it will be your miner's lamp in the dark. It will help to direct your journey and eliminate clutter.

4.   Embark on the journey. When the drumming (or music) begins, you will allow your consciousness to flow to the place of ascent you

have chosen. You will find yourself rising through many levels until you ascend to the level where your teacher is waiting for you.

5.   At the end of the drumming (or music) you will gently return to your physical focus and record the insights you have gained.

I was thrilled by how much my initial band of explorers brought back from this first journey. Here is a sampling of the travel reports that were shared in the initial workshop:

• Paula went to a special place to reconnect with an angelic guide who had assisted her in previous journeys. "A wild woman I didn't know turned up. She looked like a Viking. Her male counterpart followed and swept me up onto his horse. We went galloping off on a wild, dizzying ride. They told me this was not all going to be sweetness and light: this will be a wild ride, and I am here to experience my own death."

• One of the nurses encountered a guide who escorted her to a collection of people who resembled a MASH unit. "They were arguing and urging each other to take off in different directions. They had recently died and were just discovering that *we* decide on our conditions in the afterlife."

• Pat took off on the wings of a hawk, then realized she could fly by herself. The hawk could not accompany her above a certain level. Her guide appeared as an angelic figure, wearing wings similar to her own. She asked about this and was told, "I was you and you were me." She recognized her guide as a radiant self.

• Sandy traveled to a cave where she was tutored by a being called Kala. She did not recognize the name; later we talked about Kala as the Hindu personification of time, Kali's male counterpart, and a very appropriate adviser on death and dying. Sandy also encountered a black woman on the other side of a veil. She realized this woman was her second self. When she reached through the veil to touch her, she saw her arm turn black and become formless—and realized that she herself might also be formless. Eventually, they danced together. Then they fused, and she saw her body half-white, half-black. A cosmic struggle ensued. She felt herself being pulled, her legs stretching as she was torn limb from limb. She moved back to a witness perspective, watching this struggle from the outside.

• Lou went on a "cosmic gallop" to many locations in both the Upper World and the Lower World that suggested a range of valid traditions and techniques.

• Joan found Christ, whom she had long known to be her personal teacher. He opened his heart to her and she was enveloped in his light. "We became one. His light filled me and surrounded me." She thought she had failed to go through a more detailed agenda; I reassured her that to embody and carry that light was more than sufficient—we would all benefit from it.

EXERCISE 2: JOURNEY TO THE DEPARTED

We took a break to get ourselves grounded and back in the body by whatever means took people's fancy—stomping, snacking, hanging out with a tree. If you are experimenting with these exercises, you should do the same.

We moved on to the second of the major journeys I had planned: a journey to the departed. The approach here is the opposite of that of the trance channeler who invites the spirit of a departed person *in*, to speak through her. We were going *out*, in the shaman's way, to encounter spirits of the departed on their own ground, and to investigate the lay of the land.

Instructions for the Journey

1.   Guard your space and relax. Lie down or sit comfortably in a quiet, protected space. Follow whatever method of relaxation works best for you.

2.   Focus on a contact picture. You need to work with the image of a departed person who is connected to you—preferably (for this initial exploration) someone for whom you have benign or loving feelings. If you have dreamed of this person, call back the dream image and use this as your rendezvous point. At the start of your journey, you will try to reenter the dreamscape and initiate a dialogue with the person who appeared to you. If you do not have relevant dream memories, you may use a life memory, a portrait or photograph, or the image of the place where the departed person was buried or laid to rest as your contact picture.

3. Frame your intention. This might be expressed as follows: "I wish to visit _____ (a departed family member or loved one) in his or her present environment for our mutual growth and guidance. I will pay special attention to the location." Remember this is a journey to the departed, not a séance.

4. Be open to opportunity. If you establish contact with a departed person, you should feel free to explore any personal questions you have, from family business to continuing education beyond the physical plane. Be open to the possibility that, although you began by focusing on a particular person, another friend or relative may be the one who is most interested in communicating with you.

5. Embark on your journey.

6. Return to physical focus at the end of the drumming or music.

Here are some experiences reported by dream travelers who journeyed to departed relatives in the initial death workshop:

• Helen chose to visit her mother. Following her mother's death, Helen had been troubled by some physical disturbances in the house that could not be rationally explained. Concerned that her mother had remained "stuck" in her previous environment, Helen had performed a personal ritual aimed at helping her mother move along. In her journey, Helen was relieved to find that her mother had moved on to a new environment, but concerned that she still appeared to be "stuck."

Mom Is Glued to a Fifties TV Show

I found Mom inside a metallic container. It was shaped like a football and drifting around like a spaceship in what looked like outer space.

Mom was eating Waverly wafers and dunking them in her tea, smoking Pall Malls. All these things were favorites of hers—she died of lung cancer. She was glued to a TV show she used to like, As the World Turns.

I told Mom, "You're stuck. You need to get out of here."

"It's better than the last place I was in."

"No, no. Can't you hear Robert drumming?"

"Who's Robert? I don't see anyone."

"Follow the vibrations. Look. A hole is opening. You can go up through it and get on with your life." Indeed, a hole did seem to have opened in the ceiling of her mother's container.

"Hold on. I gotta see the end of As the World Turns. *There's only fifteen minutes left."*

• Sara journeyed upward, focused on finding two departed friends. She explored an environment in which (she was instructed) they would be required to stay until they were able to dispose of their astral bodies—which might otherwise be used by "impostors."

• Roderick found his mother. Excited as a schoolgirl, she showed him the curriculum of studies she was following at a locale that looked like a pleasant private school. Roderick noticed a large elevator and asked where it led. His mother became bashful and confused. One of her teachers explained to Roderick that she would be invited to go up in the elevator as soon as she had completed her present course.

EXERCISE 3: JOURNEY TO A RECEPTION CENTER

The purpose of the next journey is to explore how the newly departed are helped to adapt to their new circumstances. Hollywood has given us a wonderfully human and humorous version of a reception center on the other side in *Defending Your Life*, starring Albert Brooks. Different religious traditions give believers culture-specific versions: the Pearly Gates, the gardens of the Muslim paradise, the place of the white cypress with the twin springs in the Greek Mystery teachings. Robert Monroe observed modern city-dwellers who had passed on coming to terms with their new condition in a reception center that looked like a pleasant city park. I was intrigued to discover what new explorers might find.

Instructions for the Journey

1.   Guard your space and relax.
2.   Target a guide or dream image. If you succeeded in finding a guide on the other side (in the first journey exercise), you should ask your guide to escort you on that journey. If you recall a landscape

from a dream or previous journey that seems promising—like Pat's train station—you might choose to make this your target.

3.   Frame your intention. This might be stated as follows: "I wish to explore the process of transition after physical death. I will journey to a reception center where the recently deceased are helped to adjust to their new condition and are prepared for their onward journeys." You might add the following: "I will explore the conditions of this transit zone and seek insight from a guide or escort who is active on this plane—especially on whether I may be able to help in guiding ex-physicals who are lost or confused to a reception area of this kind."

4.   Embark on your journey.

5.   Return to your physical focus when the drumming ends, or at a preselected time.

Some of the explorers returned with quite stunning travelogues:

• Pat joined forces with her guide, who escorted her to an immense cathedral, Gothic in design but fashioned of translucent crystal. She was surprised by the conventional form. Her guide told her it was chosen because it suited newcomers' expectations.

Designing My Home on the Other Side

I was given a tour of a complex of buildings described to me as the Temple of Learning. I was told I would be able to teach here. I wanted to know about family members who had passed over, and I was able to visit with some of them. My father wanted me to relay a message to my mother that she would be okay, he would help her through the transition. However, she would not be joining family members in the afterlife. My father said, "You'll all be doing your own things, just as in your present life." He told me I'd get to hang out with the same kind of people who were with me in the workshop.

I wanted to know where I would be living. I was given to understand that I would be able to design my own living space. I told my guide, "I want all the colors inside my house." I saw a house constructed before my eyes, ultramodern, glass-walled, letting the light in. After all my winters in snowbelt country, I loved the prospect of living in a space that would be flooded with light in all seasons.

•   Tony's guide intervened to point him in a different direction when he set off toward a previously discovered location. He was escorted to a building with seven levels atop a mountain. On each level, different kinds of training were conducted. Some levels of this building were deep underground. On the top floor people were having a graduation party, complete with champagne. When they departed for the next stage, they became balls of golden light that shot straight up through the ceiling.

Tony was then guided to the dark side of this dimension, going out among the stars. He was instructed that he was required to contend with evil spirits—he should push them into a dark space out here. They would not be able to come back because he would be helped to force them through a one-way entry "like a heart valve."

•   Sara was intrigued by her previous discovery that we may need to move from one body to another after physical death to enter higher spiritual levels. Her travel report is firsthand confirmation of the teaching of many spiritual schools on this important theme:

Shedding Different Bodies at Different Levels

When the drumming begins, I find myself standing in front of a crystal grotto facing a pasture. My gatekeeper is waiting and I state my intent. There is a shift and I am in another place.

Beautiful gardens and pathways lead to other places. All the earthly things are there, but the colors are more intense, more real. The smells, the energy, are more alive than what we know on the physical plane.

Relatives and friends are busy greeting the newly arrived. I am greeted by my aunt and a departed friend. They both died around the same time three years ago. My aunt could not stay but promised help for future journeys. My friend stayed with me. Someone else began to explain to me that this is the first stop after going to the Light. The soul stays here for a time until the astral body dissolves. Then the soul proceeds to a place of debriefing where another body is shed. The next stop is a still higher plane where you have a chance to review the last life and see where you stand. At this point my friend relates some of the difficulties he had when he reached this stage. You continue ascending levels for different teachings, each time shedding another layer.

The layers or bodies are shed in safety when you are properly prepared to die. When you aren't ready or it is sudden, the shells can be picked up by other discarnate entities (not necessarily bad ones) and used for a time until the shell dissolves like a mask. This is not a good thing and can cause a lot of damage to the newly dead and can tie them to the earth plane for longer than necessary.

Toward the end of all the shedding, things became abstract. I saw the same place where I'd been before in a dream and was told I could go no further at this time.

This was rich experiential confirmation of esoteric teachings (clearest, perhaps, in Theosophical literature) about the shedding of different vehicles of consciousness after physical death—especially at the time of the "second death," which brings separation from the astral body or dreambody.

• Pam traveled to a guide who presided over a kind of "physics lesson." She wanted to understand whether these locales she was visiting were actually *places*. She was told the closest she can come to understanding for now was to think of a time warp.

• Rose heard Garth Brooks singing "I've Got Friends in Low Places." She was drawn downward, through a tunnel. A man on horseback appeared to escort her on a tour of a new landscape. She saw in the distance what at first appeared to be an enormous anthill. Immense lines of people wound around and around, waiting to get into a building she "knew" to be a hell. When her escort urged her toward the entry, men tried to stop her from going in. "Hey, get back in line!"

She realized these were people who had committed serious crimes. "I'm just visiting," she told them.

They did not believe her. "Wait your turn."

Her escort got her in. She inspected many retraining situations. "It was laid out like a convention center with all these booths." She was surprised to see a small altar—for the few people who are ready to pray.

She wanted to understand what happens to the worst cases. "Where's Hitler?"

She was shown a cell with immensely thick walls. From deep inside came the puny chink of a chisel.

These adventures led to animated discussion of the many-layered metaphysical universe, and the nature of heavens and hells. Pat's experience of designing her own home in the afterlife suggested that there are individual environments—sometimes overlapping with collective locales, sometimes a world in themselves—shaped by the imagination of a single consciousness. We agreed that the planes beyond the physical are both places and states of mind. In a shamanic journey or out-of-body experience, travel within them and between them is generally perceived as movement through space. More fundamentally, "graduation" from one level to another flows from the raising of consciousness and shifts in vibration.

Some of the locales we explored, such as Rose's "hell," seemed quite solid, effective jails or entirely believable habitats where people might spend a long duration without realizing that they might be able to move on. Others were much more fluid, subject to rapid alteration by a single imagination. Some were quite raw and unformed.

In the first phase of the death workshop, we also journeyed for tools to help the dying and for ways to assist departed people who may need guidance from the living. The fruits of these explorations are reflected in the next two chapters. In phase two, we followed our personal deathwalk through a deathbed meditation and a process of self-judgment to a raw encounter with our personal Deaths. I have reserved the corresponding exercises and experiences for chapter 13, entitled "Making Death Your Ally."

≈≈

CHAPTER 11

Sharing the Deathwalk

"As soon as you die, you'll find yourself in a dream just as on any other night."

"I'll tell you the truth. I don't like that. But how do you know?"

"You must have heard, I would hope, that the soul is immortal. Even though they bury your body the soul continues living. To prepare us for that life we dream . . . There is no other explanation of dreams. They are previews."

Adolfo Bioy Casares,
The Adventures of a Photographer in La Plata

When Spirit Takes the Wheel

Just as dreams rehearse us for life challenges, they rehearse us for the conditions of life after life. While many people in our society persistently slam the door on such dream experiences, leaving death as a gaping black hole, it is remarkable what insights come through when we leave the door open a crack. By encouraging others to work with their dreams, we can help them to walk the path of spirit beyond this lifetime.

Francis was an educated man in his later years who claimed that he "did not dream" before he attended a lecture I gave before a weekend workshop. The next morning, he woke from a powerful, multilayered dream that was stamped on his memory. In high excitement, he recorded his dream and rushed over in his car to our workshop space, where he signed up at the door. When I asked for

volunteers to share their dreams with the whole circle, Francis's hand
shot up. He thrilled all of us with this exciting narrative:

Spirit at the Wheel

*I am riding in the backseat of a big black limo. An invisible
spirit is at the wheel. The spirit doesn't know anything about
automobiles, and I am trying telepathically to tell it how to
drive. We need gas and pull up at a gas station. We bump right
up against the gas pump, which is also a Dumpster or trash
compactor. While we are stopped, I see a beefy guy I knew
thirty years ago peering at me from behind the pump as if he's
trying to remember who I am. We drive on to a second pump,
cutting off an ornery redneck in a green pickup who gets mad
and starts abusing us.*

*We drive round to the back door of a large building. The
spirit and I leave the car and go in through the door. When we
step into the stairwell, I drop my body and become one with
the spirit. As I go up the tight spiral stair—like a ship's stairwell—I notice that the building is actually a ship. Old and
dilapidated, like a training ship I was on in the Navy. As I climb
to a landing, I hear voices below. German tourists. Two women
followed by two men, who are impatient. They don't see me
because I'm now invisible. But one of the women stops and
stares at me as if she sees something.*

*Then all of them can see me. But they think I'm an informa-
tion machine. That's how they see me. They pull information
brochures or tickets out of my mouth and go off to read them.*

*I go on up the stairs. On a higher level, I see the ship's pilot.
He's familiar to me. But I don't know if he recognizes me or
even sees me.*

If it were my dream, I suggested, it might contain important teachings about the transitions of spirit after physical death. I notice that
after I leave my body, people come to me as a source of information.
I was interested in the transformation of a stationary building into a
seagoing vessel that (although currently anchored) could presumably
be used for a crossing. I had no doubt that this dream was a prepara-

tion for the after-death transition. As a reality check, I would want to find out if the "beefy guy" is alive or dead. All these observations drew a strong "aha" of recognition from the dreamer, who mentioned that he had a serious medical condition.

With Francis's eager consent, we turned his dream into theater, with the dreamer as casting director. The slim woman who played Spirit, turning tight spirals around the stairwell with a dancer's agility, and the tall man who stood rigid atop *my* place in the circle as the Pilot were especially convincing, giving us benign shivers.

Dreams not only prepare us for our own passage; they prepare us to help others. A New York woman dreamed that her husband was boarding a train. She ran after him, but was prevented from boarding the train. She was told she would have to wait for a later train. In a subsequent dream, she saw her husband floating away from her in a dark, rectangular box across a body of water. These dreams helped her to set aside the crusted bitterness of a sterile marriage and help her husband prepare for his journey.

A California woman dreamed she was at a school with a former boyfriend and a teacher who had died from AIDS-related disease several years before. When her friend stepped into the elevator, it went berserk, registering signs instead of numbers. Her friend grabbed at her hand, desperately telling her, "I love you." Jolted from her dream with a beating heart, the dreamer tried to contact her friend. She was unable to locate him until she learned that he had died several months after the night of her dream from AIDS-related illness. Her dream was more than a premonition of a friend's death; it came as a cry for help, foreshadowing possible confusion during the after-death transition. The dreamer, an educator who had not previously known that her ex-boyfriend was gay, later decided to volunteer to work with AIDS patients, making dreamwork a central part of her practice. Before reaching this decision, she embarked on a conscious dream journey to contact her departed friend. He told her he would help her in her new work and gave her specific and helpful information to which she had not had access in her waking life.

In many of our hospitals (where most Westerners die) death is treated as a failure, or merely the loss of vital signs. As we recover the art of dying, many of us in all walks of life—not only ministers and health care professionals and hospice volunteers—will be able to play the role of companion on the deathwalk, helping the dying to approach the next life with grace and courage and make the last seasons of this life a period of personal growth.

When a dying person is preparing to move on, one of the most helpful and human things we can do to assist her with the transition is to help her to picture a happy way of leaving a familiar environment for a journey into another dimension. Dreams, life memories, and guided meditation can all be used to help the dying to prepare for the release of consciousness from the physical plane.

Dreamwork with the Dying

Spontaneous sleep dreams may introduce images of a portal or crossing and of guides and allies on the other side who can be revisited through dream reentry or guided visualization. Such dreams are as likely to come to the helper or "coach" as to the dying person.

WATERSLIDE WORLD

Wendy's mother was in her seventies and had been living alone in another part of the United States for several years following the death of her husband. Then Wendy dreamed she was with her mother on a waterslide. They were sliding together into an enormous swimming pool, whooping it up like kids at an amusement park. Wendy's mother shot on ahead, laughing as she splashed into the clear blue water. As Wendy reached the end of the slide, a large barricade came down, blocking her from dropping into the pool. She peered round the edge of this obstruction and saw her mother swimming and frolicking in the pool, having a wonderful time.

Wendy was amazed and delighted by this scene, because her mother had never learned to swim; she had always been afraid of the water. Wendy started to step around the barricade to get into the pool. Then she heard a man's voice, telling her firmly, "You are not invited." She realized it was her father who was speaking to her. She looked down into the pool again and saw that her mother and father were sporting together. Both of them were younger. They were having a great time. When Wendy called me to share this dream, she told me she had not spoken to her mother for many weeks, but planned to phone her that evening. We both felt her dream might be preparing her for her mother's death. I asked Wendy if she intended to share her dream with her mother. "I could do that," Wendy reflected. She had often had trouble communicating with her mother. But, as she put it, "My mother believes in dreams."

I suggested that she should try to narrate her dream in a gentle, expansive way, making her descriptions as tactile and sensuous as possible: the sensation of shooting down the slide, the thrill of splashing into the water, the joy of frolicking about in the pool, the loving, playful presence of her father.

"If this were my dream," I told Wendy, "I feel it is helping me to help prepare my mother for her transition to the next life. It doesn't necessarily mean she's going to die tomorrow or next week or next year. It's *always* time to prepare for this journey, which may come long before, or long after, the time we expect."

That evening, in a lengthy, long-distance phone call, Wendy not only relayed her dream to her mother but led her inside the dreamscape, evoking the play of all the senses. Her mother loved the experience! She *felt* the smooth release into another element. She was amazed that she found herself completely at home in the water. She got happy shivers over her playful reunion with her husband. This reminded her of a dream of her own in which her husband had come to say good-bye soon after he died. He had appeared young and handsome. He had told her, "I can only stay for a moment, but I want you to know I'm living in the most beautiful place I have ever seen. It's always spring here."

I believe that the two women's dreams and the imaginal journey on which Wendy led her mother were all quite *real* experiences. Best of all, when Wendy helped her mother to step through a doorway into the next life, Wendy reminded her of something she already knew.

STEPPING THROUGH THE WARDROBE

Elibieta, a Polish laboratory assistant, dreamed she was in a friend's house. In her dream, the friend's house was notably different than in ordinary reality. Elibieta found herself walking an unfamiliar corridor, looking for a door. Where she expected to find the door, there was a wardrobe instead. When she moved the wardrobe aside, she entered a different dimension. The walls and the house disappeared, and she found her friend in a fresh new world, filled with light. The scene thrilled the dreamer, filling her with joy.

Elibieta's dream was prophetic. A year later, her friend went into a hospital for a major operation that failed to cure her illness. Afterward, the friend moved into the house of a religious order where she spent her last days. When Elibieta visited this house for the first time, she was told that the door to her friend's room was beyond a large wardrobe that had been moved into the corridor to make room for her bed. Elibieta found herself walking into a locale from her dream.

She dreamed of wardrobes repeatedly in the days that followed. On one of her visits to her friend, Elibieta found her in great pain. As Elibieta was leaving, she saw the huge wardrobe beyond the door. She turned back to her friend and shared her original dream, describing the luminous world where she had found her friend living on the other side of the wardrobe. They both got happy shivers as they explored this image. For Elibieta's friend, "stepping through the wardrobe" became a spontaneous meditation. She had been nearly blind for years prior to her final illness, but she saw these images in glowing color and depth. As she saw herself stepping through the wardrobe, she was rehearsing—in a simple, spontaneous way—for the transition that came shortly afterward, when she died peacefully in her bed.

This is a wonderful example of how working with dreams can help the dying. I was especially struck by the power of Elibieta's dream image, because the evening before she shared it with me, my youngest daughter and I had done a joint reading of the first chapters of *The Lion, the Witch and the Wardrobe*. In C. S. Lewis's fantasy for children of all ages, a wardrobe is the doorway to the Otherworld kingdom of Narnia. Elibieta could have borrowed her image from a book (though not from C. S. Lewis, who was not part of her childhood reading in Poland), and it might or might not have worked with the same power. The point is that *her* wardrobe was utterly personal and specific—*that* wardrobe, in *that* old house in Warsaw—while resonating with the depths of a universal and never-ending story.

Through the Picture

If the dying person has no strong religious beliefs, is skeptical about the possibility of life beyond the body, and has no suitable dream memories, she may still be helped by a sensitive person who can assist her to call up and reenter a beautiful memory from an earlier period of her life. This must be the *right kind of memory*. To dwell on the eve of death on familiar places and happy times among people who are still living could have entirely the wrong effect, by enmeshing the dying person in attachments to the physical world. The aim is to guide the dying person *forward,* not backward. How can this possibly be accomplished by leading that person on what sounds like a nostalgia trip?

In one of two ways. The first is to guide the dying person's mind to the image of loved ones *who have already passed on.* She may see herself dancing with her beloved husband, who died ten years before her, or bouncing on her granny's knee in the long-lost home in the Smoky Mountains. As she moves beyond the body, along the deathwalk, she may encounter these same departed loved ones. It is of secondary importance whether the figures who may now appear to her are the individual spirits of the people she knew or the forms assumed by other guides to reassure her she will be loved and protected and to speak to her according to her level of understanding.

The second kind of life memory that can be used as a springboard for leaving the body behind is an episode in which the dying person moved gracefully *into another dimension.* This is likely to be a memory of moving into the elements of water or air, since few of us have danced through fire. A beautiful example of how a memory of this kind can be used to construct a personal rite of departure is in the recent movie *It's My Party*. In this tragicomic film, Eric Roberts plays a man with AIDS who has resolved to end his life by drug overdose before he loses his eyesight and his mental faculties. In his last minutes, his friend leads him on a deep visualization of a ride they once took on a ski lift. When they got to the top, they took off and were "flying." He passes with this wonderful image of flight off the mountain.

The memory of a favorite pet can be helpful in preparing a dying person for the crossing to the afterlife. For some reason, many people in our culture seem to have fewer reservations about encountering pets that have died than about dealing with departed friends or family. In particular, dogs we have known present themselves quite spontaneously as guides to the Otherworld.

After my dog Kipling—a huge, fiercely loyal shepherd-Labrador mutt—was killed on the road in 1986, he appeared to several members of my family in important dreams. In one of my dreams, his appearance offered insight into the nature of death itself:

Across the River

I came to the edge of a river. There was an island on the far side, with lush green vegetation. I realized my dog was over there, bounding about, having a great time chasing something through the bushes. He was always a great hunter, the terror of woodchucks on the farm.

I called to him and he pointed and swiveled his head toward me. He couldn't see me. I thought he was blind, because his eyes had a milky cast. Then I realized there was a transparent screen between him and me. It covered the whole island, like shrink-wrap.

Communicating on the Soul Level

We can use the skills of active dreaming to reach people who cannot be reached by other means and share their deathwalk in a helpful and spirited way: we can learn to communicate on a soul level with patients who are in a coma, are unable to speak or reason clearly, or have suffered severe memory loss.

"I DESERVE A WINDOW"

Connie, a caring and sensitive nurse who had worked with many terminal patients, was deeply troubled by the case of an elderly coma patient who had been on life support systems for a long time. The doctors believed that there was almost no chance that Ruth would revive. For the family, hospital visits were heartbreaking; Ruth's son referred to them as "a wake that never ends." Yet for some reason, Ruth was hanging on.

Connie had attended some of my workshops and had learned to focus and expand her natural flair for dream travel. She recognized that Ruth's soul had basically left her body yet remained connected to it by a thread. So long as this thread was intact, the body would remain alive, though completely dormant, and the soul would be detained from moving into higher realms. Connie decided she would journey to communicate with Ruth on a soul level. Connie's intention was to determine why Ruth was still clinging to the vestiges of life: Did she want to come back or was something blocking her from going forward?

"When I encountered Ruth's spirit," Connie reported, "she told me she hated the shared, windowless room they had given her in the hospital. She felt she deserved better treatment. She wanted them to play the classical music she loved. She identified several tapes she wanted brought from her house. She was also very disappointed that most of her family and friends had stopped visiting her in the ward. She named several people who should come to pay their last respects. She told me that when her wishes were fulfilled, she would be ready to take her leave."

Connie persuaded the hospital to move the coma patient to a private room with a view. She called Ruth's family and asked them to bring over the tapes; Ruth's son agreed to do this at once, while expressing surprise that the nurse knew more about his mother's musical tastes than he did. One by one, the friends and family members Ruth had asked for came to pay their respects. Then Ruth passed over peacefully.

The night she died, Connie sat up in bed. "I saw a radiant ball of golden light moving through my home. I felt Ruth's presence. I was filled with joy."

"I'VE BEEN WAITING TO SAY GOOD-BYE PROPERLY"

A woman called Maya approached me during a break in one of my workshops. She was troubled by the plight of her father, a man whose condition had been diagnosed as "senile dementia."

"He's been in and out of hospital beds, and in and out of his head, for the last three years," she reported, her eyes welling with tears. "I love him but I can't stand to be near him. Is there anything I can do to help?"

I asked her father's age. When Maya told me he was eighty-four, I suggested that surely the most important thing was to help prepare him for the next life and to make sure that nothing was in his way. Maya nodded vigorously.

"If I were you," I suggested, "I would try to communicate with his higher self, on a level where he is not impaired. I would try to clarify what he wants—to come back to his body, if he needs more time, or to go forward, if he's ready."

Maya was eager to try this. She asked whether the fact that her father was living thousands of miles away might be an impediment.

"Not necessarily." I shared several experiences of working in this way across great distances.

Maya was a gifted dream journeyer and had no difficulty shifting consciousness as she leaned her back against a tree in the garden of the holistic center where we were working. She had vivid sensations of flight, and then of a joyful, animated encounter with a younger, more vigorous version of her father in a light-filled "space without walls." Her father told her he loved her and needed to lay to rest old misunderstandings. "I couldn't leave without saying good-bye properly."

Maya was deeply moved. But in a part of herself, she feared she was indulging in wishful thinking, "making things up."

Her doubts were resolved that night, when she learned that her father had passed over peacefully, less than half an hour after she had journeyed to meet him.

Shared Meditation: Joining the Light

One of the most beautiful and practical elements in Sögyal Rinpoche's application of the ancient Tibetan art of dying to modern lives is his guidance on meditation with and for those who are approaching death. He offers improvisations on the technique of *phowa*, or the "transfer of consciousness."[1] By my observation, these work quite well for Westerners providing the language and images are adapted to the personal evolution and belief system of the individual. A simple adaptation is this heart meditation:

Heart Meditation

1. Invoke the embodiment of Light and Love in the form you truly believe in, glowing in the sky above you. You may see this radiant presence as Christ or Mary or one of the Buddhas—or simply as a form of pure golden light.
2. Fill your heart with this radiant presence. See the light of its truth and compassion streaming into your heart center, washing you free from all guilt and fear.
3. See the light growing stronger and brighter at your heart center. Your consciousness is becoming a sphere of light in the place of your heart.
4. Let the light from your heart stream outward and upward like a shooting star and fly into the heart of the being of Light you have invoked.
5. See your heart-light merge with the greater radiance and dissolve into the greater Light.

A meditation of this kind is meant to be practiced until it becomes second nature. When we have mastered heart meditation ourselves, we can offer great help to the dying by guiding them through it. If they are too impaired, too scared, or too intransigent in their self-limiting beliefs to be open to this kind of practice, Sögyal Rinpoche suggests that we can still help by doing it for them.

Meditation on Behalf of the Dying

1. Visualize a radiant presence above the head of the dying person.
2. See rays of light streaming down onto the dying person, cleansing and brightening his or her whole being.
3. See the dying person rising in his or her shining body to merge with the greater Light.

All of this may be far simpler than we imagine. Brother Lawrence of the Resurrection (1611–91) a lay Carmelite brother who worked

quietly and happily in a monastery kitchen for thirty years, offers this
reassurance:

> That neither skill nor knowledge is required to enable us to go
> to God, but just a heart determined to turn to Him only, to beat
> for Him only, and to love Him only.

> That God never fails to offer his grace at our every action; but
> we do not perceive it when our minds have wandered from
> God, or if we have forgotten to ask his aid.[2]

The practice of Brother Lawrence was simply to focus his awareness, in the midst of his daily activities, on "the presence of God." He
experienced this as "an inward lifting of the heart" to a source of
boundless Love. The form in which he perceived his God will startle
those of straitjacketed faith:

> My usual method is simple attentiveness and a loving gaze
> upon God, to whom I often feel united with more happiness
> and gratification than those of a baby at its mother's breast.
> Such is the inexpressible felicity I have experienced that I would
> dare to call this state "the breasts of God."[3]

CHAPTER 12

Helping the Departed

Our service to the dead is not narrowed to our prayers,
but may be as wide as our imagination.

William Butler Yeats

What to Do When You Might Be Dead in Denver

It was snowing over the new Denver airport as I boarded the shuttle
bus for my hotel. My suitcase was flying on somewhere without me. I
had left home at the start of a warm, bright end-of-summer day—
warm enough to swim in the pool, which was still open—bound for
Boise via Chicago. Storms in the Midwest, mechanical trouble, and
missed connections had bumped me to Detroit and dumped me in
Denver snow, well after midnight, en route to a ghost airport.

Planes no longer fly from the old Stapleton field, but the look-alike
airport hotels cling like crabgrass to the perimeter of its *terrain vague*.

How do I know I'm not dreaming? I asked myself as I rode up in
the glass cage of the hotel elevator. The seasons were scrambled; I
had spent all day traveling to places that were not on my itinerary;
and I had ended up at an airport from which planes do not take off.
As a matter of fact, how did I know I wasn't dead? In dreams, I have
noticed that luggage is sometimes a metaphor for the physical body,
as well as for life burdens. Here I was, beside a ghost airport, without
my bag. Could it be I had lost my bag of meat and bones?

I called my friend in Boise. There was static on the line, but he
seemed to understand me well enough. This seemed to indicate that
I was not dead or dreaming—until I remembered that in dreams,
we quite frequently receive phone calls from the departed. What

evidence did I have that I was not one of those dead people who phone the living in their dreams?

Only the minor discomforts of the flesh: a mildly upset stomach, the pricking of stubble I pecked at with the little pink throwaway razor they had given me at the hotel reception desk. I showered until my skin shone red as a boiled lobster. The depth and texture of all these corporeal sensations were proof, surely, that I was fully inside my physical body and was therefore neither dead nor dreaming.

Yet the play of the senses (I reflected) is not confined to the physical plane. The dreambody has its own sensory array and experiences touch and smell and taste as well as sight and sound, as well as a finer range of perception mediated by finer antennae.

I resolved to dream on my problem. I tossed for a long time on an uncomfortable cusp of sleep, disturbed by the psychic litter you routinely encounter in places frequented by transients: the fantasies and nightmares of traveling salesmen, flight attendants, and (on this particular night) prison wardens, who had been in town for a conference. I watched the tawdry show for a couple of hours before I fell into a dream:

> I am flying under a snowy sky, over an airfield from which planes never take off. Below me are anonymous rooftops. I can't tell one building from another. I'm having a hard time remembering where I left my body. It's in one of these hotels, but I can't for the life of me remember which one. Something tugs at me and I decide to take a chance. I dive down through one of the rooftops and land with a huge whoomph in the body on the bed.

I opened my eyes, feeling bruised and disoriented. I recognized nothing in my environment, nothing that pertained to me. For a ghastly moment, I not only did not know where I was, I did not know *who* I was. I retained my sense of self. In a larger sense, I knew perfectly well who I was. But for a moment, I had forgotten what identity and what body I had chosen to inhabit.

I recovered from my partial amnesia within seconds, but it was a shocker. It was still percolating as the morning shuttle carried me across the high plateau toward the nested cones of the new airport terminal.

The path of the soul after death, say the Plains Indians, is the path of the soul in dreams—except that you don't get to come back (however bumpily) to the same physical body. Given my confusion, coming and going from the dream state, is it any wonder that people get lost and confused after physical death?

Why the Departed Get Stuck

The living have a crucial role to play in helping to release earthbound or troubled spirits. For one thing, some of these "ex-physicals" seem to trust people who have physical bodies more than entities that do not, because there is comfort in the familiar, because they did not believe in an afterlife before passing on—or quite simply because they do not know they are dead. "You feel more familiar to one who has just passed over," a mother was told by her departed son, in one of several similar cases reported by Dr. Robert Crookall.[1] British clairvoyant L. M. Fitzsimmons maintained that "earthbound and other spirits needing help listen and pay attention to what you have to say because, by your appearance, they realize that you have a physical body."[2]

Often they announce their condition and their need for help to the living in dreams.

By my observation, the most common reasons people get "stuck" on the other side and remain unhealthily attached to the living include the following:

1. The departed often do not know they are dead.

Swedenborg observed that "when a person enters the spiritual world, or life after death, he is in a body the way he was in the world. There seems to be no difference, so he does not feel or see any difference."

In Western society, the study of the subtle vehicles of consciousness is not exactly part of mainstream culture. So it is not at all surprising that many people who "wake up" to find themselves in a postmortem environment do not realize they are dead. They still have bodies that can experience pleasure and pain, and the world around them looks like the one they know.

Kim dreamed that a lover who had died was sprawled on the couch in her living room, watching TV. She had had previous dream encounters with him since his death, including several in which they had had sex. In the new dream, something—maybe the banality of the scene—shocked her into realizing that things were not right. She reentered the dream and asked the deceased lover, "What are you doing in my house?" He shrugged and told her, "I'm just watching TV." She initiated a dialogue. She coached him, gently but firmly, in the fact that he was no longer alive and presumably had better things to do than to hang around his old haunts. He responded by proposing sex. "You can sit on my face," he suggested with a leer. She had to get tough before he left the house.

In a dream, I found myself mentoring a large group of worldly people who were just being made aware that they had passed on:

I am in a large, pleasant assembly hall, with a platform deco-rated with flowers and ferns. Most of the people in the audience of several hundred are elderly Jewish New Yorkers, many of them deeply tanned from their retirement years in south Florida. They are very this-worldly people. They have been shocked to discover the reality of the afterlife, and they are try-ing to figure out how to relate the rules and skills they have learned to their new condition. Some insult each other in Yid-dish. I spend time with two older men—tanned, wrinkled, suc-cessful businessmen. I am astonished by the depth of my compassion and empathy for these people. I explore with them how they can apply some of their worldly gifts—humor, the art of making a deal—to their new situation. They show off the fact that I have befriended them. This gives them validation and enables them to rescue some sense of self-worth.

I recognized one of the men in this dream, the father of a woman who was a frequent participant in my Active Dreaming circles. I like to think that she and I were able to give him some practical help when he subsequently passed on.

2.   The departed cling to familiar places.

Lisa's mother had left her a piece of land, now quite valuable because of urban development in the area. Lisa wished to sell the land to have money for travel and further education, but felt she couldn't. She became confused as she tried to explain her situation to me. Little by little, I established that Lisa's mother had been a very controlling woman. Also, that Lisa had not attended her funeral and had never been to the gravesite.

Lisa reported a recent dream: "My mother is living in the shack on that land." Through dream reentry, we established that this was literally true. At Lisa's request, I journeyed to the shack and communicated with her mother directly, telling her gently but firmly that she now had more important things to do than to cling to the daughter. Lisa and I agreed on some simple rituals that would enable her to say farewell properly: a loving offering at home, a visit to the gravesite, the burial of an object associated with the mother. Powerful feelings of resolution came with this work.

3.   The departed cling to their ruling addictions and desires.

A certain kind of tavern gives me shudders. I am conscious of a swarm of dead drunks trying to get another taste—or another smoke—via the living people at the bar. Addictions and the tug of old habits frequently keep departed people from moving on into higher dimensions. In the following case study, a woman's addictions were exacerbated by those of deceased family members who had remained closely attached to her. Her courage and love enabled her to dialogue with the departed, to establish healthy boundaries, to help loved ones who had gotten stuck on the other side to find their right paths—and in the process, to triumph over her own addictions.

A TOAST FOR HONEY

Janet was troubled by a dream in which she saw herself wearing four large nicotine patches. When we began to explore the dream, she readily admitted she was a heavy smoker who had often considered quitting without much success.

I asked her if she had considered using nicotine patches.

"I wouldn't *touch* those things." She shuddered and folded her arms tightly across her chest.

The violent aversion expressed in her body language was surprising from someone who said she was still interested in finding a way to stop smoking.

I asked her to describe the "nicotine patches" in her dream in more detail.

"They're big. They're sticky and kind of gloppy. I've got one back here"—she reached over her shoulder to indicate the base of her neck. "There's another one here." As she moved her hand toward her heart, she gasped. "These things won't let me breathe."

On an intuitive hunch, I asked Janet if anyone close to her had died as a result of heavy smoking. She listed three close relations who had died within the previous ten years from lung cancer associated with heavy smoking. Janet's sister, with whom she had been especially close, had died just a year before. "I feel she's been with me ever since," Janet commented, her eyes misting. Then she remembered an uncle who had also died from lung cancer. "That makes four, doesn't it?"

Four nicotine patches stuck to her (in the dream) in a way that wasn't right. Four dead relatives, in a close-knit family, who had all been compulsive smokers, up to the end. On her deathbed, Janet's sister had told her, "I'd give anything for a smoke."

If it were *my* dream (I gently volunteered) I would try to talk to my sister—and maybe to some of the other smokers in the family who had passed on. We agreed to meet again the next day.

As preparation for this meeting, I asked Janet to bring a personal object that had belonged to her sister.

That night, I had a dream I understood only imperfectly until my subsequent meeting with Janet. In my dream, I went down in the elevator to the lobby of a large hotel, where Janet and a woman I did not know were waiting for me. Janet introduced her companion as Honey. She was a well-dressed older woman, quite formal in her manners. Her face and body were bloated, but she did not strike me as obese; I wondered if the bloating was the effect of cortisone or similar drugs. We were just starting to get acquainted when Honey dragged Janet away into a crowd of people milling by a coffee machine. I watched their heads vanish in a pall of smoke. Irritated, I went after Honey and made her sit next to me, on a settee, so she could hear what I needed to tell her.

Who was Honey? I was brooding on that as I drove to my morning appointment with Janet. On the way, I noticed a beer advertisement on a billboard. The slogan read, "A Toast with Honey," confirming my need to identify Honey.

At the beginning of our meeting, I asked Janet if she knew anyone called Honey. Janet told me this was her pet name for her departed sister. It was only used within the family, and she had not mentioned it the previous day. When I recounted my dream, Janet confirmed my physical description of her dead sister (she had been treated with drugs that caused bloating) and her old-fashioned manners. Both of us received little shivers of confirmation. I had no doubt, at that moment, that Honey *was* present. I was struck by how my dream had made it clear that I would be counseling *two* women—not only Janet but her departed sister—and that Honey might actually be my principal client.

I closed my eyes and received a clear impression of Honey. She looked like the woman from my dream, slimmed down a bit. I received a clear flow of thoughts from her. She was a loving person, deeply devoted to her family and especially to Janet. She was troubled by the realization that she might be the source of problems in her sister's life. She was ready to accept help.

I suggested to Janet that she should now try to communicate with Honey directly. What welled up from Janet spontaneously, as she talked to her sister, was beautiful and moving beyond my powers of description:

"Honey, I will always love you and I'm sure that one day we will be together again. But for now we need to follow our separate ways. You need to go forward into a new stage of learning and growing. I need to get my brain and my body clear of toxins. I don't want to carry my addictions into the afterlife. There are guides who are waiting for you—Mom is waiting—and you need to go to them *now*. You can still visit me in dreams. If you want, we'll celebrate your birthday together. We can even share a drink and a smoke, if you still need that. But only on your birthday."

As Janet's words rolled on, we both felt a quickening sense of abounding love and *resolution.* Afterward, I asked Janet to blow into the object she had brought—a ring that had belonged to Honey—and make it her intention to transfer any part of her sister's lower energy that was still with her into this ring. After she had done this, Janet said she felt immensely "lighter and brighter." I suggested that she should seal the ring in a closed container and bury it in her garden.

With shining eyes, Janet reported that she could now see a light-form she believed to be her sister's spirit gliding upward, on its proper path.

Janet had dreamed of *four* unpleasant nicotine patches. This left three to locate and deal with. I asked Janet's permission to journey on this. I soon found her father in a tavern on a street I drove along quite frequently. I was puzzled by the fact that, while I was quite familiar with that block—the drugstore on the corner, the bait shop along the way—I had never noticed the tavern. Janet told me later that the tavern had been the family's regular hangout until it closed down a decade before, just prior to her father's death. Her father was apparently hanging out in his old haunts, trying to feed his old habits, unaware that he was dead.

I was having a hard time getting through to him. Then a pleasant, red-haired woman appeared. She might have been in her twenties. She told me to tell Janet's father to turn around and listen to her. "I can get him out of here if he'll only listen."

I realized that she must be Janet's mother. I tapped the man at the bar on the shoulder. He glanced around quickly, but was still not in the mood to listen to his wife. I wondered who or what *would* get through to him. It occurred to me that a conservative, Irish-American Catholic might listen to a male priest and wondered if one might intercede. The next instant, an old-fashioned priest complete with cassock and dog's collar entered the scene. He took Janet's father by the hand and led him on board a train. The image seemed right: Janet's father was on the right line, heading out. This left two more smokers to be located—or relocated. I found brother Bill and watched as he, too, boarded the train. However, he sat apart from his father and the priest, clutching a can of beer and a pipe. I found Janet's uncle in a different location, a rural cemetery. He was watching mourners laying flowers at a grave. As I watched, his attention shifted to a nearby headstone. I realized that he was reading his own name, absorbing the finality of his own physical death. I saw Janet's mother again, in a shimmering nimbus of light. The uncle looked up and appeared to recognize her. I felt that this situation was about to be resolved in a gentle and natural way and left the two of them to get on with it.

When I reported these experiences to Janet, she resolved to construct a personal ritual of leave-taking for her three male relatives at their gravesites. Her uncle, she told me, was buried in the rural cemetery I had seen in my dream journey.

We agreed that if she was not ready to give up smoking and drinking altogether, she would take steps to ensure that when she indulged, she was doing so for herself, instead of her departed relatives. She would not smoke in her house.

This is already a happy ending, but Janet's story has an interesting sequel. Already an active dreamer with a strong spiritual orientation, Janet felt the need to check on her loved ones after they had moved on. She had a dream encounter with Honey, in what appeared to be a medical school on a higher plane, and a loving dream reunion with her mother, who assured her that her father was doing fine. They were not together (her mother explained) because they had different lessons to learn, on different levels. These dream experiences deepened Janet's sense of closure—with one important exception. She was unable to locate her brother Bill and was disturbed by my account of seeing him sitting apart on the train, with his beer and his pipe.

Janet asked me if I would try to find Bill. I told her she could probably do this herself, given the power of her love and the skills she had been developing, and that her personal experiences would be far more valuable than any messages from a go-between. Janet decided to attend a death workshop in which I encouraged participants to journey to transit stations and reception centers on the other side by the techniques described in chapter 10.

Janet journeyed to a vast open space that reminded her of St. Peter's Square in Rome. Raised Catholic and still a believer, Janet was amused—but not altogether surprised—to find herself deep inside a collective belief territory. However, when she asked for a guide who could help her locate Bill, she was approached by a male figure who looked like Mahatma Gandhi. "Gandhi" escorted her to an oversize train. She found her brother on board, still clutching his can of beer and his pipe.

"Bill was nervous," she reported. "He didn't want to come with us. I told him he could keep his beer and his pipe if he needed to, though I wasn't sure this was completely true. I yanked him by the hand. He's a big man and he was hard to move. But Gandhi kept a grip on my other hand and gave me strength to pull Bill off the train.

"Then Gandhi led us to a fountain. He directed Bill to get in. Bill was washed clean and came out looking different. Gandhi presented him with fresh white clothes in a box, like a laundry box. When Bill put them on, he changed again.

"He told me he needed to check on people we had known. I gave him a quick guided tour, flitting about through our old neighborhoods. He didn't know that a close relative had moved houses, or that the neighborhood tavern had closed down. He kept trying to give me directions but gave up when he realized everything had changed, that life had moved along since he had died.

"Now he was ready to move on. He sort of bunched himself together, imploding inward while something fell away from him like discarded clothes. I saw him shoot straight upward, like a fireball."

4. The departed are held up by unfinished business.

Breton folk wisdom holds that you must always provide proper interment for the dead or else the departed will come back to demand proper burial. During the funeral, you must try to avoid leaving the house empty; otherwise, the person who has departed may feel duty-bound to stay and watch over it.[3]

Mary's mother, an Alzheimer's sufferer, had been "out of it" for a couple of years before her death. Soon after she passed over, she started appearing to her daughter in dreams in a very different guise. She was lucid, coherent—and angry. She told her daughter that she had not been cared for or fed properly in her last months. She also insisted that her estate had been "stolen" by relatives she had never intended to be prime beneficiaries. Mary had always paid attention to her dreams and promptly hired a lawyer to investigate. The lawyer reported that the mother had been persuaded, during the last stage of her illness, to place the bulk of her estate in the hands of more distant relatives in an irrevocable trust. That night, Mary's mother visited her in another dream and told her that there were "chinks" in the trust and that it could be broken. She told her daughter firmly that she must stand up for her rights and pursue this aggressively. Based on Mary's dream guidance, the attorney was able to launch a legal action to overturn the trust. In conscious dreams, Mary reported back to her mother. Mary also resolved that, when the legal business was complete, she would stage a personal ritual of leave-taking to encourage her mother to move along her higher path.

When the living do not heed their dreams, the departed will sometimes cross into the field of physical (or quasi-physical) perception to get their message through. A sharp, cynical network news reporter I know found his definition of reality blown apart when he walked into a Manhattan office and saw Al, a producer whose funeral he had attended the week before.

"What are *you* doing here?" the reporter demanded.

Al was agitated because people at the network had not read—let alone used—some important scheduling suggestions he had written up just before his death. The memo had gone missing. He told the reporter to look under the blotter on the desk. When the reporter did so, he found the missing memo. As he did so, Al's form faded out.

Such occurrences are by no means uncommon and may—as in this case—be entirely positive and helpful to the living. (If Al had still been fretting about his lost memo a couple of years after his death, it would be a different story.)

Spirits may linger to close a deal, to collect on a debt, to settle a score, as in Deborah's story:

"YOU OWE ME MONEY"

Deborah, an antiques dealer who bought much of her stock at estate sales, was troubled by a dream of a fellow dealer who had recently died in his eighties. She had purchased the contents of his store. In her dream, she saw him lying in his coffin. The coffin was supposed to be sealed up, but in her dream it was open. She was horrified when the dead man opened his eyes. Some of his friends were present. They kept telling him, as he rose from the coffin, "Lie down and shut your eyes. You're dead." When he persisted, they got a chair for him and sat him down. He proceeded to yell at the dreamer, "You owe me money! You're selling my stuff and I haven't been paid!" She tried to explain to him that she had paid his estate. He didn't want to hear about that. He cursed and threatened, promising that if he did not get paid, he would cause unspeakable damage to the woman and her store.

She woke up terrified. Her first thought was, "He doesn't know he is dead."

The dream came in the midst of a series of troubling paranormal events at her store—things falling without apparent cause, unexplained knocks and thuds, broken glass—all involving furniture and objects she had purchased from the dead man's store.

When Deborah reentered her dream, she confronted the old man: "What are you doing? Don't you know it's time to move on?"

"I'm not ready to go," he told her. "I need more time."

Deborah found herself moving into a place of darkness and terror, a place familiar to her from experiences in early childhood. She called in light and asked for help in guiding the old man toward the light. Her call was answered. She had the impression of inexhaustible light flooding into her. She saw herself projecting light to the old man's heart area. "It's time to move on," Deborah told him gently but firmly. When he started cursing and complaining again, she shut out his words and focused on sending more light. As she beamed light into his form, she saw him rising up from the chair, then seeming to levitate. When he realized what was happening, he marveled at it. He said sheepishly, "Maybe it *is* time." She watched him rise up through several apertures, moving toward the Light.

This is a beautiful story, but it is not the whole story. As the old man lifted out of his chair, Deborah had the impression of something dark slipping away from him like an old suit of clothes. Watching over her, I had the same impression. My first image of the old man was of someone raising a mug, clutching at its handle as if terrified it would be taken away from him. It turned out the old man was a severe alcoholic. I had the further early impression of something swathed in dark, gloppy material that reminded me of mummy wrappings. As a higher aspect of the old man separated itself from this etheric stuff and rose toward the Light, a shadow being slid away: an abandoned shell that still retained some degree of life and, with that, mindless, raging bitterness and alcoholic craving. Deborah and I agreed that something must be done to contain this lower aspect of the dead man's identity. We agreed to conduct a second burial. She would take an object that had belonged to the dead man and use this as a lodging for his lower aspect, until it dissolved over time. She would bury it at the edge of the graveyard where his physical body had been interred. To assist in the transfer, she would be careful in using and displaying alcohol in her home—since the dead man's addiction was clearly one of the things that had kept him earthbound and led him to trouble the living. Afterward, she would purify her home and store by smudging and a good old-fashioned housecleaning.

5. The departed are detained by the living.

A woman was troubled by a series of dreams in which she saw her departed mother staggering under the weight of an enormous bucket. I asked her to go back inside the dream and ask her mother what was going on. Her mother told her, "I'm weighed down by all your tears. You have to stop mourning me and let me move on."

Part of setting healthy boundaries between the living and the dead is to set a term to mourning: to let our loved ones go.

We hold the departed close to the living in ways besides grief that encumber both. Certain types of séance, ritual, and psychic mediumship—amateur or professional—rely on invoking and channeling "spirit guides" on a rather low level. Call in the spirits without thorough screening and without the ability to send them away and you're in the position of someone who lives in a downtown apartment who throws open his doors and windows in the night, yelling, "Free beer." The kind of party you'll get isn't necessarily the kind of party you want.

6. Some of the departed believe they are damned.

If you have ever listened to a hellfire preacher, it will come as no surprise to you that lots of people harbor the fear that they may be consigned to an unpleasant place after death. People who are possessed by such fears at the time of death may cling to the living in the hope of avoiding damnation.

A macabre example of the complications that may ensue can be found in the record of a Jewish rite of exorcism performed by a group of rabbis in Safed in the sixteenth century. The rabbis were brought in to help a woman who had manifested signs of "possession," speaking in a man's voice in languages she had never learned. When the rabbis interrogated the occupying spirit, it proved to be that of a deceased money changer who feared a terrible fate (because of his cheating practices) at the hands of avenging angels who would bat him like a shuttlecock back and forth across the cosmos before consigning him to fiery torment in Gehenna. Rather than face this judgment, he had tried to hide himself in the body of a living person. It is not altogether clear how he got into the unfortunate woman, but the record implies it was because she had given herself over to "unclean" thoughts and practices.[4]

The Book of Wisdom counsels (1:16) that the unrighteous will be "punished according to their imagination." I think this is simple truth. I have also observed that it is possible to demonstrate to ex-physicals that if they will only *use* their imagination, they will discover that they do not have to spend eternity within the parameters of the collective belief territories.

7. Suicides may feel obliged to serve out their time.

Cara had a recurring dream. She found herself drawn, again and again, to a cemetery—"a composite of several cemeteries where my relatives are buried." In the dream, the tombs are open, and Cara looks down on the faces and bodies of family members. They are all lifeless except for her ex-husband, whose eyes are open. He starts weeping. His sobs rack his body.

Cara's ex had taken his own life. It seemed highly significant that in her dream, he was the only person in the graveyard who still appeared to be attached to his body. The others had clearly left their corpses behind and gone on somewhere else. Might this reflect how suicides often seem to stay earthbound? Cara began to wonder whether the near-suicidal bouts of depression that one of her daughters had suffered might be connected to the presence in the psychic environment of someone who had killed himself.

Cara agreed to try to go back inside her dream to seek clarity and resolution. She found that her ex was consumed with guilt for having abandoned his family. She tried to comfort him, reassuring him that all was forgiven. She woke with a happy sense of closure.

By my observation, suicides frequently suffer from a storm of self-loathing and guilt after they discover that their desperate action has not ended the pain that drove them to it. In their loneliness and distress, they reach out to the living. In extreme cases, they may even try to draw a survivor after them. They need compassionate guidance, which the living can sometimes provide—but only on condition (once again) that there are healthy boundaries. We can invoke guidance on their behalf. Sometimes, as in Jessica's case, it comes as a spontaneous gift:

NANNA AS A GUIDE

Jessica's friend Monica had died of a drug overdose in her bathtub in Sydney a year before. The coroner ruled that her death was an intentional suicide. Jessica did not attend the funeral; Monica's ashes were scattered to the waves.

Jessica had a series of chilling dreams and dreamlike experiences. In some of these, her friend appeared to be standing behind her, putting her hands around her neck. Jessica had a quasi-physical sense of this presence, even when performing onstage as an actress.

Then she had a terrifying dream in which her friend tried to drag her into a wild tidal pool among the rocks, on a storm-swept beach at nighttime. Jessica resisted, fearing she would be drowned. Her friend begged and insisted. Jessica was pulled closer and closer to the pool. She summoned her strength and broke away, declaring, "No! I won't go with you."

She woke feeling half-drowned, her life force ebbing low.

After Monica's grandmother died, Monica stopped appearing in Jessica's dreams. Jessica first spoke of "Nanna" when I perceived a woman in an old-fashioned pink suit with a matching pillbox hat, the sort of thing one might have seen at a 1950s garden party.

"That's Nanna," Jessica exclaimed. We had the shared impression that Monica's grandmother had intervened to serve as Monica's guide on the other side, though Nanna would not be playing this role indefinitely—she had agendas of her own, on higher levels.

Releasing Lost Souls

I find it quite wonderful that "ordinary" people with no special training are often able to play the role of psychopomp for the departed, even though they have never heard the word. It bears saying again: if your intentions are good, you *will* receive the help you need.

A farmer's wife had been increasingly troubled by the sense that her mother was "still around" six months after her death. The atmosphere in the house was becoming oppressive. The daughter even noticed pains in her joints that seemed to belong to a much older person and thought of her mother's constant complaints of rheumatoid arthritis. She asked for help and had the following dream:

> My mother is sitting in the rocker in the house, fussing and nag-ging, going on and on about things that don't matter. I know she doesn't belong here, but I can't get through to her until I notice my father standing behind me. He passed on almost ten years ago, though I don't think of him as being dead in the dream. He's waving to me, signaling that I should get my mother to turn around and look at him.
> "Mom," I tell her, "please turn around. Dad is waiting for you."
> "But he's dead," she snapped.
> I went over to her and made her turn around. She was flab-bergasted when she saw Dad. Then he took her in his arms and they floated up through the ceiling in a shaft of light.

The dreamer woke feeling light and happy. In the penumbra of her bedroom, she had the impression of a "ball of light" whirling across the space, vanishing through the ceiling.

What role can a nonspecialist play in releasing lost souls?

There are four key elements:

HELPING LOST SOULS

1. Set healthy boundaries.

- Make sure, for a start, that you are not feeding someone else's habits. Remember Janet's decision to quit smoking and to stop observing the family's happy hour?
- Monitor your dreams. They will give you clear insight into the situation of departed people who are relevant to you—and what may need to be done.
- Honor your departed loved ones in a sensible, appropriate way. You might want to construct a simple ritual to perform on a birthday or anniversary. When I do this, I simply light a candle and put out a bowl of water, a personal object associated with the departed person, and sometimes a favorite food or a spray of flowers.

2. Ask for help.

- It's fine if you're not entirely sure what you may need to do. There are others who do. If you are already working with power animals or spiritual guides, call them in. It is quite sufficient to call on the power of Light and Love, by any name you believe in. In dealing with unclean spirits, the name of Jesus Christ is an especially powerful name—though it may not work so well on poor Uncle Fred, who is watching the game on your TV set because he thinks it's Monday night.

3. Dialogue with the departed.

- Identify the departed person who is in your field.
- Clarify whether this person is actually aware that he or she no longer has a physical body. If you are dealing with someone who doesn't know he is dead, awakening him to the situation is often enough to get him moving in the right direction. Depending on your readiness and your connections, you can then invoke a specific guide, escort the departed person in a journey to another level, or simply encourage him to move toward the Light.
- If the departed person knows she is dead, you will need to establish what is keeping her from moving on and deal with that by

the appropriate means. Dead people often cling to agendas that will seem ridiculously petty once they become fully aware of their new circumstances. You may be able to help a departed person to arrive at that larger perspective. There may also be legitimate "unfinished business" you can help to resolve.

• Though "talk therapy" with the departed is often surprisingly effective, you should always be ready to call in additional help.

4. Consider a "second burial."

• You can't actually reason with the grasping, addictive, subrational aspect of a departed person, which so often holds spirits earthbound, enmeshing them in a thick webbing of gloppy, toffeelike strands of etheric matter. For the spirit to move on, this casing must be discarded and allowed to disintegrate, which happens naturally after the separation is made. However, the discarded "shell" has a half-life and can remain a source of confusion for the living, especially when it is animated by that aspect of the dreamsoul that is sometimes called the body of desire. None of this is difficult to grasp, once you remember that we have more than one body!

• If you have helped to release the spirit of a departed person, you may need to do something to contain and relocate the residue— the lower energy or "shell"—that lingers behind. A simple way to do this is to arrange a "second burial." You need something that will draw that energy into itself, or into which the energy can be transferred. An egg will work, providing the energy is not excessively strong. You can also work with a personal object that belonged to the departed person, or failing that, a "neutral" object such as a stone (or preferably, a fruit stone). In this case, you—or the person you are helping—should make it your intention to *blow* any part of the lower energy that may remain with you into this object. Then you should put the object in a sealed container and bury it, perhaps at the edge of the cemetery where the dead person is interred.

If you have become an active dreamer, confident of your personal relationship with spiritual guides and protectors, you may be able to do more. You may be able to journey *with* a departed person who needs guidance to a reception center or collective belief territory where he feels comfortable. Robert Monroe described his repeated experience of taking ex-physicals by the wrist and conducting them along a sort of metaphysical superhighway until they peeled off at various "exit ramps," leading to environments that fitted their tastes or religious upbringings. If you follow your dreams, you may find you are doing some of this work already.

We cannot leave this chapter without briefly entering a battle zone. Not all "lost" souls are simply disoriented, frightened, or needy. The phrase *criminal souls* would better describe those who have *chosen* to afflict the living and seek to feed on their energy and ride on their backs, to dominate their minds and even to possess their bodies. Some of these criminal souls belong to dead sorcerers who abused their skills to avoid the "second death" and continue to operate close to the earth sphere centuries after their physical deaths. Groups that experiment with occult techniques and invoke the spirits without knowing how to discriminate and *dismiss* the entities they bring through are notoriously prone to noxious influences from this quarter.

The basic ground rules here are *(a)* don't invite trouble in and *(b)* call on a specialist—in ordinary or nonordinary reality—when you are confronting a problem beyond your own resources.

CHAPTER 13

≈

Making Death
Your Ally

Here the indescribable actually takes place.

Goethe, Faust, *Part II*

The Death Workshop: Part II

Milarepa said it well: "My religion is to live and die without regrets."[1]

But who among us is without regrets? Of things done or left undone, of pain we suffered or inflicted, of moments of uncontrolled passion or of passion unsatisfied. There are people in our lives who have the gift of awakening more regrets in us than we ever knew we deserved. Ex-partners can be adept at this. They can also send us on a guilt trip that leaves us drained of the energy we might use in the effort to put things right. Once, after a conversation with a former partner that left me slumped in self-loathing, I noticed a bumper sticker on a female motorist's car that read, "I use ex-lovers for speed bumps." A confirmation from the world.

Still, if there was redemption for Milarepa, there is hope for us. Milarepa, revered as a saint of enlightenment and a prince of yogis by Tibetan Buddhists, had a notoriously successful career as a black magician before he saw the light. One of the lessons of his story is that the moment to seek release from karma is *now*—and that release is available in the instant of awakening.

If we miss that moment before death, the act of dying may offer us another opportunity—depending, of course, on the state of mind in which we leave the body. If we go out still enmeshed in old habits and patterns of thinking, we will have to deal with unfinished business somewhere further along the road (and it could be a very long road).

The Tibetan masters counsel that two things really matter at the time of death: what we have done in our lives and what state we are in *at that moment*. There is a chance of transforming karma through a heart change at the moment of death. "The last thought and emotion that we have before we die has an extremely powerful determining effect on our immediate future."[2]

So we should seek the way to deal with unfinished business *now*. Placing yourself, in your mind, at the moment of death is an excellent way to gain clarity on the issues involved and the actions required. Saint Ignatius Loyola, the warrior-father of the Jesuit order and no slouch at visualization, recommended the following means of making a sound decision:

> Suppose I am at the point of death. What course of action would I then wish to have followed in coming to this particular decision? Let this be the rule for settling the whole business.[3]

He advised that (in case this is not enough to concentrate the mind fully) we might also try the following:

> Let me ask myself how I would like to stand on the Day of Judgement. What decision would I then like to have made about this business? Knowing what rule I would then like to have kept, I will now observe it, so that then I may be filled with joy and satisfaction.[4]

This admirable prescription applies to revisiting old choices—indeed, the whole pattern of our lives—as well as to weighing new decisions.

So let us make resolving unfinished business the substance of a deathbed meditation.

EXERCISE 1: COUNTING THE BONES

See yourself stretched out on your deathbed. The moment when you will leave your physical body for good is at hand. Your vital signs have stopped. Soon your interior breathing will cease and your consciousness, with its subtle vehicles, will definitively separate from your body.

Perhaps you are alone in this space. Perhaps a nurse or hospice volunteer is in the room with you. Maybe friends and family have gathered. Someone may be praying for you, or even reminding you of the process by which you will travel to the Other Side.

Your body is going to be disposed of—buried in the earth or consigned to the fire of cremation. Maybe you have chosen to have your body exposed in a casket for mourners to visit. Even with the aid of embalmer's fluids and cosmetics, it is not something you are going to want to hang around. Soon the colors and stench of decay and liquefaction will take over. Your belly will inflate with noxious gases until the stomach bursts. Worms and maggots will be your fleshly visitors.

So you are definitely ready to move on. If you are fortunate and prepared, you may see the dawning of the Clear Light or sense the presence of a radiant guide who will speed your passage to the higher planes.

But first, on the cusp of death, you need to look back over the course of your life and ask some questions. You should answer these truthfully and allow yourself all the time you need.

EXERCISE 2: WEIGHING THE HEART

1. *Omissions*

- What do I regret *not* having done in my life?
(The answers might range from traveling to Nepal, going bunjee-jumping, or finding a great romance to doing more to help others or to use my creative gifts.)
- If I had a second chance, how would I act to fulfill this unfulfilled desire?

2. *Courage*

- When have I run away out of fear from a situation I needed to face or a test I needed to take?

• If I were presented with a similar challenge now, could I find the courage and resources to meet it?

3. Making amends to others

• What harm or hurt have I caused to other people, intentionally or unintentionally?
(Picture their faces.)
• If I could live my life again, what could I do to make amends or seek forgiveness?

4. Forgiving others

• What harm or hurt have others caused me?
• Am I now able to open my heart and forgive them?

5. Self-forgiveness

• Is there anything in my life for which I am unable to forgive myself?
• If I had more time, what could I do to put things right?

6. Grace

• Am I willing to ask for help and trust in the saving power of love?

The issue of *self-forgiveness* is a binding theme here. The "weighing of the heart"—the judgment we face after death—is likely to be an act of self-judgment, based on a thorough life review. The self that will judge, be it noted, is infinitely deeper and wiser than our ordinary personalities, our everyday selves. The judgment will determine whether we need to repeat classes and whether we will be reborn into higher or lower planes.

How do you feel after your partial life review? A little shaky? The good news is *you can rise from your deathbed*. You have been given a reprieve. Use your time wisely, to deal with as many of these issues as you can, so you can live and die without regrets.

> Now when the bardo of dying dawns upon me,
> I will abandon all grasping, yearning and attachment,
> Enter undistracted into clear awareness of the teaching,
> And eject my consciousness into the space of unborn Rigpa;
> As I leave this compound body of flesh and blood
> I will know it to be a transitory illusion.

> *Tibetan Book of the Dead*[5]

Meeting Your Personal Death

Milton demonized Death, suggesting that his other name is Satan. In later times, we have made a true devil out of Death, by pretending that he does not exist. (Remember Baudelaire? "The Devil's greatest art is to make us believe that he does not exist.")

Yet Death walks at the shaman's left shoulder. Death is the shaman's adviser.

And Death hovers at *your* shoulder now, whether or not you will turn to look or listen to the murmurings at your ear. He bobs up like the specter in a medieval masque, shadowing your moves, edging your lines with irony.

Are you ready to meet me?

Why not? You have been laid out on your own deathbed. Perhaps you have been drawn to reflect that even now, as you breathe and turn the pages, every cell in your body is constantly dying and being reborn. Who can count the little deaths that are taking place in your body as you inhale and exhale? Millions of cells are being born and devoured each time your lungs empty and fill. "What is there to fear?" as Michael Murphy's character asks in *Jacob Atabet*. "Life and death are simultaneous. We are living flames, burning at the edge of this incredible joy."[6]

Death, by any name, is a peerless teacher.

In the Katha Upanishad, Death is Yama. The youth Nachiketas, consigned to Death by his orthodox, disapproving father, enters the halls of Yama by an inner pathway whose gateway is the heart. When he arrives in this place, he at first encounters only utter darkness and emptiness, the experience of the Void. He waits three days and three nights before the bright flame of his spirit draws Death, who agrees to grant three requests. Nachiketas chooses wisely. He asks, first, that when he returns home, his father and his father's people should know him and welcome him. Next, that he should have knowledge of the secret fire that leads to the heaven world of the immortals. Yama instructs him that this secret fire is "hidden in the cave of the heart." Finally, Nachiketas wants to know what happens to those who "go beyond"—beyond not only physical death (it seems) but beyond the second death and further transformations. Yama does not want to answer this question, but the boy holds Death to his promise. The answer, again, lies in fire: the fire of the seeker's own death and transformation. Nachiketas himself is the sacred flame. The journeyer himself is the path he must walk.[7]

In complete darkness, in a cavernous space, I invited the founding members of the Death workshop to journey to the realm of their personal Death and return with his teaching. The drumbeat started at the tempo of a death march. I thought of my own encounters with Death from early childhood. Of the time I was plunged deep into the earth and lived a whole lifetime, it seemed, amongst a species of ghostly white beings—growing to manhood among them, mating with them—until I swam up to the surface, through clays and shales that gave way to a wondrously luminescent green light, to find myself a boy again, in a half-grown body beginning to heal. Of my recent visionary encounter with Sandalphon, gatekeeper between the physical and Imaginal realms, the Big Wheel, glowering dark and bright.

Edgar Cayce dreamed of Death as a fair, robust, rosy-cheeked young man who carried shears that he used to cut the psychic cord that binds the subtle body to the physical body at the crown of the head.

What would the new explorers find?

• Tony entered a "spiral flame" for his face-to-face interview with a Death that wore his own face.

• Rose found herself drawn to a pleasant rest home, watching the breeze through the open windows stirring the ferns in a planter, and recognized that Death may be as gentle as this.

• Carol journeyed far beyond her body with a Death that called herself Mercy—and came back very cold. She had met Mercy on the road, between our sessions:

My Name Is Mercy

Carol was on the highway, driving several hundred miles for a funeral, reliving memories of experiences she had shared with her friend and reflecting on the fact that two of her closest friends had died in the space of a fortnight.

She found herself speaking to Death out loud. She said, "Death, this is the second time you have touched me personally in the last couple of weeks."

Immediately she saw the image of a woman coming toward her from the sky. The woman was clothed in flowing black, with iridescent purple highlights. Under the purple-black robe, Carol saw the ripple of a white gown, trimmed in shimmering gold. The woman's face and whole being radiated light, warmth, and kindness. They looked at each other for a long moment. Then the figure vanished.

Can this be Death? Carol asked herself on a morning walk the next day, thinking about the woman from the sky. She noticed her path had taken her within an arm's reach of three mourning doves, who did not fly away as she came near them. She felt they were telling her to pay attention.

Suddenly, she saw the figure of the shining woman in black. Here comes Death, she thought.

"Want to be friends?" the woman asked.

"What is your name?" Carol responded.

"Mercy. My name is Mercy."

Carol was startled and deeply moved. From the depths of her being she said, "Yes, I do want to be friends."

• Roderick had also encountered his Death, in a dream he chose to reenter:

My Scottish Death

On the border between an elegant country estate and a wild, wooded area, I see a kilted Scots soldier with a broadsword, marching around the perimeter. I wait for him philosophically. My fate has been determined. He swings the sword up above his head and brings it down. I hear a light whooshing sound as he cuts through my body, from the crown of my head to the crotch. He makes a second, horizontal cut almost immediately, carving my body into four quarters.

Instantly, I am moving about in my second body. I return to the place where I have been staying. I feel some confusion, since I still have the semblance of a body—naked, vulnerable to cold and hunger. I wonder if I can somehow continue with the research and writing I have been engaged in here. I picture myself rising upward and am instantly levitating through the ceiling up into the attic and through the rafters.

I decide to call my wife in this dream. She comes to the phone but I can't hear her because she is speaking so softly.

I spend some time roving the night streets, watching people who can't see me. I start following them toward the entertainment district, then realize it's time to start looking for more evolved environments on higher levels. I begin to remember I don't need to hang about waiting for a guide; I can journey to these dimensions by focusing my intention.

When he reentered the dreamscape, Roderick interviewed his hitherto silent "Scottish Death."

"Who are you?"

"I am your Death. I will come at the appointed time to release you into the land of your Father."

"Why do you come to me now?"

"I come to prepare you for what awaits for you, as for all mortals, and to help you to prepare others to confront their own death with courage. I walk at your shoulder. I guard the border between the world of the living and the world of the dead. I am your guardian as well as your summoner."

"Why do you cut me into quarters?"

"I make the sign of the cross within your human form. This both releases you and protects you. Your form may not be borrowed by other entities, which may be parasites and deceivers. In quartering your body, I release your great energy to the four quarters—and unite you with your new form."

"I found myself wandering in the second body, torn between purposes."

"You are often divided like this in life. Why would it be different during the transition to the higher worlds?"

• Debbie found Kali in a special space, approached through a series of doorways. Kali described herself as "your jealous sister." Ah, Kali.

THE MASKS OF DEATH

Death wears many masks. In Hopi mythology, the god Masau'u—depicted as a skeleton wearing a mask—is the gatekeeper and mediator between the realms of the dead and the living. In the Hopi creation story, when the ancestors journey up from the underworld to inhabit the earth, it is Masau'u who welcomes them into the sunlit world. He is a friend and guide to humans and knows the ways between the worlds; he is also the lord of boundaries, fire, fertility—and humor. He can turn anything into its opposite.

The ancient Greeks had two names for their death lord. They called him Hades, which means "the unseen," and Pluto, which means "rich." The words hint at the treasures to be found in his realm. The Greek myths also warn of the need to travel these roads with great care, to avoid the fate of the hero Theseus, who lost a part of himself when it remained stuck to a bench before the throne of Hades—and of his friend Pirithous, who remained stuck there indefinitely.

Yama, the Hindu death lord, looms large in Vikram Chandra's incandescent 1995 novel, *Red Earth and Pouring Rain*. Sanjay's time is up, but because he is a marvelous storyteller he is able to strike a bargain with Death, who loves stories. So long as Sanjay is able to hold the attention of his audience—who soon fill the courtyard outside his room—he is allowed to live. As he weaves his tales, Death ceases to be an adversary. Sanjay makes stories for the joy of making stories, and when he is done, he rests his head in Yama's lap, peacefully accepting his transition to another life. By the way: Sanjay the storyteller is a white-faced monkey who is typing his memories of his human incarnations, to be read aloud by children. No writer with a sense of humor will find it hard to identify with Sanjay's plight.

It is remarkable what leaps off the page—not only the pages of a novel, but the pages of life—when the presence of Death is acknowledged.

The close encounter with Death brings courage, which Rollo May rightly identified in *The Courage to Create* as the heart of the creative endeavor. It encourages the ability to go beyond the surface vicissitudes of daily life. It brings keen awareness of a larger reality. This is clearly reflected in the experiences of survivors of near-death experiences. Kenneth Ring, one of the foremost researchers in this field, reported in *Life at Death* that 60 percent of all "returners" questioned by him said that their lives had changed; 40 percent said this had been the most important experience of their lives; 89 percent said they would gladly repeat it.

We know now what all dreaming peoples know: that the encounter does not require the physical extremity of a life-threatening illness or near-fatal accident. We move among the departed in spontaneous sleep dreams. As active dreamers, we can range far and wide through the afterworlds, observing how different aspects of the soul go to different destinations. In the process, we learn to brave our deepest fears. We encounter radiant guides and powerful spiritual allies. We discover special places to which we can return—in this life and perhaps beyond it.

I sometimes journey to a pleasant campuslike setting I first visited in a sleep dream more than ten years ago. It is a place of higher education for people who no longer have physical bodies. In my original dream, I found the "freshmen" gathered for commencement. They were mostly elderly, the women in cute white dresses with ribbons and bows. The choir sang hauntingly beautiful songs that celebrated the link between dreaming and the entry into a larger reality:

Morning, sunset, evening star—all dreams.
What cannot be known in the dream cannot be known in its
*   glory.*

The soaring beauty of their voices is with me as I write. Occasionally, in journeys to help the departed, I have tried to guide those who seem ready for those halls of weathered, ivy-draped stone, set among rolling lawns and exuberant flower beds and sparkling fountains.

When my spirit needs to soar, I sometimes ascend, in conscious dream journeys, to a world as fresh as the first day where I flew with the winged powers after leaving my astral body, as well as my physical body, behind.

And when I most need clarity, I check in with my personal Death. He/she has worn many masks. When I was a teenager in Canberra, Australia, *she* came swirling through my dreams and reveries in the terrible shapes of Kali. At the back of the history class on airless afternoons, I wrote a cycle of poems in her honor:

In the darkness, a dark woman came to me
softly as the ticking of a clock

Like Roderick, I have seen death swinging a Scottish broadsword. I have seen death as a great black bird, as a purple bruise flowering in an empty sky, as a sweet and luminous friend.

The Death I want now (to echo a splendid line of Octavio Paz) carries my name, wears my face.

PART IV

≈

The Coming of the Multidimensional Human

If we can be more conscious, this will make higher centers work. The functioning of higher centers will be in many ways miraculous.

P. D. Ouspensky, The Fourth Way

Nature shows us only the tail of the lion. But I do not doubt the lion belongs to it even though he cannot at once reveal himself because of his enormous size.

Albert Einstein

The world is not only stranger than we suppose, it is stranger than we can suppose.

J. B. S. Haldane

CHAPTER 14

Soul Remembering

> Everyone should know that you cannot live in
> any other way than by cultivating the soul.
>
> *Apuleius*

Choosing Your Birth

Birth and death are two sides of a swing door. To go beyond the gates of death is to gain access to the realms of soul where you can put yourself back in touch with the life purpose and life gifts you may have chosen before you were born. Plato's haunting account of how souls choose their *paradeigmas,* or life patterns, in the closing pages of his *Republic,* was attributed to the insights of a soldier who had died and come back. Plato taught that the things that are truly worth knowing come to us through anamnesis, or "remembering": remembering knowledge that already belongs to us, on the levels of soul and spirit. The Greek word for truth, *aletheia,* literally means "that which has not been forgotten," that which has not been consumed by the waters of Lethe.

Through dreams, which are soul experiences, soul helps us remember. A nine-year-old Long Island girl told her mother the following dream:

Carried in the Arms of Elijah

I dreamed what happens before we are born. Each of us is carried through time and space in the arms of the prophet Elijah. We forget what we have seen when we are put in our mother's womb. But it comes back in flashes as we go through life, when

*we feel something very strongly. Sometimes being with certain
people brings it back.*

According to Plato's story of Er, the soldier who died and came
back, we all play a role in choosing our births, however unlikely this
may seem when we are out of sorts with the world and those around
us. Plato attributes his account to a soldier from Pamphylia who was
"slain in battle." Ten days after the fight, Er's body was found uncor-
rupted. He returned to life two days later, atop his funeral pyre. He
had evidently survived in coma or cataleptic trance. Er told the
astonished gathering that he had been tasked by spiritual teachers in
the "world beyond" to bring back a clear description of how souls
choose their fates before birth.

He described how he had made a soul journey to a "mysterious
region" where he saw two openings in the earth and two in the heavens, with "judges" sitting between them. Souls of the just who had
departed were sent to the right and upward; those of the unjust were
sent to the left and downward—all wearing "tokens" of how they
had lived their lives.

Through the other pair of gates, souls descended from above or
ascended from the earth, prior to embarking on a new life on earth.
In this transit zone, they swap stories of reward or punishment, pro-
portionate to their good or bad deeds in previous lives. Then they
journey to the place of the Axis Mundi, "a spot whence they dis-
cerned, extended from above throughout the heaven and the earth, a
straight light like a pillar, most nearly resembling the rainbow, but
brighter and purer." Everything revolves around this pillar. "From
the extremities was stretched the spindle of Necessity, through which
all the orbits turned." Er perceived this as a vast interplay of vortices,
or whorls,

as if in one great whorl, hollow and scooped out, there lay
enclosed, right through, another like it but smaller, fitting into
it as boxes that fit into one another, and in like manner another,
a third, and a fourth, and four others, for there were eight of
the whorls in all, lying within one another, showing their rims
as circles from above and forming the continuous back of a single whorl about the shaft, which was driven home through the

middle of the eighth. . . . The staff turned as a whole in a circle with the same movement, but within the whole as it revolved the seven inner circles revolved gently in the opposite direction to the whole, and of these seven the eighth revolved most swiftly.[1]

Each whorl has its color (the outermost "spangled") and distinctive musical note. The Fates help to turn it: Clotho (who sings of things that are) turns the outermost circle, Atropos (who tells what will be) turns the inner circles, Lachesis (who deals with what is past) alternates in helping each.

The returning souls are brought before Lachesis. A "prophet" takes lots from the lap of Lachesis and explains how they must choose their next life experience: "No divinity shall cast lots for you, but you will choose your own deity." He casts the lots among them, and they see the numbers they have drawn. Then he places "patterns of lives far more numerous than the assembly" on the ground before them. They will take turns to choose according to the numbers they have drawn. Every possible life experience—including those of birds and animals—is here. The consequence of each choice is on the head of the chooser, and its full implications are not always apparent. The life of a great prince is accompanied by horror and the murder of his sons. The life of an ordinary man, on the other hand, holds charms for Odysseus, who has had enough of the dramas of the hero's life. Orpheus chooses to come back as a swan; he remembers how he was once torn apart by women and wants to avoid having to deal with them again.

When they have chosen their birth, the souls are again marshaled before Lachesis.

She sent with each, as the guardian of his life and the fulfiller of his choice, the genius that he had chosen, and this divinity led the soul first to Clotho, under her hand and the turning of the spindle to ratify the destiny of his lot and choice, and after contact with her the genius again led the soul to the spinning of Atropos to make the web of its destiny irreversible, and then without a backward look it passed under the spindle of Necessity.[2]

They cross the Plain of Oblivion in dreadful, stifling heat. They camp by the River of Forgetfulness, "whose waters no vessel can contain," and all are required to drink from it. Some drink too deep and forget everything they have experienced. Some drink only sparingly and will return to earth with the mixed blessing of remembering what they were before. They drift into sleep, and as they dream, there is thunder and a quaking in the earth, and the souls are "wafted upward to their birth like shooting stars." Some arrive clear-eyed and focused, remembering who they are. Many bring back only a gust of memory, like an image from a fading dream. Most remember little or nothing of who they are and what they are meant to become.

Er could tell the Greeks all this because his guardian daimon did not permit him to drink from the waters of Lethe. Yet even so, he cannot explain how he returned to his body. Man is an animal that forgets and remembers and forgets again.

This is one of the most important sacred teaching stories of the West, though it is rarely taught in our schools and colleges, let alone as part of a common culture. The myth of Er has parallels in other traditions.

The Yoruba say that the individual soul, or *ori,* goes before the high god Olodumare before it joins a physical body. The *ori* kneels down before Olodumare to receive its destiny. It comes into the world to fulfill this destiny:

What the *ori* comes to fulfill
It cannot but fulfill it.

This personal destiny is known as *iponri,* which means "the *ori*'s portion or lot." The more fortunate and evolved souls choose their own destiny at the feet of the high god. Most souls accept their fate, with only limited ability to negotiate the details. A third category have their destinies "laid on their backs" and come into the world reluctantly.

In the Yoruba version, when a soul has received its destiny from Olodumare, it embarks on its journey toward physical birth. When the soul arrives at one of the gates between the worlds, it must answer the questions of the Gatekeeper, the *oni'bode.*

GATEKEEPER: Where are you going?
JOURNEYER: I am going into the world.
GATEKEEPER: What are you going to do?
JOURNEYER: I will be born to a woman named X and a man named Y, in the town of Z. I will be an only son. . . . At the age of . . . I will . . . and will die in . . . and will be mourned by all and given proper burial.
GATEKEEPER: *To*. It is sealed.[3]

The destiny is doubly sealed—at the feet of the high god and at the gates between the worlds.

When souls come into this world, most forget their contract with the high god: the destiny that has been assigned to them.

Can the destiny be changed? It can sometimes be changed for the better by divine intercession, especially with the help of Orunmila, the austere lord of divination who cannot be bribed. It can be changed for the worse through the interference of forces of evil. A destiny can be aborted through human weakness and impatience.

One of the two most important insights, in the Yoruba version, is that "an unhappy destiny can be rectified if it can be ascertained what it is."[4] There is a story of a father who traveled to Ajiran—a town reputed to be a gate between the worlds—to discover why his children died young. In what was clearly a soul journey, he previewed the probable death of his surviving son from snakebite and was able to use his foreknowledge to prevent this from coming to pass.

The other vital Yoruba insight is that we have an ally in heaven who is in no way alien to ourselves. This ally can help us remember our destiny—and coach us on how to fulfill it or modify it. The *ori* has a "double in heaven," a personal daimon. When the Yoruba offer you the blessing "May *ori* go with you," they are actually saying something like, "May you walk with your guardian angel, your own Higher Self."

Soul-remembering, in some of the Yoruba stories, is the key to weathering life's ups and downs with grace and tenacity. There is a tale in the Odu—the verse recitations that accompany Ifa divination—of a celebrated royal drummer who decided to commit suicide at the peak of manhood after suffering many misfortunes. He fainted during his suicide attempt.

The drummer's soul now comes face-to-face with a Gatekeeper who demands, "Why do you appear unbidden at the gate?"

He recounts his troubles. The Gatekeeper shuts him up in a room and tells him to listen carefully.

He hears footfalls as the people who are going to be born in the world come before the Gatekeeper. He listens as they recount their destinies.

"Have you been listening?" the Gatekeeper demands. "This shows how one's life is ordered."

The would-be suicide is reminded that what happened to him on earth happened in accord with his destiny.

The Gatekeeper shows him a house full of goods and a pen full of cattle that were to be his in the next year of his life, according to his destiny. "But through your impatience, you have forfeited everything."

The drummer wept and protested so strongly that at last Olodumare granted him an extension—ten more years in which to enjoy his predestined riches.[5]

Journey to the Source

So much of the harm we inflict on ourselves and others stems from the fact that we do not remember who we are. How do we embark on the journey of soul remembering?

By working with spontaneous dreams, which are the language of soul. By learning to operate in the twilight zone, when our "double in heaven" can communicate with us clearly. By rising on the planes to commune with a master teacher on a higher level. By traveling backward through the scenes of our present life journey, back through the womb itself, to discover where we were and what we knew before we took on physical bodies.

A Buddhist technique of recollection called "traveling against the fur" goes even further. You begin by finding yourself in the present moment. You allow your awareness to travel backward through the scenes of your life ("against the fur") until you are back in the womb. You step through the womb, into the zone you inhabited before entering this life experience. You travel back through all your previous life experiences until you come to the point where the first life bursts into the world, setting time into motion—to the border beyond which time does not exist because nothing is yet manifest. By the time you return to that Ur-point, you are expected to have mastered and transcended the memories and emotions of all the lives you have reentered, and to have moved beyond sterile speculation about the nature of ultimate reality. A supremely enlightened being remembers all of his "previous" lives but refuses to draw moral or metaphysical conclusions from this.[6]

Soul Families

As you begin to practice the art of soul remembering, you are likely to become aware that you are born within a spiritual family: that your present life experience is intimately connected to those of people living in different times and different dimensions. You may be fortunate enough to find soul mates who are living in your present reality. Sometimes soul families arrange reunions at an agreed rendezvous in space and time. A California woman learned about this through a remarkable dream. In this dream, she was an observer. She was certain she knew the people whose stories were being played out. But she could not identify them (not yet, anyway) in waking life.

YOU CAN TAKE IT WITH YOU

The members of a family of souls have decided to reincarnate together. They are resolved to live their entire lives together in the same place, a midsized town in New England.

As they find prospective parents, the returning souls appear to their mothers in dreams. One of them speaks as follows: "I am the soul of your unborn child. I am returning at this time with many others. I expect you to raise me in the town where you are living. Then you may retire to Florida if you wish, but I am not to be removed from this town." The gist of the other dream messages is similar.

One soul appears in his mother's dream as a distinguished gray-haired man. He identifies himself as her unborn child. He tells her, "I was a doctor in my last life. I will be a doctor again in this one. I will expect you and Dad to put me through medical school."

He gives her a health advisory. Living inside her, he has detected an anomaly in her heartbeat. It could easily be treated, but unless it is taken care of, it could result in difficulties during the delivery. (He clearly has a vested interest in this matter!) He describes the test she should undergo and reassures her that her doctor will know just what to do.

The scene shifts to south Florida. The soul family appear, as a group, in the dream of an elderly woman. A successful mystery writer, she lives in a luxurious condo on the bay in Miami. In the writer's dream, the members of the soul family explain what they are doing. They tell her she will be joining them in the New England town during a "second wave" of reincarnations.

The elderly writer is far from pleased. Obviously she will have to die to come back in a new body. She complains that she has worked hard to get where she is now. She enjoys her life as it is and does not want to give it up.

Her dream visitors tell her she will enjoy her next life even more. They show her the town they have selected and tell her that her future mother has already been chosen. The prospective mother is an artist who has already gained some recognition locally. Her paintings are selling well in the largest gallery in town. The artist lives in a big house on a salt pond, and the boathouse is her studio. In her dream, the Miami writer inspects a room that is filled with "water light."

In the last part of *her* dream, the dreamer watches the writer wake up in her Miami condo, struggling to remember and make sense of her experiences during the night. The writer recalls the name of the New England town she was shown in her dream and grabs her atlas to see if it really exists. When she locates the town in her atlas, she calls her travel agent and makes arrangements to fly to the Northeast.

The dreamer watches as the Miami writer collects a rental car at the airport, drives to her dream town, and cruises the streets until she finds the art gallery. The writer scans the paintings on display until she finds a canvas and a name that correspond to her dream memories of her prospective mother. The gallery owner gives her the artist's home number. "I love your work!" the writer gushes on the phone. She is soon invited to visit the artist's studio.

She finds herself in a scene from her dream: in the boathouse on the salt pond. Future Mom, flattered by the interest of a well-known author, thinks she has made a sale. But the writer has another agenda.

Now convinced that she "dreamed true," the writer flies back to Miami and visits her lawyer's office. She changes her will, leaving everything to the New England artist who may be her future mother.

"Maybe I can take it with me," she reflects.

This thrilling and richly layered dream report has the narrative structure of a marvelous "finished" story—though it comes virtually unedited from the dreamer's raw experience. With little effort, a screenwriter could adapt it for a superior episode of a TV series like *Twilight Zone*.

But the dreamer felt she was watching "actual happenings, perhaps some way in the future."

I believe that this dream contains quite accurate insight on the process by which souls are introduced to their prospective biological parents. It raises the stunning possibility that a second consciousness inside the body—that associated with the fetus in the womb—can offer a pregnant woman practical guidance on health and delivery (and should be approached as an active participant in the whole process). It suggests that we are born into a spiritual family, as well as a biological family.

The dreamer was not sure why this dream had come to her, but felt that she might be connected with the "soul family," or that one of its members would one day appear in her waking life. She was living in California, but felt she might one day be drawn to that New England town and would know it from the dream.

Exploring Other-Life Experiences

Belief in reincarnation is common to most of the world's spiritual traditions. It was shared by some of the early Church Fathers—especially in Alexandria, where the influence of Basilides and his fellow gnostics ran strong—though it was later condemned by the bishops. I have been interested in the theme since my early childhood because of those recurring dreams of an RAF pilot who was shot down and executed a few years before my birth, and because of my frequent contacts, in dreamlike states, with personalities whose earthly homes seemed to be in other times and places.

A mild belief in reincarnation is probably useful. But we need to remain open-minded about how the process actually works. When the law of karma (the belief that we must reap the consequences of our actions in previous lifetimes) is used to explain birth defects, poverty, and life handicaps, it can breed callous indifference to the plight of the less fortunate. There are other issues that I notice quite frequently in my practice:

CHECKLIST: WHOSE LIFE IS IT?

1.   "Past-life memories" are often the memories of dead people who remain attached to the living. I have had heart-to-heart talks about this with therapists who practice past-life regression; some recognize this problem as a source of much confusion. (I wish they would say so on the record!) I observe such confusion quite frequently in my workshops. For example, a troubled young man announced that he "knew" that many of his problems stemmed from the fact that he had been a Ku Klux Klan member involved in burnings and lynchings in the nineteenth century. When we looked into his case, we found that he had picked up a hitchhiker: a dead person whose memories the young man had confused with those of a previous life. Before this discovery, the young man had made little progress—by his own admission—in working off his "negative karma." On the contrary, he had been inclined to act out some of the personality traits of the other character, adopting an excessively controlling and aggressive style toward others, this time in the name of spirituality, rather than white supremacy.

2.   "Past-life memories" are often teaching stories. They may spring from many sources, including the lives of people to whom we are closely related within a biological or spiritual family. Scenes from other lives, glimpsed in dreams or dreamlike states, can provide valuable insight. Sometimes they help us to image our relationships with other people in a revealing way, or to define key challenges we are facing in life. However, their teaching value may be reduced if you jump to the conclusion that you lived all these episodes in

chronological sequence and are bound to the iron wheel of karma as a result.

3.   What part of us is reborn? We are body, soul, and spirit. In our genes, we carry the memory of the entire history of our species since we crawled out of the primeval swamp. In our enduring spirit, we carry the spark of the divine. Though the soul that makes the bridge and enters into incarnation may retain—or recover—the memory of other life experiences, it may not be identical to the entity that animated those other bodies.

4.   What if it is all happening *now?* In the world of spirit, as in dreams, there is only *now.* From this perspective, if I "was" the druid who refused to become the willing sacrifice in Scotland more than a thousand years ago, then what I do or fail to do in my present life will affect him, as much as his actions will affect me. If there is causality at work, it will flow both ways. And glimpses of another life experience you may have had—or be having, in a parallel reality—may come just as easily from the future as the past.

You may have had dreams or waking insights that contain specific or insistent traces of a possible past-life experience, like my dreams of the World War II pilot. A woman in one of my drumming circles has been dreaming since childhood of a romantic tragedy played out in Crete, in Minoan times. For a time, she wondered if she was condemned to relive this story in modern guise. She came to a clear resolution. She would accept the high drama and sense of personal destiny that came with her Minoan dreams, while being careful not to reenact an ancient tragedy. Above all, as she describes it, "I realized I must lead my own life, not hers."

We must live into our own times. It is important not to saddle ourselves (or others) with responsibility for what may have happened during another life experience. A woman in one of my workshops glimpsed a "past-life" experience in which she saw herself burned at a stake by a circle of cowled inquisitors that included her husband. This neatly dramatized the way she now felt about her partner, and his defensiveness in the face of her spiritual quest. But to jump from that insight to the accusation that "the SOB is trying to do me in like he did before" would be of doubtful value to either party in the relationship!

Suppose you have already lived through many lifetimes, as ancient Celts, like modern Hindus (and many other peoples) believe. Too much knowledge of how you used or abused the opportunities of those life experiences could inflict crippling pain or guilt or feed feelings of hatred and revenge, if it returned to you before you were truly ready for it. If reincarnation is a fact, then we need to have developed the grounding and humor required to integrate the memories we may be able to draw from past (or future) lives. Curiosity is fine, but timing is important. If you want to look into these areas for yourself, here is a simple exercise that does not ask you to cage yourself in any preconceived notions and focuses on gaining access to knowledge that may be helpful to you *now*.

EXERCISE: EXPLORING ANOTHER LIFE EXPERIENCE RELEVANT TO YOU NOW

1.   Relax in a protected space.
2.   Focus on your intention. Your purpose is to explore another life experience that will be helpful for you to know about now. Don't specify whether is a "past" or "future" life, or whether it is your personal experience or that of somebody else. Be open to possibility— and remember that it is arguably more important to communicate with our ancestors from the *future* than with those from the past.
3.   Find a place. The location you will use may have come to you in dreams, in twilight states, or in previous journeys. If this is the case, you will let yourself glide back into the remembered image. If you enjoyed your visit to the House of Time, this imaginal locale offers you many portals for traveling backward—or forward— in time.
4.   Look at how you are dressed. This will give you a clue to your identity and the period. Better still, look in a mirror or reflecting surface.
5.   Let a scene unfold. Consider how the people or situations that appear may be relevant to you now. Do you recognize anyone? Pay close attention to the eyes of people you encounter.
6.   Ask for the lesson. What lesson can you derive from this experience that is relevant to the challenges and opportunities that currently confront you? The lesson may come to you with a powerful

image. For example, I once found myself in vivid scenes from the life of a *strategos,* or military commander, in ancient Macedonia. I saw him throw his weapons into the sea—which I took as a message to evolve beyond my "warrior side" and seek peace and healing.

7.   Consider whether this experience feels like your own. At this point, it is appropriate to ask whether the life you are exploring belongs to you or to someone who is clearly distinct. Given the openness of the initial question, you may find you have actually been looking into the life of another person who is living now. I once found myself inside the body of a black basketball player who seemed to be very much alive! Don't prejudge your experience.

Dialogues with the Higher Self

Life is a process of remembering and forgetting, forgetting and remembering.

The theme of the forgotten mission is beautifully conveyed by the "Hymn of the Soul" in the gnostic Acts of Thomas. The hero is sent from the East into Egypt in search of the Pearl beyond price, which may be his own Higher Self. Drugged by the food and drink of the country where he now finds himself, he forgets who he is. From the distant land from which he has come, the king and queen and "all the princes of Parthia" send a message to awaken him to the memory of who and what he is and recall him to his forgotten mission.[7]

The same theme resonates, in modern dress, in Doris Lessing's allegorical novel *Shikasta.* An envoy is sent to Earth from a higher civilization in a distant galaxy. To reach his destination, he must pass through a vast waiting area, a plane of mists and illusions, where souls wander between incarnations. On Earth, the envoy succumbs to the miasmal conditions; he forgets who he is and why he has come. A new envoy must be sent to remind him.

Our true spiritual teachers do not forget. When we open ourselves to the possibility of remembering who we are and what we might become, they communicate clearly. To receive their knowledge—and recover the knowledge that belonged to us before we came through the tunnel of the birth canal—we must be in a corresponding state of consciousness. As Anaïs Nin remarked, "We do not see things as they are; we see them as *we* are."

Ordinary consciousness is a candle bobbing on a dark river, casting an inconstant circle of light across the water, in which an occasional creature from the deep can be glimpsed indistinctly. The river is vast, flowing into a boundless ocean. This is the sea of the greater Self. We cannot see it by the light of our daily trivial mind, which scarcely combs back the darkness.

One of the most beautiful images of the Higher Self that I have seen is among the major arcana painted by Jo Gill for the Servants of Light tarot deck, conceived by Dolores Ashcroft-Nowicki. The tarot trump is number 17, the Star. The card shows a naked woman, standing on the earth and yet still asleep. Half her body is immersed in the astral sea. Above it rises a circular Rainbow of Promise. She is watched by unsleeping eyes. A shining star, high above, sends a beam of light through the crown of her head to her heart. The light is the gift of her truest teacher, the Higher Self, which is trying to awaken her to who she is and what she may become.[8]

It is in twilight states that you are most likely to discover and forge a relationship with your life teacher, beautifully described by the Persian Sufis as the "soul of the soul." The Persian mystics also speak of the "angel of the philosopher," the "invisible master," the "witness in Heaven," and "the Gabriel of my being." Another name for the guide who comes to those who are ready, on the horizon of dreams, is Khidr, the "master of those who have no worldly master."[9]

If you have now learned to maintain relaxed awareness in the twilight zone, on the cusp of dreams, you are ready to use this opportunity to dialogue with your own Higher Self. The medieval Church contemplatives used a similar technique that they called Conversations with the Soul. Hugh de St. Victor evokes the essential practice:

> I will speak in secret to my soul, and in friendly conversation I will ask her what I should like to know. No stranger shall be present. We will talk alone and openly to each other. Thus I need not be afraid to ask even the most secret things and she will not be ashamed to reply honestly. Tell me, I ask you, O my Soul, what is it you love above everything?[10]

True spiritual evolution surely progresses through a closer and closer alignment with the Higher Self. A quantum leap is achieved through *fusion* between the focus personality and the Higher Self. The larger person now communicates with a Higher Self on a higher level than before.

The previous evolution of consciousness has taken humans from the conditions of the group soul—comparable to animals, fish, or even insects—toward individuation. The next phase of evolution can take our species as a whole to a new plane of consciousness and being. We are invited to participate in the emergence of a new species.

The invitation may come in ways that are terrifying to the little self, which clings to its little things.

One of my favorite teaching stories was popular with the gentle, ascetic philosophers of Vedanta, precisely because its raw, primal quality is calculated to shock the hearer out of conventional pieties. It is a story about you and me: about the relationship between the little self and the big Self.

THE PARABLE OF THE WANNA-BE GOAT

The she-tiger is prowling the woods. She is hungry. She is pregnant and has two lives to feed. At the edge of the forest, she discovers a herd of goats, grazing on the plain. She advances toward them cautiously, keeping downwind. But her big belly makes her clumsy. When she makes her spring, she dashes her head against a protruding boulder and is killed. Her cub is born posthumously. When the goats come back, they find a blind, mewling, helpless newborn. They take pity on it and decide to raise it as one of their own. They teach it to eat grass and to bleat like the herd. The cub is always the odd one out in the herd, the butt of many jeers. But it does its best to fit in.

Until one day the Bengal man-eater comes stalking through the woods. He has just eaten a gazelle for breakfast, but he is always hungry. His spring is impeccable. The goats all flee—except for the wanna-be goat. The tiger inspects the cub in astonishment. "What are *you* doing here?"

"Maaaaah," bleats the wanna-be goat.

"We don't bleat," growls the man-eater.

Confused, the cub nibbles grass.

"And we do not eat grass!" roars the man-eater. "We are *not* vegetarians!"

The tiger seizes the cub by the scruff of the neck and carries him to a reflecting pool, to show him his true face.

When the wanna-be goat sees his true face, he squeals in terror.

Enraged and disgusted, the man-eater grabs the cub and drags him back to his lair, where he is hoarding the remains of the gazelle he had for breakfast. He pries open the cub's jaws and forces down some of the raw meat. As the blood trickles down the wanna-be goat's gullet, he opens his jaws. And he *roars*.

Whereupon the tiger says, "Now that you know who you are, we can begin to discuss how you ought to behave."

The message is savagely clear. The reason we can hope to succeed in our hunt for the Higher Self is that, while we fancy we are the hunters, the big Self—the tiger in the soul—is hunting us. The hunt is pursued through events in the outer, as well as the inner, world. As the alchemists observed, in a statement that stunned Jung into formulating his theory of the *objective psyche,* "The soul is only partly confined to the body, just as God is only partly enclosed in the body of the world."[11] If we persist in denying the voice of the Higher Self, it will keep after us in any way that will get our attention—in tiger skins or ET outfits, through wild coincidence and bizarre anomalies, even by clawing apart the fabric of space-time.

CHAPTER 15

≋

Alien Encounters
and Spirit Callings

An unspeakable horror seized me. There was a darkness,
then a dizzy, sickening sensation of sight that was not like
seeing; I saw a Line that was no Line, Space that was not Space;
I was myself and not myself. When I could find voice, I shrieked aloud
in agony, "Either this is madness or it is Hell." "It is neither," calmly
replied the voice of the Sphere. "It is knowledge; it is Three
Dimensions: open your eye once again and try to look steadily."

A. Square discovers a higher dimension in Edwin Abbott's Flatland

Bleedthroughs from Other Dimensions

Our physical reality is surrounded and permeated by the vigorous,
thrumming life of the realms of spirit and imagination to which we
return, night after night, in dream. There is *no distance* between the
Otherworld and its inhabitants and our familiar, sensory reality;
there is a difference in frequency.

The nearness of the Otherworld is hard for us to grasp. In the Tal-
mud is the legend of the four sages—evidently proficient soul travelers—who journeyed to heaven. One of them was called Ben Zoma.
When Ben Zoma came back, he went round telling people, "Between
the upper waters and the lower waters are but three finger-breadths."
He was trying to explain that the distance between heaven and
earth—between the "upper and lower waters" God divided to create
the firmament (Genesis 1:7)—there is *no distance* worth talking about.
People thought Ben Zoma had lost his mind. Later commentators

concluded that he *did* lose his mind and cited his story as a reason why meditation and soul travel should be proscribed.[1]

Madness lies in the collapse of boundaries, in the overthrow of all borders between ordinary and nonordinary reality. Yet the border cannot be a Maginot Line. Put an armed perimeter between yourself and all experiences of a larger reality and you'll find yourself facing "hostiles," just as people who slam the door on their dreams find themselves fleeing from nightmares.

Just as we can make Otherworld journeys, Otherworld beings can visit us, to shake us out of the consensual hallucination that there is only one world, but also to confirm the reality of experiences in other orders of reality by bringing a gift or a marker into this one. After making a healing journey for a patient at a distance that seemed to have produced powerful and beneficial results, a therapist was asking herself whether she had truly made a difference. Then a bleedthrough from another dimension gave her shivers of confirmation:

The Tree Man

A friend asked me to pray for her father, who was scheduled for open heart surgery. I decided to journey in spirit to see if I could be of help. I talked with Bill's spirit the night before the surgery, and based on his wishes, I concluded that he would probably not leave his body permanently at this time. I saw and felt myself applying therapeutic touch to his body.

He remained in intensive care in critical condition longer than the surgeons had hoped. They had not been able to clear all of his arteries. Oxygen levels were too low, and there were problems with blood gases.

I wondered if there was something I could do. I journeyed again, calling on my guides. We go to Bill and I talk to his spirit. He is considering leaving. His body is weary. His heart is weary. Yet there are things he wants to get in order before leaving his family. My guides are pouring forth loving light. My guide gives me a small tree and instructs me to place it in Bill's heart. I lovingly place the tree in his heart with the intention that it will bring healing, and especially that it will oxygenate his blood.

The next day, I received word that he had had a better night, his blood gases were improving, and he was being moved from intensive care.

Out walking soon after this, I noticed a man with a cane on the sidewalk next to my apartment building. As he walked past some pine trees, he moved into a tree trunk and disappeared. I was astonished because I thought the man was in the flesh. He looked ordinary. Yet he clearly went into the tree.

The therapist observed that her glimpse of the "tree man" would have been even harder to explain to outsiders than her experience of distant healing. "But the only person I needed to convince was myself. Since then, I have had a greater ability to trust myself and just *do* what I am called to do as a healer."

A nurse shared an equally powerful experience with me. In a waking dream, a beautiful Otherworldly woman beckoned her across the street from her house. The nurse was not sure whether she should go, but her dog was with her and she decided to trust his instinct. When the dog ran toward the strange woman, the nurse followed. At this point, she noticed that the lower part of the stranger's body was that of a deer.

Travels with Deer Woman

The deer woman takes my hand and we are flying together. She takes me back through my childhood, and through other critical passages in my life. I realize she is guiding me through a complete life review. When we return, she hugs me and tells me to trust in my gifts to heal and to help lost souls.

When she woke, the nurse was astonished to find deer pellets on the floor of her bedroom. Though she lived near the woods, her room was on the second floor and she thought it was highly unlikely that a deer would have climbed the stairs! She called family members in to confirm her find.

Not often recognized in the huge corpus of literature on alien encounters is that every night of the year, dreamers encounter Otherworld beings who would certainly rate as "aliens" (by the standards of ufology) if dreams were recognized as real experiences. These dream visitors sometimes leave physical tokens of these encounters. It seems that because our society has denied the reality of the dreamworld, the dreamworld is breaking through into our reality. Terence McKenna may be right when he announces that "the waking world and the world of dream have begun to merge" and that this will result in a transformation of our species.[2] Since we so often insist that what is "invisible"—i.e., cannot be seen with ordinary eyes—is unreal, we are getting more and more bleedthroughs from hyperreality. This is surely one aspect of all the alien encounters and UFO sightings, as of the proliferating visions of the radiant goddess figures that the pious identify as the Blessed Virgin Mary (even though they rarely call themselves by this name).

Encounters with a "true and invisible order" are puncturing holes in our definitions of subjective and objective, internal and external, 3-D and multidimensional, leaving us struggling to find new paradigms, as Jung struggled in his later years to describe an *objective* psychic reality—"an alien country outside the ego," a world invisible but fully present to this one. In fact, we don't need to invent new models. We have had them all along, above all in the shaman's understanding that the dreamworld is the real world. We need to recover what we have lost, which will amount to an act of cultural soul retrieval. While we cling to the notion that what is real is merely what can be experienced with the senses or tested with lab equipment, bleedthroughs from hyperspace are steadily sapping the foundations of our consensual reality.

The process was brilliantly anticipated in a jewel of precognitive fiction by Jorge Luis Borges entitled "Tlön, Uqbar, Orbis Tertius." A volume from the encyclopedia of an unknown planet—Tlön—is found in a bar, the legacy of an eccentric expatriate English mathematician. The detail and rigor of this work suggest that Tlön is a "complete cosmos." In Tlön, thoughts are things. Academics and experts debate whether Tlön "really" exists or is the invention of a secret society of scientists and metaphysicians.

Then objects from Tlön spill over into physical reality. A cone of impossibly dense metal, unknown on earth but a symbol of the gods on Tlön, spills from the belt of a drunken youth on the night of a flood. Then all forty volumes of the hitherto suspect Encyclopedia of

Tlön turn up in a Memphis library. At this point, consensual reality begins to unravel.

> Almost immediately, reality gave ground on more than one point. The truth is that it hankered to give ground. . . .
> Contact with Tlön and the ways of Tlön have disintegrated this world.[3]

Extraterrestrials or Interdimensionals?

Go through a good collection of alien encounter and "abduction" stories, such as John Mack's *Abduction*,[4] and you are likely to conclude that some larger reality is irrupting into consciousness on a rather grand scale—whatever interpretation you place on the source of these encounters. Are we dealing with extraterrestrials or interdimensionals? Are the physical-seeming experiences people report, sometimes with trembling shock, actually their fogged memories of experiences they had in their dreambodies? This is my personal suspicion, supported by the many accounts of "floating" and "flying" and the character of some of the minor injuries reported after the encounters, which are typical of what is sometimes described as astral repercussion. (If the dreambody is bruised or buffeted, marks may be transferred to the physical body.) As for the aliens encountered, they often seem less like star travelers than spirits or elemental forces of the very Earth we inhabit.

Take the first case in Mack's collection. While walking a coast path in Maine fittingly called the Marginal Way, Ed has a flashback to a strange episode in his life that unfolded nearly four decades before. He remembers himself aged sixteen, sleeping outside (in the backseat of the family car) in nature, near the ocean. He is feeling "horny"; there is a lot of pent-up sexual energy with all those teenage hormones kicking in. Ed recalls "drifting off." Then he experiences "tingling" sensations at the base of his neck. Next he is "floating" and finally flying over land and water to a "bubble" at the sea's edge. He is scared by the presence of strange beings. But he is welcomed by a slender, Otherworldly woman with silver-gold hair. She is wearing a silvery "tunic" and a medallion. She lets him have sex with her. When she has appeased his sexual cravings, she and her companions begin a kind of intensive training. They instruct Ed to "talk to the earth" and "listen to the anguish of the spirits." They show him the distorted psychic forms generated by human negativity and the consequences of man's persistent despoliation of the environment.

Whatever kind of "aliens" these might be, they certainly do not appear to be aliens from *out there*. While Ed talks of "alien doctors," the Otherworld beings talk of "spirits" and repeatedly demonstrate their connection to elemental forces of nature and their talents as shape-shifters. If they are "alien" in any way, it is only because we have become so alienated from the worlds of nature and dreaming.

Ed seems to believe that because his memories are so intensely *real,* they must relate to a physical experience. Active dreamers know better. His own account—with the tingling and floating and flying—strongly suggests that he made a journey outside the physical body. Certainly he knew crawling fear and warm sensuality and orgasmic pleasure, but he knew all these things (in all probability) in his dreambody. As a whole, Ed's story has all the elements of a lost ritual: of a puberty rite or adolescent vision quest. He goes to a liminal place, at a liminal time, where his adventures begin to unfold when he enters a twilight state of consciousness. In many traditional cultures he would have been *deliberately* separated from the community at this time to undergo a major rite of passage involving an encounter with the spirits in their own realm. Our society is skimpy with such rites of passage, especially when they open onto spiritual depths. But Ed managed to set the stage by himself, by entering a physical and psychic borderland where the spirits could reach him. At least, that is what a shaman might say. It seems Ed was not able to do much with the experience until many years later and still could speak about it only in "techie" language. Ed is not to blame for that. The society in which he was raised gave him no model and no vocabulary for a spirit calling.

In the second case in Mack's collection, a woman called Sheila starts experiencing "dreams" that combine powerful *vibrations* ("as if electricity is flowing throughout my whole body") with a sense of physical paralysis—possible OBE markers—shortly after her mother's death. Sheila's mother died after a botched operation that followed a long and traumatic illness. The torment for mother and daughter did not end with her death. Sheila was horrified to discover that her mother's body was left lying in an open vault for three days covered only by a thin layer of earth. These facts seem to me to be central to Sheila's subsequent experiences. To any student of folklore, as well as anyone who has tried to help the departed, they immediately suggest an ancient motif: the grief or anger of the unburied or misburied dead. Unfortunately, this aspect of the story is not explored by Mack. He briefly notes (but does not investigate) material that surfaced in previous hypnosis. Sheila was haunted by visions of a living skeleton, a curling iron, a sinister "piecrust-colored rectangle" with slits—a possible metaphor for the open vault under the thin crust of earth—that filled her with dread. All these images seem to point to the presence of the departed mother in her field.

Previous psychiatrists had tried to dope (as well as dupe) Sheila into dismissing her experiences as "only" dreams. To his credit, John Mack does her the human service of accepting that in some sense her experiences may be *real* as he leads her through the hypnotic regressions. But once again, the "alien abduction" scenario does not help us to understand what *kind* of reality we are dealing with, or to address its challenges. Sheila reports seeing skinny, silvery "peoplelike" beings in her room. Are these ETs, or spirits of the departed—possibly including her mother? She "remembers" being shown a huge stained-glass window under a dome. Is this a UFO, or a church? Could it be one of the locales in which the departed are helped, according to their belief systems, to adapt to the conditions of the afterlife? The transition from Sheila's world to the realm of the "aliens" is through "gray stuff." Is this the memory of an "abduction," or of pushing through an energy membrane between dimensions?

In one of the most interesting cases in Mack's collection, a man has the good sense to refuse to be defined as an "abductee." Carlos is a fine arts professor and artist with some Scottish ancestry. He has a history of life-threatening illness that may have loosened the connection between the physical body and the dreambody. Under hypnosis, he describes going back into his body at age one: "I felt I was sliding into it like you put on socks and shoes and trousers." He also remembers a small "angellike" creature who appeared the night he watched an aurora borealis—and later of being able to lift into the air "in a mirror image of the small creature" and to fly about in this form.

He attributes his healing from pneumonia to the "beaming" of light energy into his body by "alien" creatures.

He goes to the Bay of Seals on Iona in 1970 and sings Gregorian chants to the seals to test the legend that they contain the souls of monks slain in Viking raids; a seal swims close in and shadows him for half a mile as he walks the beach.

The following night, after dancing with abandon for a couple of hours, he goes down to the beach and sees a huge luminous "pink bubble" on the waters. It approaches and envelops him. He is transported to a scene in which he sees himself as an "orphan boy" in Columba's time, during a Viking raid.

When he returns to Iona twenty years later, Carlos has a thrilling experience he describes as "lightfall." He sees a column of peach-colored light descending into the sea, creating a great circle of sparkling light that he perceives as a "tunnel" to something in the clouds above. The light enfolds him—he loses consciousness and memory and finds himself a hundred yards away along the beach when he wakes up. Under hypnosis, he recalls ascending through the "tunnel of light" into a "ship." He describes a variety of creatures—smaller light beings like the one he saw in childhood, a dominant "female," scary robotic insectoid critters—and a projection screen that is also a window.

Under hypnosis, Carlos remembers a painful examination and crystal surgery leading to healing and transformation into a body of light.

Carlos not only refuses to be called an alien abductee, he refuses to apply the term *alien* to the beings he believes he encountered. He refers to them as "light beings" and "Earth gardeners." He maintains that experiences like his offer a "paradigm of initiation." I believe he is right.

I considered going through all the case studies in John Mack's book to determine whether *any* of the experiences reported truly conform to the notion of an "extraterrestrial" visitation or an "alien" abduction—and whether other models of understanding might offer better ways to help people who are disturbed or traumatized by such episodes than does simply adopting or dismissing the ET scenario. I was delighted to find that Carlos had done a good part of my work for me.

To get to the truth of these things—to help people whose reality system has been shattered by experiences that violate physical laws and linear conceptions—we need to go back to Paleopsych 101. We need to recognize that spirits are real, that there are real worlds beyond the physical universe, and that we can visit them in embodied form and receive visitors from them. Hypnotic regression, with its questionable crop of "memories," is not the best way to clarify an experience that may or may not be an "alien encounter." Through the techniques of Active Dreaming, we can go back into the image or the memory—fully conscious and fully protected—and see for ourselves. The dreamgate is also the stargate. When we have gotten these basics straight, we can proceed to discuss *in which reality* a *real* event took place. We can move on to consider when and why beings from higher dimensions (who are infinitely closer to us than beings from "outer space") might choose to materialize and dematerialize in our little 3-D world.

Visitors from Hyperspace

We no longer have an agreed model by which to understand or explain encounters with visitors from a larger reality. In this respect, to quote Sir Edward Tylor again, we have indeed "fallen from the high level of savage knowledge." Indigenous peoples recognize many kinds of Otherworld beings and many passages between their realms and ours. They understand that the distance between dimensions is really no *distance* at all. Handsome Lake, the Seneca prophet, says the distance between our surface world and the world of the spirits is exactly as wide as the edge of the maple leaf. Dreaming peoples evolved a science and diplomacy of interdimensional travel. Unlike so many of our ufologists, they know this is a two-way traffic; we not only receive visitors from hyperspace, but we ourselves can journey to other worlds. Dreaming peoples also know that we must be able to close the doors between the worlds as well as open them, since not all beings from other dimensions are benign.

A spokesman for one of the premier gatherings of UFO watchers, the U.S. Mutual UFO Network, announced in 1987 that after studying thousands of cases, the organization had concluded that just four types of aliens are visiting Earth: a humanlike entity, a small humanoid, and two of their creations—a robot and an "experimental animal."[5]

We see what we are able to see. Perhaps we see that which we are. What a telling judgment on our condition it would be if we could see only—from the vast panoply of beings and forms in multidimensional reality—the four comic-book figures approved by the Mutual UFO Network! But thankfully it is not so. With their eyes open or closed, in their physical bodies or their dreambodies, people see beings of light and space invaders, shape-shifters, birdmen, giants and dwarfs, gods and daimons, spirits of the departed, spirits of stone and stream, cones and towers of pulsating energy, lightfalls, fiery trees, "a window that opened on the inside of a star."[6] "The fairies of the air are different from those in the rocks," as an old Celtic woman told Evans-Wentz.[7]

We are not alone. Once again, we are relearning what was common sense to our paleo-ancestors, and to many generations after them. We must get beyond the sterile black-and-white controversy between skeptics and UFO believers who think that extraterrestrials are coming among us in physical spaceships to conduct genetic experiments and/or colonize the planet. In the vast literature on this subject, Jacques Vallée, to my mind, has made the most important single contribution. Vallée argues that UFOs may be "neither objects nor flying." They don't necessarily come from anywhere in space. They are not necessarily extraterrestrial. Similar sightings have been made throughout human history and have been explained according to the paradigms of each culture—as the manifestations of gods and spirits, as the work of magicians or fairies.[8] Why do these things appear to us now, with such frequency? Paracelsus maintained that "everything God creates manifests itself to man sooner or later. . . . These beings appear to us in order for us to become able to understand them." And, in understanding them, to revise our definitions of reality and reopen our accounts with possibility.

In a third-century Buddhist sutra, the *Gandavyuha,* there is a fascinating account of how "enlightened beings" seek to guide us to higher consciousness and an expanded view of the nature of reality. It is the perennial task of certain beings, by virtue of their spiritual development, to help others to move beyond the restrictions of ordinary awareness in order to awaken to the full potential of mind. To perform their task, these teachers need to operate partly within the field of these same restrictions. To bring insight to where people live, they have to share their lives and their social and cultural environment. For this reason, the identity of the teacher is often deliberately obscured, as he or she adapts to the needs and circumstances of the society in which he or she operates. Yet these teachers retain the ability to be "beyond the world even while in the world," and retain the knowledge that "the world as we know it is only a description." Acting from this knowledge, they are able to "transform or suspend the deep structures of the description at will."[9]

How does this relate to UFO sightings and alien abductions? Perhaps in this way: that we have become so grossly enmeshed in material reality, so wedded to technological models, so divorced from the Dreaming, that higher consciousness must pursue us in forms adapted to our limited conceptions of what is real. As Jung observed in his essay on flying saucers, "anything that looks technological goes down without difficulty with modern man."[10] UFOs and "alien robots" *look* technological—until you look closer and discover that they behave more like ghosts or spirits. Can you hear someone saying, "Now that we have got your attention, we can begin to work on your definition of reality"?

You don't really know where you are unless you have traveled someplace else. So let us enrich our perspectives on this theme by considering those of three societies where journeys through hyperspace were well understood.

The Vedic Science of Interdimensional Travel

"The social organization of the ancient Vedic peoples allowed for regular contact with higher beings," to quote Richard Thompson's splendid book on this theme[11] As a result, Vedic literature contains a rich zoology of hyperspace. The Puranas refer to four hundred thousand humanlike races that live among the planetary systems, within contact range of humans. Some of these beings—gods, demons, and others—are more evolved than humans; some are less so. Some are friendly to humans, others detest the human race. Some intervene in human affairs, for good or bad; others are sublimely indifferent. Whatever their differences, most of these beings have something in common: they are more powerful and more intelligent than humans.

In the Vedic sources, these humanoid species are attributed special powers, or *siddhis,* that are magical to ordinary humans but may be developed by an advanced yogi or seer. They can communicate across vast distances by pure thought. They can fold time and space and travel from one point in the cosmos to another without being impeded by physical objects or the laws of physics. They practice teleportation: they are capable of transporting physical bodies from one place to another without crossing the intervening space. Though the Sanskrit sources do not use a term that can be directly translated as "dimension," it should be noted that the power of teleportation *(prapti-siddhi),* the ability to move through physical objects *(viyahasa),* and the power to materialize or dematerialize at will *(mano java)* would all be characteristic of multidimensional beings playing hide-and-seek with a species embedded in a 3-D reality. One further attribute of our visitors from hyperspace, in the Vedic accounts, is that they are prodigious shape-shifters, able to show themselves in many forms.

The Vedic cosmos is multilayered. There are fourteen inhabited realms, or *lokas,* seven below the earth, and seven above it.[12] As you will already know if you have become an Active Dreamer, you will bump into a ceiling or impenetrable wall as you go upward—until you are able to adjust your frequency to go higher. It is easier to travel "down" than "up," although beings from the higher levels rarely choose to descend into the miasma of the sublunar planes. The highest level is Brahmaloka, the realm of Brahma. Below this are levels inhabited by sages who cultivate transcendental knowledge and consciousness. Below them is Svargaloka, the realm of the Devas, or gods, whose wars with lower forces impact humans.

Some beings actively rebel against the cosmic hierarchy and sometimes interfere dramatically in human affairs. Between gods and humans are intermediate races that are neutral or hostile to man.

The higher orders of beings use *vimanas,* vehicles whose flight patterns will interest students of UFO sightings. They fly through the air, sometimes visible, sometimes invisible. They can move in any element. They turn at impossible angles. They appear in the sky "like whirling firebrands" and disappear in less than the blink of an eye.

They can change the weather, producing twisters, lightning bolts, hailstones.

In the Vedic accounts, visitors from hyperspace appear to humans for many different reasons. Some come to help and guide, some to meddle. Sexual attraction plays a large role in the epic stories and is a leading cause of alien abductions; the daughter of the Naga king kidnaps Arjuna after she becomes infatuated with him.

Visitors from hyperspace also show up because they are called in. The Bhagavata Purana contains a riveting scene of a ritual at the court of a king. As the priests vibrate mantras, gods and Gandharvas and celestial seers gather to join in the ceremonies.

Scottish Crossings

Robert Kirk, a seventeenth-century Anglican vicar at Aberfoyle in Scotland, wrote a remarkably detailed account of the Otherworld, its inhabitants, and their intercourse with living human beings. Kirk's Secret Commonwealth is not another collection of folklore and popular beliefs but a rigorous study, scientific by the standards of its day, that is clearly grounded in experience. Its main interest today is that it describes a "secret way of correspondence" with the invisible world: a means of crossing between ordinary and nonordinary reality at will.[13]

Kirk subtitled his work "An Essay of the Nature and actions of the Subterranean and for the most part Invisible People, heretofore going by the names of Elves, Fauns and Fairies and the like." By "subterranean," he does not mean creatures living in dark, gloomy places in the bowels of the earth. Their realm is full of light, though it is not lit by any sun. They live in "cavities" and may pass wherever air may go. The earth is "full of cavities and cells," and everywhere is inhabited; there is "no such thing as pure wilderness in the whole Universe."

Though invisible to most humans, the inhabitants of these realms are not disembodied. They have "light changeable bodies, like those called Astral, somewhat of the nature of a condensed cloud." They are best seen at twilight. They shape-shift and can make their "bodies of congealed air" appear and disappear at will.

The fairies are "of a middle nature betwixt man and Angel," like the daimons of the ancient world. They are mortal, in the sense that they pass from their existing state, but they live far longer than a human life span. They are strongly connected to the earth and special places within the earth. They tend to show themselves in the costume of the country and speak its language. Kirk discusses rival opinions in his parish about whether the "good people" are spirits of the departed, clothed in their subtle bodies; "exuded forms of the man approaching death"; or "a numerous people by themselves." He suggests that all these descriptions may be valid for different phenomena. Just beyond the borders of everyday perception is a vast and varied population.

Encounters with the fairies can be dangerous. They are known to abduct humans into their realm. Those who enter the Otherworld willingly may have a hard time getting back. Some inhabitants of the invisible realm are hostile to humans, and some seek to feed on the energy of the living.

However, the peoples of the Secret Commonwealth take a close interest in human affairs, and our lives are closely related to theirs. One of Kirk's most intriguing observations is that each of us has a double who is fully at home in the Otherworld. The old Scots Gaelic term for this double is *coimimeadh* (pronounced "coy-me-may"), which means "co-walker." Kirk improvises a series of synonyms for the double, including: *twin, companion, echo,* "*Reflex-man,*" and *living picture.* The double resembles the living person both before and after she or he dies. The double survives physical death, when the co-walker "goes at last to his own land." When invited, the co-walker will make itself "known and familiar." But most people are unaware that they have a double. Since it lives in a different element, it "neither can nor will easily converse" with the everyday waking mind.

Your double may be seen by others. Kirk gives several examples: of someone's double entering a house shortly before the person himself arrived; of sightings of the double of a person who had just died or was soon to die; of the perception of the subtle form of a lover or spouse standing close to the loved one; of a woman who observed her second self walking ahead of her as she left her home. Kirk also offers clues to the possible influence of the co-walker—

even unrecognized and unperceived—in a person's life. He cites the Scots belief that someone who eats great quantities of food without putting on weight is being joined in the gourmandise by a "joint eater" or *geirt coimitheth*. Maybe there is a tip here for a new weight-loss program!

Rereading *The Secret Commonwealth* while I was preparing this book, I asked for dream guidance to clarify exactly what Robert Kirk means by "co-walker." In my dream, I acquired a suede coat identical to the coat I most often wear when flying around the world or traveling to my Active Dreaming workshops. In my dream, I carried both these garments, swapping them according to circumstances. The dream confirmed my suspicion that Kirk is writing about the dream double; unfortunately, he tells us little about dreaming, where the double is most easily perceived.

Kirk speculates that everything may have its double—a tantalizing hint of the existence of what I have called counterpart reality.

How can we know the truth about these things? Through the art and science of *seeing*. Robert Kirk describes the practice of the Scottish seer as he was able to understand and enter it. The seer is able to make spirits visible to himself and others. He is able to cross into the Otherworld and return at his choosing. Kirk includes a curious report of a seer who was seen to vanish, body and soul, from a certain spot and reappear an hour later some distance from the point of his crossing. The gift of seeing runs in certain families, but many of the most powerful seers receive their calling directly from the spirits. Their initiatory visions are often wild and shamanic; they fall into "fits and Raptures." The gift of seeing brings the ability to look into subtler orders of reality and perceive things "that for their smallness or subtlety and secrecy are invisible to others" even though they are intermeshed with them. The seer is accompanied by an inner light that can be focused and directed, "a beam continually about him as that of the sun." Kirk's description of the *taibhsear*'s "beam" closely parallels Inuit accounts of the "shaman-light" of the *angaqok*.

Kirk provides an interesting account of a seer's initiation. He winds a cord of human hair around his middle in the shape of a helix. He bends down and looks backward between his legs. The object of his gaze may be a funeral procession, moving over a border crossing.

Or it may be a hole in a tree—like the hole left in a fir tree when a knot has gone.

Kirk describes how a seer can provide a layman with temporary access to the Sight. The apprentice places one foot on the seer's foot, while the seer lays a hand on the apprentice's head, so that the would-be seer is enclosed within the *taibhsear*'s body space as well as his energy field. As he looks over the seer's right shoulder, the apprentice is suppose to see "a multitude" of beings rushing toward him through the air.

The gifts of seeing include the ability to fold time and space. Kirk cautions—as any good practitioner would—about the difficulty of interpreting and working with some of these sightings. He recounts the case of a woman with the Sight who foresaw a seaborne attack on her island in the Hebrides but was confused about whether the soldiers in the boat were hostile or friendly and even whether they were coming or going—with good reason, since they had stolen a barge from her island and were rowing toward it with their backs to the shore.

As a man of the Church, Kirk goes to great lengths to argue that there is nothing ungodly about "correspondence" with Otherworld beings, quoting reports of visionary experiences in the Bible. He also contends that it is as "natural" to encounter the inhabitants of the Otherworld as it is to go fishing; both involve moving into another element. He reassures us that we are dealing with "an invisible people, guardian over and careful of man," whose "courteous endeavour" is to convince us of the reality of the spiritual world and of "a possible and harmless method of correspondence betwixt men and them, even in this life."

According to local tradition, Robert Kirk paid for his knowledge. He was reputedly taken by the fairies in 1692 into a fairy knoll across a little valley from his church; villagers were still pointing out the site centuries later.[14] Were the fairies annoyed with him for revealing their secrets? Or had they fallen in love with him? Maybe the tale was concocted by people who wanted to "spook" their neighbors into keeping away from personal exploration of the unseen. Some say the fairies took Kirk's body and soul; some say only the soul. A related tradition says that he had a means of coming back from the Otherworld that depended on the actions of a cousin to whom he announced it in a dream. But the cousin lost his nerve when he saw the clergyman's double appear in the church at a baptism. So Robert Kirk remained on the other side.

When the Key to the Dreamgate Was Stolen

Bora circles are sacred ceremonial grounds of Australian Aborigines. In the East they consist of larger and smaller circles connected by a path. The smaller circle represents the Sky World, where Biame has his home. It is forbidden to noninitiates. The larger ground, representing Earth, is open to the community.

A sacred teaching story tells of a time when the god Biame left the Earth to return to his camp in the Sky. He called the Kadaitcha, an ancient clan of sorcerers, from the heavens to take his place and watch over human affairs. They were welcomed by the tribes and assumed the forms of men. Their chief, Kobbina, made his home under the red rock (Uluru) that is Biame's altar and took a wife from the court of the Moon spirit. She bore him twin sons, Koobara and Booka.

A time came when Biame needed Kobbina's counsel. The god called the chief of the Kadaitcha to journey to his camp in the Sky World. Kobbina had to choose which of his sons would watch over the people in his place. He chose Koobara. The rejected twin, Booka, who was ugly, squat, and violent, flew into a rage and killed his father. In the melee, his mother also perished.

Biame, watching from on high, decided to intervene when he saw the evil twin's followers routing the other members of the clan. Koobara's forces rallied as they sensed the god descending from the Sky World through the astral planes. Booka fled the field, bent on preventing the god from manifesting on the Earth plane.

In a vast cavern under the red rock was a stone platform holding the Rings of Bora. These nine sacred circles of stones were Biame's doorway into the world of men. Booka attacked the altar with a desperate frenzy. To work his destruction, he had to overpower the Four Sisters of the Wind, the guardians of the sacred site. The Sisters were no match for Booka's violence. The evil twin and his followers stole the key to the circles, an egg-shaped stone called Kundri. It is the heart of the Rainbow Serpent. Now the Bora rings are locked and Biame is shut out of his Earth garden.

The renegades rape and blind the Sisters of the Wind. The Earth is now separated from the Sky World, and the stage is set for the desolation of the South Land by invaders whom Booka supports.

Yet Biame reaches, even now, from the Sky World to renew contact.

My version of this Aboriginal myth is based on a beautiful retelling by Sam Watson in the prologue to his novel *The Kadaitcha Sung*.[15] It is a haunting evocation of the tragedy that befalls men when they lose the Dreaming. "Those who lose the Dreaming are lost," as the Aborigines say. The dreamgates are also the portals to higher worlds. And dream travel is the road to hyperspace.

CHAPTER 16

≋

Starwalking

What is outside is also inside; and what is not
outside man is not inside. The outer and the inner
are one thing, one constellation, one influence,
one concordance, one duration . . . one fruit.

Paracelsus

Dreamgates Are Stargates

What is alien is what is "other." And what is most profoundly *other,*
for many of us, is our own larger Self. The reality we encounter is our
mirror, but our perception is fogged. We fail to recognize how the
thoughts and feelings we send out develop a life of their own, like
unacknowledged children. We disclaim any relationship with our
shadow selves—the aspects we have denied or rejected—to the point
where we end up being stalked by them, in the dreamworld *and* the
surface world, like the character portrayed by Roger Moore in the
old movie *The Man Who Haunted Himself.* Worst of all, we regard
as utterly "other" the messengers from the big Self who are forever
trying to get us to look squarely at the mirror and see our own true
face. And to remember that our spirits are starborn.

It is fascinating to see what happens when people who have been
terrified by encounters with alien intruders can be helped to revisit
the experience as conscious dreamers, in a state of full awareness.
Many find—as the snake dreamer in chapter 4 found—that power
and self-knowledge are waiting beyond the fear. Has not Death
taught us that the way to such power lies *through* the terror? So does
the way to the stars.

Joyce had been terrified since childhood by a succession of intensely *real* experiences in which she was torn from her familiar environment by "space aliens" who somehow transported her to a "mother ship" where she was subjected to painful "surgical penetration." When she described these episodes in a dream group, she initially balked at the suggestion that she might be reporting *dreams.* "These things were *real*," she insisted. She shivered, folding her arms tightly over her chest. "This stuff really happened."

I had no doubt that, in some order of reality, her experiences had indeed taken place, though her memories might be fragmentary and garbled. Given the force of her emotions, this did not seem the time to get into ontological discussions. I simply asked Joyce if she had a question about her abduction experiences.

"Why me?" she said without hesitation.

I asked if she would be willing to try to go back to a locale she remembered—with the aid of shamanic drumming—to answer that question. Joyce was understandably scared. I reassured her that she would go escorted by a partner and "bodyguard." A frequent flier in the group—a tall "warrior woman" who had mastered formidable challenges of her own, in both worlds—volunteered for this role.

To her amazement, Joyce found a portal opening as soon as the drumming began. "I whizzed through a kind of ribbed tunnel. It was like an elevator lying on the horizontal. I shot right inside the mother ship. Except it didn't look anything like a conventional spaceship. It was a sphere, full of patterns of light. The aliens were also made of light. They seem to be able to put on bodies as we put on clothes. I felt safe and welcome here. They told me this is a place of rendezvous, and I can come back in dreaming. I wanted to know why they hurt me. They told me that without penetration there is no birth—of life or understanding. They told me I have the same powers they have whenever I'm ready to use them."

Joyce has become a happy star voyager, inside the dreaming. What she had previously encountered, she now believes, was molded into the images of her fears. These experiences are happening in a realm where thoughts are things in the most literal, palpable fashion. The beings she encountered and revisited are transpersonal. In relation to her normal self, they are "other" and "out there." In the larger scheme of things, within the limitless realm of Mind, they are in no way alien: different but not separate, separate but not different.

Maureen reported many encounters with "aliens" who appeared in her house at night. Some had "saurian heads, like turtles," but wore loose-flowing clothes; these seemed to be engaged in their own business and paid no attention to Maureen. Others were gray-blue, "like ectoplasm." On closer inspection—and subsequent interrogation—one of these proved to be a departed family member who had remained place-bound. One of Maureen's most interesting sightings was of "a very human-seeming woman in a blue top and red shorts" who kept her back turned. Several days after the dream, as she dressed to go jogging, Maureen suddenly realized that *she* was the "human-seeming woman" in the blue top and red shorts; it seemed she had caught a glimpse of her future self.

Maureen's sightings reflect the fact that from time to time we tune in—usually quite unintentionally—to frequency bands beyond the spectrum of ordinary consciousness. We pick up different audio-visual signals, some quite unrelated to us. We also see what is living with us in our immediate environment on frequency bands that are usually invisible to normal sight. Remember that the distance between you and the spirits is the width of the edge of the maple leaf. If you want to verify these statements for yourself, *right now,* you should relax into the twilight state and start scanning your psychic environment. You might see yourself switching channels or dialing up—as if on a shortwave radio—into higher energy bands. Alternatively, you could play a game suggested by my psychic friend Chuck Coburn.[1] This should be used only for identifying or contacting *higher* entities.

EXERCISE: IDENTIFYING HIGHER ENTITIES IN YOUR FIELD

1.   Be open to the possibility that beings from other dimensions are close to you at this moment. You are separated from them not by space but by frequency levels.

2.   Make it your intention to identify (and if appropriate, to communicate with) a *higher* entity in your field. See its rate of vibrations slowing down, as leaves settle after a windstorm, until you begin to perceive it.

3.   Identify what you have brought into your field of perception.

I have noticed that among Active Dreamers, experiences of "alien abduction" seem to be relatively infrequent, and Otherworld beings are rarely confused with "aliens from outer space." This may be because Active Dreamers have much richer personal mythologies than the population at large and are at home in the imaginal realms. In preparing this chapter, I went back through my own journals. I found *hundreds* of experiences that could be classified as "alien encounters" in the current sense of the phrase. Some involve contact with intelligences associated with other star systems and planetary spheres, even with other galaxies, and travel to these systems. They are *real* encounters—sometimes thrillingly so—but they are taking place in a separate reality. I believe that we can have physical encounters with beings from other dimensions, as the Phoenicians saw gods descending to earth from winged disks, and as the Israelites saw a prophet carried upward in a chariot of fire. I believe it is entirely possible that we have had physical visitations by beings from "outer space" and will have more of them. I see no reason why our species should not one day develop a technology equal to the inventions of science fiction that could teleport physical bodies to other points in the galaxy or (as in *Sliders*) to parallel worlds.

But to become a star voyager, you don't have to hope you will still be around if and when NASA comes up with a multidimensional space shuttle. The dreamgates are open.

Are you interested in a voyage to another star system? The great spiritual lineages each have their own method of star voyaging. In ancient Egypt, this is the journey on the Boat of Ra to the Sun Behind the Sun. For the Taoist masters, it is starwalking—a kind of cosmic hopscotch among the constellations.[2] The dream people of Mount Etna journeyed into the volcano to come out among the stars. We are going to learn now from the ancient dreamers of West Africa who say not only that we are starborn but that we can journey back to our source.

The Journey to Sirius B

As part of their most secret religious tradition, the Dogon of West Africa have preserved—perhaps for thousands of years—a body of knowledge about the Sirian star system that was only accessible to modern astronomers within the last generation.

In Dogon belief, the most important star in the sky is Sirius B, which can only be seen through a powerful telescope. They call this dwarf star *po tolo*. *Tolo* means "star." *Po* is the Dogon name for the smallest grain they know—a tiny cereal grain called *fonio* in West Africa and *Digitaria exilis* by botanists. The Dogon also describe Sirius B as "the egg of the world." They say that it gave birth to everything that exists in the universe, that life on Earth was seeded from this star.[3]

The starseed legend is intriguing in the light of current scientific knowledge and speculation about the birth and death of stars. In the eyes of science, "a star is a nuclear furnace, burning hydrogen and creating nuclear 'ash' in the form of waste helium."[4] It is also an exquisite balancing act between the force of gravity, which tends to crush the star, and the nuclear force, which tends to blow it apart.

A star matures and ages as it exhausts its nuclear fuel.

The furnace shuts down when a yellow star builds up too much waste helium. Gravity starts to crush it. The temperature rises until it may become hot enough to burn helium, shape-shifting into a *red giant*.

When the helium is used up, the furnace shuts down again, gravity takes over, and the red giant shrinks to become a *white dwarf*, a miniature star with the mass of an entire star squeezed to the size of Earth.

If the star is massive enough (many times bigger than our sun), most of the elements in the white dwarf will continue to be fused into heavier elements, until you get down to iron—at which point no more energy can be squeezed out and the furnace shuts down permanently. Now heat rises to *trillions* of degrees, the iron core collapses, and the surface layer of the white dwarf explodes, releasing a supernova, the greatest burst of energy known in the physical universe.

The immense force of the supernova releases a tremendous shower of stellar debris: starseed. It mixes with other gases. Second-generation stars are born from this fusion. This is the origin of the "heavy" elements in our bodies that our sun was not hot enough to forge. As Michio Kaku writes, "The heavy elements in our bodies were synthesized in a supernova that blew up before our sun was created . . . a nameless supernova exploded billions of years ago, seeding the original gas cloud that created our solar system."[5]

For the Dogon, however, the source of this cosmic event is not nameless. Its name is *po tolo,* the seed-star, or *aduno tal,* the Egg of the World.

The Dogon know that the orbit of Sirius B is egg-shaped or elliptical. They know that Sirius A is one of the foci of this orbit, *not* its center. They know that the orbital period of this "invisible" star is approximately fifty years. They seem to have known all these things long before modern astronomers.

They describe Sirius B as both "infinitely tiny" and the heaviest thing in creation. They say it is composed of a metal, *sagala,* which is a little brighter than iron and so heavy "that all earthly beings combined cannot lift it." These perceptions have also been confirmed by recent astronomers, who report *(a)* that Sirius B is a white dwarf, the smallest kind of star (apart from collapsing neutron stars, which are totally invisible), and *(b)* that Sirius B is composed of superdense matter that exists nowhere on earth. White dwarf stars do not give out much light, but have a fantastically powerful gravitational field. The density of Sirius B is calculated to be sixty-five thousand times that of water, while the density of our sun is about equal to that of water.

The first photo of Sirius B was taken in 1970, by Irving Lindenblad of the U.S. Naval Observatory in Washington, D.C.

The big question is, how did a preliterate African people acquire such exact astronomical detail about a star that cannot be seen with ordinary eyes?

There are two reasonable explanations. The first is that at some point in history—maybe thousands of years ago—some people in West Africa received a visit from travelers who were familiar with the Sirian star system. These visitors might have come from the star system itself, a theory pursued by Robert Temple in his fascinating and prolix book, *The Sirius Mystery.*[6] They may have come from another dimension. Or they may have come from another time; they might even have been human astronomers from the future.

The second hypothesis—to me the most interesting—is that the Dogon know these things because their shamans have been to Sirius and have seen how things work. This is the clear implication of Dogon tradition, as reported by anthropologists Marcel Griaule and Germaine Dieterlen.[7] According to Dogon oral history, in early times their shaman-kings, or *hogons,* were ritually sacrificed every seven years. It was believed that the soul of the *hogon,* released from the body, would journey to the invisible seed-star in a cosmic return of energy. No doubt it was also hoped that the shaman-king would be able to intercede with higher powers on behalf of his people. A priest-king who was both craftier and more adept than his predecessors managed to avoid this cycle of blood sacrifice in an interesting way. With the help of his son, he "feigned death," possibly by going into deep trance in the fashion of some renowned shamans and yogis. He "lay dormant" for several months. Then he appeared before the *hogon* who had been chosen to succeed him. He announced that he had made a soul journey to the seed-star, the Egg of the World. He drew star maps, defining its orbit. He convinced his listeners that he had been and seen, sharing specific information that would only become known to Western science many centuries later, as well as insights into the spiritual process of manifestation that remain beyond the reach of science. After this soul journey was reported to the elders, the seven-year slaughter ceased; priest-kings were permitted to rule for the whole duration of the orbit of Sirius B.

Return to the Womb of Life

I was intrigued by the Dogon legend of a shaman-king who made the return journey to the star from which life on Earth was seeded and brought back proofs. How did he do it? And in which reality? If a West African shaman could do it, can we do it, too?

An artist friend sent me a hand-painted mandala, without explanation, suggesting only that I might like to experiment with it when I had time. Up in the middle of the night, I stared at the image. The form of the mandala was a hollow disk, composed of twelve concentric bands of color. At the center, against a black field, was a red triangle. Inside the triangle was a swirl of deep blue-green. I half-closed my eyes, letting my focus blur. Instantly, the 2-D image became a window. I found myself peering down a cosmic tunnel at a blue-green planet. I realized I was looking at the planet Earth, as if from a vast distance. When I "zoomed in" to get a better look, I found myself looking at men with spiral tattoos on their faces, who were gazing up at the skies. Were they Maoris? Why were they in the picture?

Unable to answer these questions, I rotated the mandala until the triangle was pointing downward. The view through the window shifted dramatically. It was as if I was looking the other way through the tunnel, back into the source of germination, into a cosmic womb that was indescribably dense and fecund, pullulating with new life. I thought of the Dogon accounts of the Egg of the World. Maybe it looked something like this.

I called my artist friend and reported my impressions. "Not bad," she commented. She explained that she had painted this mandala in consultation with an elder of the Maori people of New Zealand. She informed me that the Maoris also believe that life on Earth was seeded from the Sirius star system. The mandala had been designed as a visual portal for journeying between the two realms. My impressions suggested that it works.

Excited by this fresh discovery, I decided to conduct an experiment with the help of the seasoned travelers in one of my advanced Active Dreaming programs. With the aid of shamanic drumming, we would embark on a journey to Sirius B to explore the legend—shared by other indigenous peoples, including the Hopi—that we are its starseed.

To prepare for this experiment, I journeyed to seek guidance from an intelligence I associated with another star system as well as a higher dimension.[8] I returned with these instructions:

"Set Your Course for Sirius"

Begins now a new story, for each telling makes all completely new and each hearer is as fresh a discoverer as any Columbus.

It begins with the argonauts of hyperspace: that is, the voyage through dimensions beyond the physical. In this way intelligent life comes to the Earth environment, as it has come to other systems. The voyage begins with Sirius, though we prefer to call this system by another name: A-KAR-MA-TET. This means "the Womb of Life."

The vessels for the journey are infinitely light, as bright and radiant as spinnings of starlight. The captains take on human form only in the final stages, prior to landing. The time required for the journey is inconceivably long and as sudden as thought. The process is easier to understand from the Fifth Dimension, easier still from higher levels, but these escape fluent translation.

Set your course for Sirius.

The legends may be tracked through the folk memory and mythology of many peoples. Remembered in some of these tales is the viability of the return journey. Though the original vessels are broken, the gateways still exist and the course settings can be learned. There are physical locations on Earth where this is easier.

Picture this:

An orb within a doorway, composed of opaque, fine material. Its color is blue-gray. Above and beyond it, the midnight sky of outer space, sprinkled with stars. Stretch your consciousness to touch the orb. You feel its gentle resistance; it stretches like a membrane. Adjust your density and let yourself flow into the sphere. It encloses and protects you. This will be your vessel for the journey.

Inside, you have the impression of controls, perhaps of other beings in holographic form. The controls are not panels or switchboards, but patterns of light that form designs slightly reminiscent of Greek mosaics.

Settle yourself comfortably. The navigational guidance system is activated by thought. Use it.

Your mind on my purpose.

Before embarkation, ensure the physical and psychic security of your launch site. Empowered thought forms—elementals—will normally be sufficient for this purpose. But care is required because there are rival forces in the cosmos *and not all of them wish you well.*

The conditions of interdimensional travel are quite different from linear journeys, though for ease of explanation they will be remembered and described in terms analogous to travelogues. The warp-shift is an acceleration within. You may have the sense of implosion, of becoming inconceivably small, or of journeying through a pinhole at your own center.

All the worlds may be explored within the sphere you have entered. *The name for this orb is the Kara Senduri, which means "the Heart of Voyaging."*

Take your place where there is no place.

Set your course for a star system in outer space that is within. This is how it begins.

In subsequent workshops, we used several visual keys to establish a flight path to the Sirius star system. We stood outside under a wintry night sky and saw how the belt of Orion points like an arrow at the blue-white glow of the bright star of Sirius. We meditated with the Maori-designed mandala. We practiced becoming inconceivably small and journeying to the stars through the space at the heart of an atom. And we developed the image of the "blue-gray orb" to the point where we were able to use it as a vessel for group expeditions.

Some of the early voyagers brought back literal-seeming reports of reconnoitering the dead wreck of a neutrino star drifting among cosmic dust in outer space. Most found themselves entering a deeper order of reality that brought a deep sense of awe. The most articulate among us struggled for words to contain these experiences. They spoke of being inside a cosmic "seed," of joining a "ripple" that reached throughout the cosmos, of "entering the plane where thought begins to manifest creation." Some reported encounters with higher intelligences. One woman described a gathering of superior beings she described as "the Council of Light"; they gave her a "bundle" of information that had to be carefully unfolded.

We agreed to a dream rendezvous. The night before the next class, we would all try to meet in the Kara Senduri, the "ship for Sirius," and try to discover more about this vessel and its possible uses. In my own dream journey, I had a highly tactile sense of entry into the sphere; the surface was rubbery and springy. Inside, I had clear impressions of several members of the group, especially Debbie, Lou, and Gail. Others seemed wispy, not fully there. I noted that other beings had joined us. They had silvery, opalescent bodies. One of them gave me a cylinder about eighteen inches long and four to five inches in diameter, encased in a sheath. When I removed the sheath, the surface of the cylinder resembled a map or the projection of a landscape, with areas of blue sea. Light blazed from the core of the cylinder through gaps or holes, symmetrically arranged. Holding this object, I felt myself being recharged and energized. I realized I could use this object to project light, to defend myself (I thought of the *Star Wars* image of a "light saber") or to recharge my batteries at any time. At the same time, it seemed to me I was looking at something like a map of the world projected through a further dimension. What one might expect to see projected onto a sphere was here projected onto a cylinder that might be its 5-D counterpart. The model reflected the curvature of space-time and offered a key to the oneness of inner and outer space.

As we embarked on our journey together, other impressions came flooding in. There were strong Egyptian motifs. Were we traveling in a high-tech version of the Boat of Ra, in which Egyptian star voyagers set their course for the Sun Behind the Sun, another esoteric name for Sirius, or its metaphysical counterpart?

I went to the next class with high anticipation. Lou spoke immediately of seeing me holding a "tube" with light coming from inside through "diamond-shaped" apertures. Gail spoke of her vision of a "light saber." Several members of the group spoke of feeling that they were on board an "Egyptian" starship, with a helmsman at the rudder, escorted by guides in "silver-gray bodies."

As an experiment in shared dreaming, this could clearly be rated a success. Did it bring us to any firm conclusions about Sirius B? We are still exploring and still struggling with the difficulties of translating this kind of experience into coherent language. The "sphere" we have used has proved a viable vessel for adventurous group travel, like the "spirit canoes" of the shamans of the Pacific Northwest. If someone unprepared saw us journeying in a blue-gray sphere, would he think he had seen a flying saucer?

≋

CHAPTER 17

The View from the Fifth Dimension

Perception has a destiny.

Ralph Waldo Emerson

5-D Vision

There is rising support among physicists for a paradigm long familiar to shamans and seers: that our physical universe is embedded in hyperdimensional space. Superstring theorists float the idea that the cosmos was *ten*-dimensional before the big bang, when it fractured into the fast-expanding, four-dimensional universe we now inhabit and a six-dimensional universe that contracted at awesome speeds. As Michio Kaku relates, "This theory predicts that our universe has a dwarf twin, a companion universe that has curled up into a small six-dimensional ball that is too small to be observed."[1]

But not too small, perhaps, to be *experienced*. In the Upanishads, the sage instructs Svetaketu to look for the secret of reality in the apparently empty space at the heart of a tiny seed.[2] A Birmingham woman has an encounter with "aliens" who speak an archaic form of English; they tell her they are "projections" and instruct her that "the Deity itself dwells at the heart and core of the atom."[3] In one of my experiments in journeying beyond the body, I found myself becoming inconceivably small and traveling to another world through the space between subatomic particles.

What would it mean to be able to re-vision our world of physical extension and linear time—if only for an instant—from higher dimensions and *see* the larger pattern? It would surely lead us to a radical redefinition of reality, scrapping the frog's-eye view ably satirized by Michael Murphy in *The Future of the Body:* "To a frog with its simple eyes, the world is a dim array of greys and blacks. Are we like frogs in our limited sensorium, apprehending just part of the universe we inhabit? Are we a species now awakening to the reality of multidimensional worlds in which matter undergoes subtle reorganizations in some sort of hyperspace?"[4] I agree with Murphy that full awakening may bring a quantum leap in the evolution of our species, including physiological changes, the widespread development (or recovery) of advanced psychic abilities, the adoption of shamanic modes of healing as mainstream practice, and our return to the values and practices of a dreaming society.

Claude Bragdon evokes the difficulty of grasping multidimensional reality: "It is here—in us and all about us—in a direction toward which we can never point because it is at right angles to every direction we know. Our space cannot contain it, because it contains our space. . . . We are embedded in our own space, and if that space be embedded in higher space, how are we going to discover it?"[5]

We already know the answer: through dream journeys into hyperspace, or through the irruption of beings from hyperspace into 3-D reality.

In his novel *Perelandra,* C. S. Lewis beautifully evokes the process by which beings from higher dimensions can make themselves perceptible to those who have reached a sufficient degree of attunement to see them at all. The first appearance of the eldils—"hypersomatic" beings associated with the planetary spheres—is as a faint light, bringing "almost imperceptible" alterations in the visual field. When they first attempt to show themselves to Ransom in a form he can recognize, he is terrified by "darting pillars filled with eyes, lightning pulsations of flame, talons and beaks and billowing masses" rushing through cubes and hexagons into a black void. Ransom asks them to put on forms better suited to human sensibilities. Now he sees rolling wheels, "concentric wheels moving with a rather sickening slowness one inside the other." When the eldils shape-shift for the third time, the human observer sees humanoid giants: "Whenever he looked straight at them they appeared to be rushing towards him with enormous speed: whenever his eyes took in their surroundings he realized that they were stationary." Their bodies are "burning white" but their heads are surrounded by "a flush of diverse colors" that Ransom later finds he cannot name. He concludes that when "hypersomatic" beings choose to appear to us, "they are not in fact affecting our retina at all, but directly manipulating the relevant parts of our brain." This produces the sensations we would have if our eyes were capable of receiving colors in the spectrum that are actually beyond their range.[6]

Visionary fiction—Borge's story "The Aleph," Charles Howard Hinton's Victorian "scientific romances," C. S. Lewis's cosmic trilogy—comes as close as anything in print to describing what the experience of seeing in 5-D might be like. In a twilight state, after waking before dawn, I found myself looking through a kind of window into a space that contained a whole world. People, objects, jungles, cities, and oceans were all there together in a kind of orderly heap—not superposed, but coexistent in a way that defied spatial conceptions.

To see things in this fashion can be dizzying for the ordinary mind. In his parable *Flatland,* Edwin Abbott evokes the "unspeakable horror" that may seize a consciousness accustomed to living in a world of limited dimensionality when confronted with manifestations from hyperspace.[7]

Yet the next stage in the evolution of human consciousness—I am convinced—will involve the development of widespread abilities to see into the larger reality and maintain multiple levels of awareness in the midst of everyday life.

While drumming for one of my Active Dreaming groups, I experienced an expansion of consciousness of the kind I am talking about. I found myself watching the circle from every angle at the same time, as if my perception were operating simultaneously at every point around the periphery of a sphere that contained the whole scene, including my own body. Within this sphere, as I monitored the movement of subtle energies as well as physical bodies, it struck me that this might be what the view from the fifth dimension is like. I was awed by the reflection that there are beings for whom this kind of vision is quite routine, that they intersect with our lives and take a close interest in our affairs.

The Spiritual Secrets of Manifestation

While much of our science and many of our cultural paradigms are rooted in the most abject materialism, the return of the Dreaming is reawakening more and more people to the perception—shared by all dreaming traditions—that the events and structures of our physical reality are emanations from a deeper reality.

The Aborigines of the northern Kimberley ranges say that in the beginning, there was only earth and sky. In the earth was the Great Mother Ungud, in the form of a great snake. In the sky was Wallanganda, the All-Father, in the form of the Milky Way. The sky-god threw water on the earth; Ungud made it deep. In the night, as they dreamed, life arose from the watered earth in the shapes of their dreams.

From the sky-god's dreaming a spiritual force went forth as images that he projected on the faces of rocks and the walls of caves. These images can still be seen, painted in reds, whites, and blacks. Some say a mystical bird was the original painter, grasping the shapes of the sky-god's dreams in his own dreaming. After the paintings were done, Wallanganda reproduced their forms in the bodies of living beings, which he sent out across the land.

The paintings are the spiritual source of living beings. In the Kimberley rock paintings, Wondjina figures do not have mouths or eyes because these are the gift of Ungud. The Wondjina spirit—associated with rainmaking and fresh water—lives beneath the paintings in the waters under the earth, creating "child-germs," spirit children. In a dream, a father-to-be will find one of these spirit children. In another dream, he will put it into his wife. It assumes human form in her body. At death, this part of the soul returns to the water hole from which it came.[8]

Though the names may seem alien or exotic, this is a story about you and me. It reminds us that the process of manifestation begins with a movement or intention on the spiritual planes that is projected toward physical reality through images—the *facts* and events of the imaginal realm. By entering the imaginal world through dream travel, we can become active participants in this process and cocreators of the circumstances of our lives on Earth. As we learn to work with the hidden order of events, we will come to recognize that it also reveals itself through the play of synchronicity in everyday life. As evolving beings, we will come to take dreams more literally and waking life more symbolically.

Living by Synchronicity

Synchronicity is a wonderful matchmaker. If you meet someone as the result of a chance encounter, or a series of unlikely incidents, that already marks the new person as "significant" in your life. Try to remember how you met your current partner, and what precisely led you to your present job. I am constantly asking people how they came together, and I hear some intriguing stories.

"I met my partner because a child's red balloon bonked each of us on the head at a county fair," Robin told me. They were complete strangers, each visiting the fair for the first time. The bouncing balloon seemed to promise fun, but was also, perhaps, a caution about not leaving things up in the air.

Sometimes the striking event or coincidence that flags the other person as special comes after the first meeting. I had had a couple of cursory meetings with my wife, Marcia—then a publicist in New York—in other people's offices before she remarked, quite casually, that she had once dreamed the result of the Kentucky Derby. That enlisted my fullest attention. I promptly reached into my pocket and pulled out all the cash I had on hand, which was $60. I handed it to Marcia and told her to put it on the winner in that year's Kentucky Derby, which was all of a week away. In the next week, Marcia did not dream the race result, but she got a feeling about the winner. The horse she liked was a long shot, the only filly in the Derby. She hesitated about betting my money at the OTB, partly because the horse was called Genuine Risk, which brought out her mixed feelings about the chemistry that was starting to develop between us. At the last moment, minutes before post time, she trekked to the betting parlor and put my money on Genuine Risk. She hedged on the race and the relationship by putting her own money on a horse called Withholding. Genuine Risk romped home, at thirteen to one, and we took the risk of going out together.

I have learned the importance of being open to the unexpected, especially when I am traveling. I often find surprising opportunities when travel plans go awry: when there are seating changes, baggage mix-ups, even delays and cancellations. I have met wonderful people because of missing a bus or being held up at an airport or train station. Here is one example:

A SEATING ASSIGNMENT NEXT TO BALZAC

The spirit of Honoré de Balzac, the French novelist, seemed to preside over a series of coincidences that started with a dream.

In the dream, I was intrigued by a book I saw on a shelf in a store filled with curiosities, including recordings of native ceremonies made by early explorers. The title of the book was a tongue twister. I wrote it down as *Choao,* which looked Portuguese but was not quite right.

A couple of days later, I strolled into the Book Barn in Watervliet, New York, one of my favorite used-book stores. On the counter was the Penguin Classics translation of Balzac's novel *Les Chouans.* Dan Driggs, the store owner, told me it had just come in, with a couple of cartons of old books he had accepted in trade; he let me have it for a dollar.

Reading Balzac's opening chapters that night, I was enthralled by the Frenchman's ability to capture a whole society in its time and place. I admired the way he swooped over a whole landscape, richly envisioned, before homing in on the characters whose lives were to be made or unmade within it. I wished for some of the same panoramic vision, to pull together the big cast of characters and events I was seeking to describe in a historical novel I was working on at the time.

I was grateful to the Library Angel (as Arthur Koestler described the benign agency that produces the right book at the right time) for delivering the book from my dream, and the flow of literary inspiration that ensued. But the chain of coincidence was not yet complete.

Several months later, after boarding a New York–bound plane at Schiphol airport in Holland, I found myself changing my assigned seat twice. Members of a sports team were traveling together. One of them had taken the window seat assigned to me by mistake. I told him to stay put; I was glad to take his aisle seat, with my long legs. Then one of his friends, in the seat directly behind me, asked if I would swap with him. This also suited me fine. But by now I had the sense that something of an unusual kind was ready to take place.

I found myself seated next to a man about my own age who was traveling with his teenage daughter. He was reading Balzac (*Eugénie Grandet*) in French—not a usual sight on modern aircraft, and all the more striking because, as it turned out, my neighbor was German, not French. We struck up a conversation that touched on some of the deepest issues in my life at that time and resulted in an extraordinary gift.

My neighbor was struggling, as I had been, to maintain a close relationship with a daughter in the face of the pain and division caused by the breakup of an earlier marriage. He was preoccupied—as I had become, working in Europe with the dreams of Germans and Dutchmen—with the survival of the ghosts of the Nazi past and the horrors of World War II. Finally, in addition to his love of Balzac he had a passion for Rilke. He wanted to share this with his daughter, who had been raised in the United States and did not know German.

Before I brought out my own travel reading to show him—a portable set of Stephen Mitchell's graceful translations from Rilke—my neighbor excused himself from further conversation by telling me, "There is something I must do for my daughter." He proceeded to write out from memory a long Rilke poem in his native language. He then composed a free translation into English, covering several pages at impressive speed. He showed me his work as he went along, and we discussed some of the English expressions. The poem ("Aus den Stundenbuch"), previously unknown to me, caught me up in its spell, not least because one of its themes is the numinous quality of the chance encounter.

Encouraged by my enthusiasm, my new friend made me a second copy of his translation, which runs in part:

> And sometimes there comes a serious traveler
> who moves like a light through our hundred minds
> and shows us, through our shivers, a new way.

When coincidence piles on coincidence in this fruitful way, it brings more than a passing shiver, or a single message. It brings the sense that everything has meaning, everything is connected, within a universe that is dynamic, spirited, and interrelated. This borders on the experience of grace. Certainly, I felt blessed by a state of grace in that moment, with those words, freshly minted, trembling in my hand.

EXERCISE: DREAMWORK WITH EVERYDAY LIFE

When we use coincidences as homing beacons, we tap into a hidden order of events beyond surface reality. When we accept that everything that enters our field of perception has meaning—and that everything is connected—we put ourselves in resonance with a larger reality and open our lives to the flow of natural magic.

Here are a few games you can play any day of your life that will expand your awareness of synchronicity and symbolism in your outer environment:

1. Write a dream report on a day in your life.   Any day will do, today or way back, special or blah. Write a quick summary of the main events, and anything else that leaps out at you. Write fast. Don't edit and try not to pause until you are done. Don't worry about muddling names or details; you do that in your dream journal all the time, and this is not your office calendar.

Jot down any associations that come through strongly as you are writing.

You now have the story of a day in your life. Give it a title. Don't fuss over this; keep moving at speed.

Add any sketches, doodles, or souvenirs—a matchbook from that restaurant?—that catch your fancy.

Now work with your day report as you have learned to do with dream reports. Explore symbols. Note recurring themes. (Late again? Always getting involved with the wrong type of man?) Look for puns, visual and verbal. Track your social self: What do you do or not do with certain people that is out of character?

Draw a moral or motto from the events of the day. Decide how you will act on it from now on.

2. Matchmaking.   Make a short list of the people who are most important in your life. Try to remember how you met them, and if there were any events in your early relationship that flagged them as special—or maybe as people you should guard against. If you have been keeping a dream journal, go back through it and see if any of your first encounters with significant others were heralded by dreams and whether there might be guidance for you now from this source. Think about the role of chance encounters in your life. Are you open to a chance encounter now?

3. Homing beacons.   Start a running log of coincidences that come to your attention. Consider how these coincidences may shed light on your current actions and expectations. When coincidences pile up thick and fast, like repeat messages, you are clearly being asked to pay attention to something. If you get three speeding tickets on a single trip for dinner—as once happened to a guest who drove to my home from New York City—you are plainly being given a warning that may apply to more than your driving.

THE JONI MITCHELL TEST

A San Francisco woman whose personal life had been on hold decided to seek dream guidance. Liz asked for a dream to help her find the right man. In her dream, she encountered a Roman Catholic priest complete with cassock and dog collar. Raised a strict Catholic, she was less than thrilled. I thought I'd outgrown all that, she moaned inwardly. But the priest turned out to be human and humorous; she rather liked him. "Life is full of pain," he counseled her. "You must enjoy it while you can." He escorted her up to the top of a cathedral so she could get a better view of things.

Intrigued, she went back inside the dream, climbed to the top of the steeple, and looked down. As she studied the cityscape below her and the river winding through it, she realized she was looking down at Dublin, a city she had visited a few years before. She was not sure whether the dream contained the answer to her question, but she decided to honor it by going to a local Irish pub where they often had good music. At the pub, she met a man she liked, but had reservations about going out with someone she had run into at a tavern. He told her about a music album he liked, and she decided that she would get the CD and apply what she called "the Joni Mitchell test."

She would go out with the guy if she found they liked the same music. She had never heard of the group he had mentioned. Her potential date told her she couldn't miss the CD because of the people in "thigh-high boots" on the cover.

Back at the office, Liz got caught up in her work and forgot about the album until she was passing a record store on her way home. When she went in, she found she could not remember the title of the album or the name of the group. But there on the shelf, facing her at eye level, was a picture of people in thigh-high boots on the cover of a CD. She purchased the album and took it home. When she put it on the player, she found herself humming along with the first couple of songs. The third song gave her goose bumps. She had recorded this number off the radio ten years before. She had been using it for mood music—it always seemed to bring her to a happy place—but had never been able to identify the performers. She grabbed the CD and studied the cover. Behind the figures in thigh-high boots she recognized the cityscape of Dublin and the River Liffey, as seen from the top of a church steeple. She was looking into her dreamscape.

Did she go out with the man she met in the Irish pub? What would you have done? They had some good times together and decided that was enough. Liz no longer felt stuck in her relationships. The interweavings of dreams and synchronicity had opened her life to natural magic.

The Doorkeeper of Dreams in San Francisco

The taxi pulled up at the curb outside the Triton, a wondrously funky hotel at the edge of San Francisco's Chinatown. I reached for the door handle, but the Triton's doorman, a tall, imposing figure in a long tailcoat, was faster. I gaped at the pattern of moon and stars against the midnight blue cloth. It looked like a blowup of some of the artwork on the cover of my book *Conscious Dreaming,* which I was in town to promote. I snatched up a copy of the book.

"You are wearing the jacket of my book," I told the doorman.

"Oh, no," he responded. "Your book is wearing *my* jacket."

The exchange gave me delicious shivers. In that instant, the doorkeeper jumped into the numinous guise of his archetype: the sometimes tricksterish figure who presides over our crossings and passages in life. And I knew that my day in the Bay Area was likely to follow a logic beyond the publicist's schedule that appeared to rule my hours.

My first appointment was at the Embarcadero cinema, where I was due to meet a columnist who had invented an interesting format. He liked to invite authors and other likely suspects to watch a movie that would then become the focus for an interview. According to my schedule, we were set to watch a new film, *I Shot Andy Warhol*. This seemed to be unrelated to a dream that had lingered from the previous night. In my dream, I was in a rain-swept city by the sea, entangled with a willowy blond woman who desperately craved my affection. When I finally embraced her, she remarked, "It's because of the *umbrellas.*" Waking, I could not find a counterpart for the willowy blonde in my current life, though she strongly reminded me of Catherine Deneuve.

On to the Embarcadero, where I discovered that the program had changed. Instead of watching *I Shot Andy Warhol,* I was being taken to see the new release of the French classic *The Umbrellas of Cherbourg,* starring Catherine Deneuve. As we shook hands, the columnist, David Templeton, explained he had picked the Deneuve movie because of its "dreamlike" quality. As the movie credits rolled, I found myself back inside the previous night's dream.

For any contemporary viewer, *The Umbrellas of Cherbourg* is dreamlike on less personal levels. The scenes are lit in hot pastels— flamingo pink, curacao blue, key lime green—more evocative of *Miami Vice* than a blustery northern seaport circa 1960. Every snatch of dialogue is sung—in a foreign language, with subtitles. The symbolism is thuddingly Freudian, heavy on close-ups of gasoline hoses and filling tanks, long-neck decanters, and umbrellas being extended and retracted.

I was chortling over all of this when I froze in my seat, suddenly conscious that I had been sucked into an older and deeper dream. By this point, the hero of the movie—an Everyman fittingly called Guy—was achieving his lifelong dream: ownership of an Esso gas station. The camera dwelled on the deliciously rounded shoulders of the gas pumps. I realized I *knew* that vintage gas station. I had pulled up at one of those pumps in a powerful dream, more than a year before. This was the dream:

I have pulled into a gas station to fill up my tank. It is a period Esso station, like something from the fifties, with rounded, platinum-colored pumps, almost art deco style. I overshoot the pumps because my engine is overcharging. I have to back up to fill my tank. Now there's a problem with the trigger on the nozzle of the hose. I have to jiggle it to get the gas flowing. I notice the numbers on the gauge are rising very, very slowly. But when I'm done, I know I have plenty of gas for the journey.

The content of the dream may not seem dramatic. But I knew it was important because I woke from it *charged* with energy, certain that it contained a vital message.

Now a Freudian like those who clearly had a hand in the making of *Umbrellas* might have had a field day with the possible sexual metaphors in this dream—and had it been someone else's dream, he might have been on the right track. But I have noticed that in my dreams, visits to the gas station (when not entirely literal) usually have to do with money and material resources. As it happened, I had a major issue of this type to resolve in my waking life. My agent had recently taken the manuscript of *Conscious Dreaming* to an editor and a house we both felt were right for the book. The editor was enthusiastic about the book, but had offered only a modest advance. The question I faced was whether to go with this editor or shop my manuscript around at other houses in the hopes of getting a larger advance.

As I mulled over my dream of the period gas station, I realized I could distill its message in a few phrases: "I've been overcharging. I need to back up. It may not look like I'm getting enough gas to fill the tank, but there's plenty for the journey."

I called my agent, Stuart Krichevsky, and told him the dream and the message I had derived from it. We agreed to "back up." By the end of the day, Stuart had confirmed the details with Leslie Meredith and I had shared my dream of the "period gas station" with her. Because of this dream, *Conscious Dreaming* was published by Harmony/Crown. A year after the dream, Crown sent me to San Francisco on the first leg of a book tour—and into the cinema where I reentered the landscape of my dream.

I was in a philosophical mood as I strolled back up the hill to the Triton for the next of my interviews. Was my gas station dream a memory from the future, an experience my 1996 self (the one who had just been to the moviehouse) had relayed back to my 1995 self? Maybe the whole of my waking life was enfolded in a deeper matrix. Maybe events that are experienced sequentially by the brain and the physical body can be witnessed *simultaneously*—with all their possible variations—from dimensions beyond 3-D and beyond linear time. Maybe this is possible through dreaming.

The hotel doorman stood guard in his coat of moon and stars.

"Thank you for sharing my dream," I greeted him.

"Ah," the doorkeeper corrected me, "you are sharing *my* dream."

Notes

≈

Introduction: You Are Born to Fly

1. "The Pre/Trans Fallacy," in Ken Wilber, *Eye to Eye: The Quest for the New Paradigm* (Boston and London: Shambhala, 1996).
2. Ibid., 2–7.

Chapter 1: Becoming a Frequent Flier

1. See A. Irving Hallowell, "Ojibwa Ontology, Behaviour and World View," in S. Diamond, ed., *Culture and History: Essays in Honor of Paul Radin* (New York: Columbia University Press, 1960), 207–44.
2. Mudrooroo, *Aboriginal Mythology* (London: Aquarian, 1994), 50–52.
3. Sri Aurobindo, *Letters on Yoga* (Pondicherry, India: Sri Aurobindo Ashram, 1970), 1024.
4. Marc de Civrieux, "Medatia: A Makiritare Shaman's Tale," in David M. Guss, ed., *The Language of the Birds* (San Francisco: North Point Press, 1985), 74.
5. See my essay "Missionaries and Magicians: The Jesuit Encounter with Native American Shamans on New England's Colonial Frontier," in Peter Benes, ed., *Wonders of the Invisible World* (Boston: Boston University, 1995), 17–33.
6. Lawrence C. Watson, "Dreaming as World View and Action in Guajiro Culture," in *Journal of Latin American Lore* 7, no. 2 (1981): 239–54.

Chapter 2: The Gateway of Images

1. See Andreas Mavromatis, *Hypnagogia: The Unique State of Consciousness between Wakefulness and Sleep* (London and New York: Routledge, 1987), 186–216, for a survey of creative breakthroughs in the twilight zone.

2. Mary Watkins, *Waking Dreams* (Dallas: Spring Publications, 1985).

3. Raymond de Becker, *The Understanding of Dreams* (New York: Bell Publishing, 1968), 153–54.

4. Iamblichus, *On the Mysteries,* trans. Thomas Taylor (San Diego: Wizards, 1984).

5. Physiologists will tell you that the stuff of inner light shows— "ideoretinal light, luminous dust, entoptic light, eigenlicht"—is the "excitation of optic neurons arising from within the retina without benefit of light from the external world"; cf. M. J. Horowitz, *Image Formation and Cognition* (New York: Appleton-Century-Crofts, 1978), 25. Mystics will tell you this is the dawning of the inner light. The Inuit will tell you it is the birth of the *angaqok*'s shaman-light, "a mysterious light which the shaman suddenly feels in his body, inside his head, within the brain, an inexplicable searchlight, a luminous fire, which enables him to see in the dark, both literally and metaphorically speaking, for he can now, even with closed eyes, see through darkness and perceive things and coming events which are hidden from others." Cf. Knud Rasmussen, *The Intellectual Culture of the Iglulik Eskimos,* trans. William Worster (Copenhagen: Report of the Fifth Thule Expedition, VII; 1, 1930), 112.

6. The name of the temple of Thoth at Khemennu (the City of Eight) was Het Abdit, literally the "house of the net." G. R. S. Mead suggests that "this Net was the symbol of a certain condition of the inner nature which shut in the man into the limitations of the conventional life of the world, and shut him off from the memory of his true self"; cf. Mead, *Thrice Greatest Hermes: Studies in Hellenistic Theosophy and Gnosis* (York Beach, Maine: Samuel Weiser, 1992), 1:41. Mythologically, the net may also be the web of life or the Veil of the Goddess. The Egyptian goddess Neith wears a weaver's shuttle on her head. The inscription at her temple at Saïs reads, "I am all that has been and shall be and no mortal has ever revealed my robe." To go beyond the veil is to go beyond the ordinary human condition. It is possible that Neith, with her veil and her weaver's shuttle, personifies the human energy web, spun from fine threads or lines of force or light; see chapter 5.

7. See Emily Peach, *The Tarot Workbook* (New York: Sterling, 1990).

8. Caitlin Matthews, *The Celtic Book of the Dead* (New York: St. Martin's Press, 1992); Athon Veggi and Alison Davidson, *The Book of Doors: An Alchemical Oracle from Ancient Egypt* (Rochester, Vt.: Destiny, 1995).

Chapter 3: Through the Dreamgates

1. Artemidorus, *The Interpretation of Dreams: Oneirocritica*, trans. R. J. White (Park Ridge, N.J.: Noyes Press, 1975).

2. Wampanoag elder Maniquontat retells stories of Moshup (or Maushop) in *The Children of the Morning Light* (New York: Macmillan, 1994). For a vivid early account of the clay walls of Gay Head, see Albert C. Koch, *Journey through a Part of the United States in the Years 1844–1846,* ed. Ernst A. Stadler (Carbondale: Southern Illinois University Press, 1972).

3. Robert Crookall, *The Study and Practice of Astral Projection* (Secaucus, N.J.: Citadel, 1979).

4. Cited in D. Scott Rogo, *Leaving the Body* (New York: Fireside, 1993). This is one of the better studies of alternative methods for journeying beyond the body, though (like many of the others) it is weak in the areas of conscious dreaming and shamanic soul-flight (the old-fashioned ways!). My favorite book in this area remains Robert Monroe, *Journeys out of the Body* (New York: Anchor, 1977).

5. See Gareth Knight, *The Treasure House of Images* (Rochester, Vt.: Destiny, 1986).

6. William Buhlmann, *Adventures Beyond the Body* (Harper San Francisco, 1996).

7. Rabbi Zalman Schachter-Shalomi with Howard Schwartz, *The Dream Assembly* (Nevada City, Calif.: Gateways, 1989).

Chapter 4: Wings of the Shaman

1. On the fall of the Dreaming Tree, see Mudrooroo, *Aboriginal Mythology,* 51–52.

2. Based on de Civrieux, "Medatia," in Guss, *The Language of the Birds*.

3. *The Eye of the Storm: Eight Contemporary Indigenous Australian Artists* (Canberra: National Gallery of Australia, 1997).

4. On "feathered sages," see Berthold Laufer, *The Prehistory of Aviation* (Chicago: Field Museum of Natural History, 1928).

5. See Michele Jamal, *Deerdancer: The Shapeshifter Archetype in Story and Trance* (New York: Arkana, 1995).

6. The *Cad Goddeu* ("Battle of the Trees") may be the work of the sixth-century "Scottish Merlin," or Myrddin, whose battles took place in the now-vanished Forest of Caledon.

7. On cats as familiars, see M. Oldfield Howey, *The Cat in Magic* (London: Bracken Books, 1993).

8. A. Irving Hallowell, *Culture and Experience* (Philadelphia: University of Pennsylvania, 1955), 178. See also John A. Grim, *The Shaman: Patterns of Religious Healing among the Ojibway Indians* (Norman and London: University of Oklahoma Press, 1987).

9. An Algonquian shaman called Pigarouich was said to have been given in a dream a power song that he used to call animals; Reuben Gold Thwaites, ed., *The Jesuit Relations and Allied Documents (JR)* (Cleveland, Ohio: Burrows Brothers, 1896–1901), 14:133. Father Jerome Lalemant reported that dream messengers came to the Hurons "now in the form of a raven, or some other bird, now in the form of a serpent . . . or of some other animal, which speaks to them and reveals the secret of their good fortune, either in the recovery of their health when they fall sick, or in the successful issue of their business" (*JR* 17: 153–55).

10. Cf. Joseph McMoneagle, *Mind Trek* (Charlottesville, Va.: Hampton Roads, 1993).

11. Nikolai Tolstoy, *The Quest for Merlin* (Boston: Little, Brown, 1985), 139. The Gaelic word *tuirgin*, which literally means "circular birth," is defined by *Cormac's Glossary* as "a birth that passes from every nature into another . . . a transitory birth which has traversed all nature from Adam and goes through every wonderful time down to the world's doom."

12. In the Welsh cycle of legends, Gwydion is the most famous of all magicians, with the power to create palpable illusions. As a punishment, he was transformed by Math into three animals in succession, with gender shifts: into a stag, a sow, and a wolf. His connection with the animals helped Gwydion to accomplish a classic feat of soul retrieval. He followed a sow to find his nephew after Llew was gravely wounded and his soul took flight from his body in the shape of an eagle. Gwydion sang three *englyns* to call back the soul of his nephew.

Chapter 5: Paleopsych 101

1. James Hillman, *The Soul's Code* (New York: Random House, 1996).
2. See my article, "Blackrobes and Dreamers," in *Shaman's Drum* 28 (summer 1992).
3. "You will never find out the limits of the soul [psyche] by going, even if you travel over every way, so deep is its report" (Heraclitus fragment xxxv). There is an excellent commentary in Charles H. Kahn, ed., *The Art and Thought of Heraclitus* (Cambridge: Cambridge University Press, 1987), 126–30.
4. Frederic W. H. Myers, *The Human Personality and Its Survival of Bodily Death*, 2 vols. (London: Longmans, Green, 1903), 1:247.
5. Ibid., 1:249.
6. Edward Tylor, *Primitive Culture* (London: John Murray, 1871).
7. There was widespread belief in a "pneumatic body"—a link between body and soul—in the first centuries of the Christian era. In the Gospels, Holy Spirit is a fluid substance, breathed into people—a concrete force Simon Magus tried to purchase (Acts 8:18). St. Augustine recognized subtle bodies and *materia spiritualis,* "spiritual matter."
8. The garment of the soul is the Kabbalist *malbush;* cf. D. P. Walker, "The Astral Body in Renaissance Medicine," in *Journal of the Warburg and Courtauld Institutes* 21 (1958): 119–33. On *malbush* in Luria's Kabbalism, cf. Gershon Scholem, *Kabbalah* (New York: Schocken, 1974), 150–51.

9. The Taittriya Upanishad describes five *atmans* (often referred to later as the five *kosas*, or "sheaths"):
   1. The body is the outer covering. It is described as *annarasamaya*, or "formed by the juice of food."
   2. The breath-soul is called *pranayama atman*, "formed by life-breath." This is the center of animal vitality.
   3. The imaginal body, *manoyama atman*, i.e., "composed of *manas*," which can be translated as imagination, will, or desire.
   4. The mental body or "knowing self" (*vijnanamaya atman*).
   5. The "soul of bliss," *anandamaya atman*.

10. In Greek, *ochema* means both "vehicle" and "vessel." It has the same root as *ocheo*, "to carry." Chariots and boats appear again and again in ancient myths and scriptures as vehicles for the gods, for mystical journeys, and for journeys to the Otherworld.

    The pagan emperor Julian, like the prophet Elijah, is supposedly borne aloft in a fiery chariot. In our dreams, we update the imagery, substituting rocket ships, jet planes, and UFOs for chariots of fire, just as medieval artists showed Elijah traveling to the upper world in a farmer's cart.

11. See Harold Saxton Burr, *Blueprint for Immortality: The Electric Patterns of Life* (London: Neville Spearman, 1972).

12. See A. E. Powell, *The Etheric Double* (Wheaton, Ill.: Quest Books, 1969).

13. Egyptian inventories of the vehicles of consciousness include a physical body *(khat)*, a soul *(ba)*, a heart *(ab)*, a double *(ka)*, an intelligence *(khu)*, a power *(sekhem)*, a shadow *(khaibit)*, a spiritual body *(sab)* a name *(rem)*, and a glorified or celestial body *(sahu)*. The precise meaning of each term is unclear from the sources; confusion prevails even in modern attempts to differentiate the *ba* from the *ka*.

    Death is sometimes described as "going to one's *ka*." The Book of the Dead points the way "for you and your *ka*."

    Kings and other powerful people are believed to have more than one *ka*. The god Re is said to have fourteen *ka*s (as well as seven *ba*s).

    It is unclear whether *ka* is "higher" or "lower" than the *ba*, which seems to be breath-soul and blood-soul as well as bird-soul. But what is clear is that at death they go to different places.

14. Jean Houston, *The Possible Human* (Los Angeles: Jeremy P. Tarcher, 1982).

15. For an exhaustive cross-cultural of literature on the subtle bodies, see J. J. Poortman, *Vehicles of Consciousness*, 4 vols. (Utrecht: Theosophical Society, 1978).

16. A. E. Powell, *The Astral Body and Other Astral Phenomena* (Wheaton, Ill.: Quest Books, 1991), 1.

17. The Greek term *augoeides* means "possessing splendor, brightness, or radiance."

18. In the *Odyssey,* it is the eidolon ("image") or *skia* ("shade") of Herakles that Odysseus encounters in Hades. In his higher spirit, the hero has gone to live with the gods (XI:602–5). Porphyry explains that for the immortal soul "being in Hades" means being linked to a spirit-body just as "being on Earth" means being linked to a physical body. In the Orphic traditions, Hades extends from the subterranean level of Tartarus through all of space to the moon and has many, many levels. See G. R. S. Mead, *The Doctrine of the Subtle Body in the Western Tradition* (London: John M. Watkins, 1919). The spirits who inhabit the moon are described in Plutarch, *De facie quae in orbe lunae apparet;* see his *Moralia,* vol. 12 (Cambridge, Mass.: Harvard University Press, 1995), 1–223.

19. On Olympiodorus's perceptions of the subtle body, see E. R. Dodds's important essay "The Astral Body in Neoplatonism," appended to Dodds's translation of Proclus, *The Elements of Theology* (Oxford: Clarendon Press, 1992).

20. Paul appears to acknowledge the existence of the astral body in I Corinthians 15:40–44. There is a clear hint that this perception is based on *experience*. In the famous passage of II Corinthians 12:2–4 he seems to be writing of himself in the third person:

"I know a man in Christ who fourteen years ago was caught up to the third heaven—whether in the body or out of the body I do not know, God knows. And I know that this man was caught up into Paradise—whether in the body or out of the body I do not know, God knows—and he heard things that cannot be told, which man may not utter."

21. Poortman, *Vehicles*, 2:94.

22. Ibid., 2:101. When Catholic author Alfons Rosenberg wrote about the "psychical body" of man in *Die Seelenreise* (1952), the Church responded by placing his most important works on the Index of proscribed books.

23. Hildegard of Bingen sees the soul taking possession of the body of the child "like a fiery globe" during the mother's pregnancy. She speaks of soul repeatedly as having the shape of a sphere. She also speaks of soul as "breath" or "aerial" and recognizes "seven levels" of embodied being. See also Gabriel Uhlein, *Meditation with Hildegard of Bingen* (Santa Fe: Bear & Co., 1982).

24. Augustine is also credited with "the earliest lucid dream report in Western history." The details are in Morton Kelsey, *God, Dreams and Revelation* (New York: Augsburg, 1974), 264–65. The hype is in Stephen LaBerge, *Lucid Dreaming* (New York: Ballantine, 1987), 21. The claim ignores the vast body of literature on dream travel and soul-flight in the ancient world.

25. On Padre Pio as a bilocator, see Patricia Treece, *The Sanctified Body* (New York: Doubleday, 1989), 329–44.

26. Many instances of bilocation are recorded in Butler's *Lives of the Saints,* and the Roman Catholic Church includes the phenomenon in its acknowledged charisms.

27. Machaelle Small Wright, *Dancing in the Shadows of the Moon* (Jeffersonton, Va.: Perelandra, 1995).

28. Charles Williams, *Descent into Hell* (Grand Rapids, Mich.: Eerdmans, 1980). On Williams's life and esoteric studies, see Gareth Knight, *The Magical World of the Inklings* (Shaftesbury, Dorset: Element, 1990).

29. Michael Harner, *The Jivaro* (Berkeley: University of California Press, 1984).

30. Often at his initiation, the Aboriginal spirit man receives a spirit snake as his ally; he can use it to gather information and travel to places where he cannot go in his normal form. The spirit snake may itself be the magic cord the shaman uses to travel to the Sky World. See A. P. Elkin, *Aboriginal Men*

of High Degree (New York: St. Martin's Press, 1977) and Mudrooroo, *Aboriginal Mythology.*

31. James Barr, "Of Metaphysics and Polynesian Navigation," in *Avaloka* 3, nos. 1–2: 1–8. See also John Perkins, *PsychoNavigation* (Rochester, Vt.: Destiny Books, 1990), 46–58.

32. The Taoists recognize two basic souls, each of which has multiple parts: the *hun* has three parts, while the *p'o* has seven. In addition, five *shen* live in the liver, lungs, heart, spleen, and kidneys, each symbolized as an animal: dragon, tiger, red bird, phoenix, and stag. The number of *shen* associated with different parts of the body is multiplied many times in Taoist medical treatises. Cf. I. P. Couliano, *Out of this World: Otherworldly Journeys from Gilgamesh to Albert Einstein* (Boston: Shambhala, 1991), 74–76. The seminal work on Chinese beliefs about multiple and separable souls is J. J. M. de Groot, *The Religious Systems of China,* vols. 4–6 (Leiden: E. J. Brill, 1901–10).

33. On Aristeas, see J. D. F. Bolton, *Aristeas of Proconessus* (Oxford: Clarendon Press, 1962). Maximus of Tyre left the following account of Aristeas' soul travels: "There was a man of Proconessus whose body would lie alive, yes, but with only the dimmest flicker of life and in a state very near to death, while his soul would issue from it and wander the sky like a bird, surveying all beneath—land, sea, rivers, cities, nations of mankind, and occurrences and creatures of all sorts; then returning into and raising up its body, which it treated like an instrument, it would relate the various things it had seen and heard in various places." Maximus, *Philosophumena* x.

34. On Proclus and the "golden chain," see Marinus of Samaria, *The Life of Proclus,* trans. Kenneth S. Guthrie (Grand Rapids, Mich.: Phaes Press, 1986).

35. Sri Aurobindo on the *siddhis,* or special powers: "We need not shun the *siddhis* and cannot shun them. There is a stage reached by the yogin when, unless he avoids all action in the world, he can no more avoid the use of the *siddhis* of power and knowledge than an ordinary man can avoid eating and breathing; for these things are the natural action of the consciousness to which he is rising." Sapta-Chatusthaya in *Collected Works* (Pondicherry, India: Sri Aurobindo Ashram, 1970–76), 27:366.

36. Paramhansa Yogananda, *Autobiography of a Yogi* (Los Angeles: Self-Realization Fellowship, 1983).

37. In the epic Mahabharata, the *suksma atman* is described as journeying outside the body—while its owner sleeps—feeling and seeing as during waking moments. It travels on "fine roads" through zones that correspond to the senses, the wind, the ether, the Manas, the Buddhi—and finally rises to reach the highest *atman;* cf. verses 11188–93.

38. The story of Shankaracharya's body-hopping has parallels in tales of Tibetan practitioners of *phowa* (the transfer of consciousness); cf. Alexandra David-Neel, *Magic and Mystery in Tibet* (New York: University Books, 1965).

39. On soul-flight in European witchcraft, see Carlo Ginzburg, *Ecstasies: Deciphering the Witches' Sabbath,* trans. Raymond Rosenthal (New York: Penguin, 1992). The account of the Benandanti is in his brilliant earlier work *The Night Battles* (1966), trans. John and Anne Tedeschi (Baltimore: Johns Hopkins University Press, 1992).

40. Frederick Buechner's *Godric* (San Francisco: Harper & Row, 1980) is based on the life of the twelfth-century Godric of Finchale. Adamnan, *Life of Columba* (Lampeter, Wales: Llanerch facsimile, 1988), reflects the importance of soul travel in early Celtic Christianity.

41. On Kabbalist meditation and soul travel, see Aryeh Kaplan, *Meditation and Kabbalah* (York Beach, Maine: Samuel Weiser, 1985), and especially the class transcripts in *Innerspace: Introduction to Kabbalah, Meditation and Prophecy* (Brooklyn: Moznaim Publishing, 1991).

42. See Abraham ben Hananiah Yagel, *A Valley of Vision,* trans. and ed. David B. Ruderman (Philadelphia: University of Pennsylvania Press, 1990). Yagel (1553–1624) wrote this work at age twenty-five.

43. Frederik van Eeden, "A Study of Dreams," in *Proceedings of the Society for Psychical Research* (1913), 27–67.

44. Robert Monroe, *Ultimate Journey* (New York: Doubleday, 1994), 10.

Chapter 6: The Otherworld and the Imagination

1. Henry Corbin, "Mundus Imaginalis, or the Imaginary and the Imaginal," in *Swedenborg and Esoteric Islam,* trans. Leonard Fox (West Chester, Pa.: Swedenborg Foundation, 1995).

2. Ibid., 9.

3. Ibid. The Alam al-Mithal is as vast as the imagination. Ibn al-Arabi describes its content in chapter 8 of the *Futuhat.* There are many worlds within this world, with different forms and rules—a moment in one may be a year in the other. There is a world of gold and a world of saffron, where the women make the houris of paradise look like frumps. Cities and houses can be built by pure intention and imagination.

4. Henry Corbin, *Spiritual Body and Celestial Earth: From Mazdean Iran to Shi'ite Iran,* trans. Nancy Pearson (Princeton: Bollingen, 1989), 126ff., 131ff., 160–63.

5. Ibid., 118. The City of the Hidden Imam—Hurqalya—exists in the Alam al-Mithal. It can be visited only in visionary dreams. See Corbin, "The Visionary Dream in Islamic Spirituality," in G. E. von Grünebaum and Roger Caillois, eds., *The Dream and Human Societies* (Berkeley and Los Angeles: University of California Press, 1966).

6. Moshe Idel, *Studies in Ecstatic Kabbalah* (Albany, N.Y.: SUNY Press, 1988), 73.

7. Ibid., 74. These quotations are from a fourteenth-century kabbalistic collection known as the Likutei HaRan, possibly compiled by Rabbi Isaac of Acre.

8. Sandalphon, the "master of images," is frequently counterposed to Metatron, the Angel of the Countenance, who reflects the brightness of the godhead. "One rules from the earth to the heavens in their entirety, and he is Metatron, and one rules the earth and all that is upon her, and he is Sandalfon. One brings souls to the body, Metatron, and one brings the imprint and form to the fetus and determines whether it be male or female, and he is Sandalphon" (*Sefer HaTemunah,* cited in Idel, 85).

   Sandalphon is called the Wheel (Ofan), as in Ezekiel's "wheels." He is "the secret of the bull and the secret of the forest and the power of the night." He is a gatekeeper who can block man's ascent to higher realms of spirit beyond the astral planes. "Sandalphon keeps the gate and binds and shuts all the supernal gates" (*Sefer Sha'arei Zedek*, cited in Idel, 78).

The chanting of the Divine Names that is the Kabbalist's preferred tool for shifting consciousness is within Sandalphon's gift; he is the Prince of Prayer.

"In his hand is the ability to clothe the light of the Most High King, and to enclothe the prophets at the time of their prophecy, their spirits [enclothed] with the ray of the Spirit, and their bodies with the brightness of his body" (cf. Gershon Scholem, *Tarbiz* 16 [1945]: 202–3). Here Sandalphon seems to exercise another intriguing function, that of some kind of astral clothier. He issues the prophets proper outfits for their travels around the imaginal realm.

9. Samuel Taylor Coleridge, *Biographia Literaria* (London: Everyman, 1963), 167.

10. W. H. Auden, "Making, Knowing and Judging," in *The Dyer's Hand* (London: Faber, 1963), 54–55.

11. There is a marvelous commentary on Dante's arrival at St. Peter's Gate in Helen M. Luke, *Dark Wood to White Rose: Journey and Transformation in Dante's* Divine Comedy (New York: Parabola Books, 1989).

12. Here is an excerpt from my dream journal for the night of January 30–31, 1997:

More Guidance from Yeats

I am walking in the woods, reflecting on a method of activating the creative imagination devised by Yeats. This involves setting off patterns of harmonic vibrations between pairs of spheres. These are made of a very fine, translucent material, possibly glass or crystal. I see some of these pairs arranged in an arc, as on the edge of a much larger sphere.

Some refinements on this system have been added by an assistant to Yeats. Yeats explains he has formal responsibility (in my dream) for devising visualization exercises for members of the Golden Dawn.

He offers a paradox, stating that something must be described by both of a pair of opposite terms, or by neither.

I knew nothing about the sphere projection of the Tree of Life, as "refined" by Florence Farr, until researching this dream. I was astonished to find a drawing in a book by Mary Greer that closely corresponded to my dream image of the spheres arranged in an arc; cf. Mary K. Greer, *Women of the Golden Dawn* (Rochester, Vt.: Park Street Press, 1995), 256–67.

Significantly, Florence Farr was instructed by her spiritual guides to practice dream incubation. She was told, "Sleep now and dream of the answer to your question" (Greer, 261). She eventually abandoned ceremonial magic to follow the path of dreaming and individual vision.

13. See Dion Fortune, *The Magical Battle of Britain* (Bradford on Avon: Golden Gates Press, 1993).

14. See Francis King, ed., *Astral Projection, Ritual Magic and Alchemy: Golden Dawn Material by S. L. MacGregor Mathers and Others* (Rochester, Vt.: Destiny Books, 1987); and Dolores Ashcroft-Nowicki, *The Shining Paths* (Wellingborough, England: Aquarian, 1983).

15. An excellent source on traditions of Scottish seership is Anne Ross, *The Folklore of the Scottish Highlands* (New York: Barnes & Noble, 1993).

Chapter 7: Journeys of Initiation

1. Mircea Eliade, *Rites and Symbols of Initiation* (New York: Harper & Row, 1975), xii, x.

2. Carl Kerenyi, *Eleusis: Archetypal Image of Mother and Daughter* (Princeton: Bollingen, 1991), 82–83.

3. See R. J. Stewart, *The UnderWorld Initiation* (Wellingborough, England: Aquarian Press, 1985).

4. Cf. Richard L. Thompson, *Alien Identities* (Alachua, Fla.: Govardhan Hill Publishing, 1995), 283–84.

5. Plutarch's accounts of the Trophonius initiation are in two essays: "On the Demon of Socrates" and "On the Spirits Who

Live in the Face of the Moon." Translations appear in Plutarch, *Moralia* (Cambridge and London: Harvard University Press, 1994, 1995), vols. 7 and 12 (respectively).

6. According to Pausanias, Trophonius was remembered as a great architect—and a resourceful thief and a fratricide. He and his brother Agamedes built a treasury for a king called Hyrieus, constructed so they could enter through a secret passage by removing a stone and steal the treasure at night. The king set traps. When Agamedes was caught, Trophonius supposedly cut off his head so he could not testify against him. Then the earth gaped and swallowed Trophonius in the grove of Lebadea (near Chaeronea, on the road to Delphi). Cf. Pausanias, *Description of Greece*, trans. Arthur Shilleto (London: George Bell and Sons, 1886), 211ff. The superficial details of this savage story make it impossible to grasp why Trophonius would be revered both as oracle and initiator. They conceal deeper mysteries. The treasure may be that of the soul.

7. The nature of the spirits associated with the moon may suggest that "the human being who earnestly strives to be good within the limits of his present opportunities will have a larger sphere of activity open to him as a Daemon in the Afterworld." John Oakesmith, *The Religion of Plutarch* (London: Longmans, Green, 1902), 173.

8. For Apollonius' visit to the Cave of Trophonius, see Philostratus, *The Life of Apollonius of Tyana*, 2 vols., trans. F. C. Conybeare (Cambridge, Mass., and London: Harvard University Press and William Heinemann, 1969), 2:381–83.

9. There were seven degrees of initiation in the mysteries of Mithra. Each had its vestments and headgear, including animal masks or "counterfeit heads." By the third century, cloth or paper masks were generally substituted for the animal pelts of earlier times. At the fourth grade—Leo—you put on a lion mask and became a full participant, a member of the inner circle. The Mithraics celebrated communion with consecrated loaves, marked with a cross, and wine, wearing their masks. They celebrated Natalis Invicti on December 25, which was recognized by the Church as the birthday of Christ only in the

fourth century. See Franz Cumont, *The Mysteries of Mithra,* trans. Thomas J. McCormack (New York: Dover, 1956).

Their downfall was the exclusion of women (although Mithraic sisterhoods appeared before the Empire became Christian); it is interesting that such strongly Mithraic elements came through in the dream of a modern American *woman.*

10. Peter Kingsley, *Ancient Philosophy, Mystery and Magic: Empedocles and Pythagorean Tradition* (Oxford: Clarendon Press, 1995), delves with a rare blend of scholarship and intuition into the stories of Empedocles' mystical leap into the mouth of Etna.

11. See Dion Fortune's introduction to *The Cosmic Doctrine* (London: Society of the Inner Light, 1995), where she also explains that a spontaneous dream experience opened the gate to her encounters with the Masters.

Chapter 8: Creative Journeys

1. Arthur Koestler, *The Act of Creation* (London: Arkana, 1989).
2. Henri Poincaré, "Mathematical Creation" (1913), in P. E. Vernon, *Creativity* (Harmondsworth, England: Penguin, 1978).
3. Albert Einstein, letter to Jacques Hadamard, in Bernard Ghiselin, ed., *The Creative Process* (New York: New American Library, 1952).
4. Jean Cocteau, "The Process of Inspiration," in Ghiselin, *Creative Process.*
5. Caitlin Matthews and John Matthews, *The Encyclopedia of Celtic Wisdom* (Shaftesbury, England, and Rockport, Mass.: Element, 1994).
6. Steve Wilson, "The Irish Bardic Tradition," in Philip Carr-Gomm, ed., *The Druid Renaissance* (London: Thorsons, 1996).

Chapter 9: Healing Journeys

1. Jean Houston, *The Possible Human* (Los Angeles: Jeremy P. Tarcher, 1982).
2. Robert Graves, *The Greek Myths* (Harmondsworth, England: Penguin, 1960), 1:173–78.

3.   Mead, *Thrice Greatest Hermes*, 1:327.

4.   Miranda Green, *Symbol and Image in Celtic Religious Art* (London and New York: Routledge, 1989), 156–61.

5.   Mircea Eliade, *Shamanism: Archaic Techniques of Ecstasy* (Princeton: Bollingen, 1974), 288–97.

6.   Joseph Campbell, *The Way of the Animal Powers* (San Francisco: Alfred van der Marck/Harper & Row, 1983), 1:176. On the survival of shamanism among the Buryat, see Kira Vam Deusen, "Buryat Shamans and Their Stories" in *Shamanism* (Journal of the Foundation for Shamanic Studies) 10, no. 1 (spring/summer 1997).

7.   W. K. C. Guthrie, *Orpheus and Greek Religion* (New York: Norton, 1966).

8.   Eliade, *Shamanism*, 367–68.

9.   E. S. C. Handy, *Polynesian Religion* (Honolulu: Berenice Bishop Museum Bulletin, 1927), 81ff.

10. Thwaites, *Jesuit Relations* 10:149–53; cf. Moss, "Blackrobes and Dreamers." For other Native American accounts of the journey to the Land of the Dead to rescue lost souls, see Ake Hultkrantz, *The North American Indian Orpheus Tradition* (Stockholm: Ethnographical Museum of Sweden, 1957).

11. Morton Smith, *Jesus the Magician* (Harper San Francisco, 1981).

12. Cf. R. K. Narayan, *Gods, Demons and Others* (Mysore: Indian Thought Publications, 1967); Roy C. Amore and Larry D. Shinn, *Lustful Maidens and Ascetic Kings* (New York and Oxford: Oxford University Press, 1981); and Sri Aurobindo's poetic interpretation *Savitri: A Legend and a Symbol* (Pondicherry, India: Sri Aurobindo Ashram, 1984).

Chapter 10: New Maps of the Afterlife

1.   Sögyal Rinpoche, *The Tibetan Book of Living and Dying* (Harper San Francisco, 1992).

2.   Maggie Callanan and Patricia Kellet, *Final Gifts* (New York: Bantam, 1993).

3.   Signe Toksvig, *Emanuel Swedenborg: Scientist and Mystic* (New York: Swedenborg Foundation, 1983). The best general intro-

duction to Swedenborg's work is Wilson Van Dusen, *The Presence of Other Worlds* (New York: Swedenborg Foundation, 1985).

4. Wilson Van Dusen claims that "Swedenborg explored the hypnagogic state more than anyone else has before or since" (*Presence*, 23).

5. Emanuel Swedenborg, "Journal of Dreams #52." (The translation in the Van Dusen edition differs slightly.) All references to Swedenborg's works follow the standard paragraph listings, uniform in all editions. All his writings are available from the Swedenborg Foundation, 139 East 23rd Street, New York, N.Y. 10010.

6. Swedenborg, "Journal of Dreams #54."

7. Swedenborg maintained in his later writings that "there is no spirit or angel who was not born a man" ("Divine Love and Wisdom #257"). When this well-known quotation is studied in context, it is plain that Swedenborg refers to entities who are using subtle bodies that preserve the memory of human life. He calls such vehicles "cutaneous coverings." Swedenborg also communicated with spirits by mental telepathy, especially at the dinner table: "I also spoke with spirits by ideas alone, without words, and they understood as well as with words, by my merely representing from internal sight" (Swedenborg, "Spiritual Diary #2251").

8. Swedenborg, "Spiritual Diary #2542."

9. Swedenborg, "Spiritual Diary #5099."

10. Swedenborg, "Conjugal Love."

11. For Swedenborg's views on the clergy, see R. L. Tafel, *Documents Concerning Swedenborg* (London: Swedenborg Society, 1877), doc. 6, 59. For his conflicts with Swedish ministers, see Toksvig, *Emanuel Swedenborg*, 331ff.

12. Swedenborg, "Word Explained #7387."

13. Swedenborg, "Word Explained #6905."

14. Tafel, *Documents*, doc. 252.

15. Toksvig, *Emanuel Swedenborg*, 324–25.

16. Swedenborg, "Arcana Coelestia #68."

17. Monroe, *Ultimate Journey*, 120–21.

18. Ibid., 130.

19. Robert Monroe interview in Nevill Drury, *The Visionary Human* (Shaftesbury, Dorset: Element, 1991).

Chapter 11: Sharing the Deathwalk

1. Sögyal Rinpoche, *Tibetan Book*.
2. Brother Lawrence of the Resurrection, *The Practice of the Presence of God,* trans. Donald Attwater (Springfield, Ill.: Templegate, 1974).
3. Ibid.

Chapter 12: Helping the Departed

1. See Robert Crookall, *The Study and Practice of Astral Projection* (Secaucus, N.J.: Citadel, 1979).
2. L. M. Fitzsimmons, *Opening the Psychic Door* (London: Hutchinson, 1933).
3. Anatole LeBraz, *The Celtic Legend of the Beyond,* trans. Derek Bryce (Lampeter, Wales: Llanerch, 1991), 46–51.
4. Hayyim Vital (1542–1620) gives a detailed account of the spirit possession and attempted exorcism of the woman of Safed in his *Sefer haGilgulim,* the "Book of Transformations." One of the witnesses to the exorcism rite was Alkabez, the author of the Sabbath hymn "Lekha dodi" ("Come, my friends"), still sung in temples on Friday evenings. A partial translation of Vital's account appears in Raphael Patai, "Exorcism and Xenoglossia among the Safed Kabbalists," in *Journal of American Folklore* 91, no. 361 (1978): 823–33. For other tales of the dybbuk as possessing spirit, see Howard Schwartz, *Gabriel's Palace: Jewish Mystical Tales* (New York and Oxford: Oxford University Press, 1993).

Chapter 13: Making Death Your Ally

1. For Milarepa's instructions on preparing for death, see Garma C. C. Chang, trans., *The Hundred Thousand Songs of Milarepa* (Boston: Shambhala, 1989), 2:556–57, 567–69.
2. Sögyal Rinpoche, *Tibetan Book,* 224.

3. Saint Ignatius Loyola, *The Spiritual Exercises,* trans. Thomas Corbishley (Wheathampstead, England: Anthony Clarke, 1987), 65.

4. Ibid.

5. Francesca Fremantle and Chogyam Trungpa, *The Tibetan Book of the Dead* (Boston: Shambhala, 1975).

6. Michael Murphy, *Jacob Atabet* (Los Angeles: Jeremy P. Tarcher, 1977).

7. Juan Mascaró, trans., *The Upanishads* (Harmondsworth, England: Penguin, 1967), 55–66. Cf. Sri Krishna Prem, *The Yoga of the Kathopahishad* (London: John M. Watkins, 1955).

8. Alain Daniélou, *Hindu Polytheism* (London: Routledge & Kegan Paul, 1964), 272.

Chapter 14: Soul Remembering

1. Plato, *Republic,* X.616–17, trans. Paul Shorey, in *Collected Dialogues,* 840–41.

2. *Republic,* X.620–21.

3. E. Bolaji Idowu, *Olodumare: God in Yoruba Belief* (New York: Wazobia, 1994), 174.

4. Ibid., 181.

5. Ibid., 180.

6. Cf. the Buddhist techniques for remembering previous existences described in Mircea Eliade, *Yoga: Immortality and Freedom* (Princeton: Bollingen Series, 1973), 180–85.

7. M. R. James, *The Apocryphal New Testament* (Oxford: Oxford University Press, 1950), 411–15. His mission accomplished, the hero resumes a mysterious robe of light.

8. Cf. Dolores Ashcroft-Nowicki, *Inner Landscapes* (Wellingborough, England: Aquarian Press, 1989), 36–37.

9. Khidr, "the Verdant One," appears in the eighteenth sura of the Koran, entitled "The Cave." For Jung's essay on Khidr, see *The Archetypes and the Collective Unconscious,* 135–47.

10. Watkins, *Waking Dreams,* 20.

11. Michael Sendivogius, *De sulphure,* cited in Jung, *Psychology and Alchemy* (Princeton: Bollingen Series, 1968), 279.

Chapter 15: Alien Encounters and Spirit Callings

1. There is an elegant retelling of "The Four Who Entered Paradise" in Howard Schwartz, *Gabriel's Palace: Jewish Mystical Tales* (New York and Oxford: Oxford University Press, 1994), 51–52.

2. Terence McKenna, "New Maps of Hyperspace," in *The Archaic Revival* (Harper San Francisco, 1991).

3. Jorge Luis Borges, *Fictions* (London: Calder Jupiter, 1965), 33.

4. John Mack, *Abduction: Human Encounters with Aliens* (New York: Scribner's, 1994).

5. Cited in Peter Hough, "The Development of UFO Occupants," in Hilary Evans and John Spencer, eds., *UFOs 1947–1987* (London, 1987), 127.

6. Cf. Jaques Vallée, *Dimensions* (New York: Ballantine, 1989), 144, 152.

7. W. Y. Evans-Wentz, *The Fairy Faith in Celtic Countries* (New York: Citadel, 1990).

8. For a practitioner's view of the evocation of kindred phenomena, see Franz Bardon, *The Practice of Magical Evocation: Instructions for Invoking Spirit Beings from the Spheres Surrounding Us* (Wuppertal, Germany: Dieter Ruggeberg, 1984).

9. Thomas Cleary, trans., *Entry into the Realm of Reality* (Boston: Shambhala, 1989).

10. C. G. Jung, "Flying Saucers: A Modern Myth of Things Seen in the Skies," in *Civilization in Transition* (Princeton: Bollingen Series, 1978).

11. Richard L. Thompson, *Alien Identities* (Alachua, Fla.: Govardhan Hill, 1995).

12. Ibid., 203–4.

13. R. J. Stewart, ed., *Robert Kirk, Walker between Worlds: A New Edition of The Secret Commonwealth* (Shaftesbury, England: Element, 1990).

14. Evans-Wentz, *Fairy Faith*, 89–90.

15. Sam Watson, *The Kadaitcha Sung* (Ringwood, Victoria: Penguin, 1990).

Chapter 16: Starwalking

1. Cf. Chuck Coburn, *Funny You Should Say That* (Redway, Calif.: Seed Center, 1995).

2. In ancient texts the Taoist adept is promised "he will have a garment of feathers, will ride on a lightbeam or saddle a star." He is to become a master of the "art of ascending to heaven in full daylight," able not only to ride to the sky with the aid of cranes, wild ducks, flying tigers, or dragons, but to shape-shift into light or a cloud. See Isabelle Robinet, *Méditation taoiste* (Paris: Dervy, 1979), 68–69, 249–50. Taoist methods of starwalking include calling in the spirits of the stars and traveling through astral gates associated with different constellations, especially the Dipper. See Michael Saso, *The Teachings of Taoist Master Chuang* (New Haven: Yale University Press, 1978).

3. Cf. Robert K. G. Temple, *The Sirius Mystery* (Rochester, Vt.: Destiny, 1987), especially chapter 1.

4. Michio Kaku, *Hyperspace* (New York and Oxford: Oxford University Press, 1994), 218.

5. Ibid., 221.

6. Temple, *Sirius Mystery*.

7. Marcel Griaule and Germaine Dieterlen, "Un Système Soudanais de Sirius," in *Journal de la Société des Africainistes* 20, no. 1 (1950): 273–94. See also Marcel Griaule, *Conversations with Ogotemmeli: An Introduction to Dogon Religious Ideas* (London and Oxford: Oxford University Press, 1970).

8. I made the original journey that opened this channel of communication in 1988, traveling through the heart of an atom. I published a brief description in *Conscious Dreaming*, 126–27.

Chapter 17: The View from the Fifth Dimension

1. Michio Kaku, *Hyperspace*, 27.

2. Chandogya Upanishad, 6:12–13. See Robert Ernest Hume, trans., *The Thirteen Principal Upanishads* (Oxford: Oxford University Press, 1921).

3. Cited in Patrick Harpur, *Daimonic Reality* (London: Penguin Arkana, 1995).

4. Michael Murphy, *The Future of the Body: Explorations into the Further Evolution of Human Nature* (Los Angeles: Jeremy P. Tarcher, 1992).

5. Claude Bragdon, *Explorations into the Fourth Dimension* (1916) (Lakemont, Ga.: CSA Press, 1972), 16, 37.

6. C. S. Lewis, *Perelandra* (1943), reprinted in *The Cosmic Trilogy* (London: Pan, 1989), 326–27.

7. Edwin Abbott Abbott, *Flatland* (1884) (New York: Harper & Row, 1983).

8. Andreas Lommel, *Die Unumbal: Ein Stamm en Nordwest-Australien* (Hamburg: Museum für Volkerkunde, 1962), 10–12. Cf. Campbell, *Way of the Animal Powers,* 1:141.

Bibliography

≋

I published annotated bibliographies on dreaming, dreamwork, and shamanism in *Conscious Dreaming,* and I refer the reader to these for my suggestions on further reading in these fields. The present bibliography identifies works that have been especially helpful in my exploration of these key areas: the history and practice of dream travel; the nature of the dreambody and other vehicles of consciousness; the workings of creative imagination and the geography of the imaginal realm; the art of dying; "alien encounters"; and the evolution of consciousness toward the multidimensional human. We are privileged in our time to enjoy unprecedented access to the recorded traditions of many societies, including guidebooks to the universe that were long held secret by spiritual orders. We are challenged to test them carefully, draw on them responsibly, and bring them together into a new synthesis.

Abbott, Edwin Abbott. *Flatland: A Romance of Many Dimensions* (1884). New York: Barnes & Noble, 1983.

Achterberg, Jeanne. *Imagery in Healing: Shamanism and Modern Medicine.* Boston: Shambhala, 1985.

Adamnan. *Life of Saint Columba.* Felinfach, Wales: Llanerch, 1988.

A.E. (George Russell). *The Candle of Vision: Inner Worlds of the Imagination* (1918). Bridport, Dorset: Prism, 1990.

Apollonius of Rhodes. *The Voyage of Argo.* Trans. E. V. Rieu. Harmondsworth, England: Penguin, 1971.

Arden, Harvey. *Dreamkeepers: A Spirit-Journey into Aboriginal Australia.* New York: Harper Perennial, 1995.

Arrien, Angeles. *The Tarot Handbook.* Sonoma, Calif.: Arcus, 1987.

Ash, David, and Peter Hewitt. *The Vortex—Key to Future Science.* Bath, England: Gateway, 1995.

Ashcroft-Nowicki, Dolores. *The Shining Paths.* Wellingborough, England: Aquarian, 1983.

————. *Highways of the Mind: The Art and History of Pathworking.* Wellingborough, England: Aquarian, 1987.

Atwater, P. M. H. *Beyond the Light.* New York: Avon, 1994.

————. *Future Memory.* New York: Birch Lane Press, 1996.

Aurobindo, Sri. *Letters on Yoga.* Pondicherry, India: Sri Aurobindo Ashram, 1970.

————. *Savitri.* Pondicherry, India: Sri Aurobindo Ashram, 1984.

Barber, Paul. *Vampires, Burial and Death.* New Haven: Yale University Press, 1988.

Barrett, William. *Death-Bed Visions* (1926). Wellingborough, England: Aquarian, 1986.

Bentov, Itzhak. *Stalking the Wild Pendulum.* Rochester, Vt.: Destiny, 1988.

Besant, Annie. *Death—and After?* Adyar, Madras: Theosophical Publishing House, 1991.

Bohm, David. *Wholeness and the Implicate Order.* London: Ark, 1985.

Bolen, Jean Shinoda. *Gods in Everyman.* San Francisco: Harper & Row, 1989.

————. *The Tao of Psychology: Synchronicity and the Self.* San Francisco: Harper & Row, 1982.

Bolton, J. D. F. *Aristeas of Proconnesus.* Oxford: Clarendon Press, 1962.

Borges, Jorge Luis. *Fictions.* London: Calder Jupiter, 1965.

————. *A Personal Anthology.* London: Picador, 1972.

Bosnak, Robert. *Tracks in the Wilderness of Dreaming.* New York: Delacorte, 1996.

Bradley, Marion Zimmer. *The House between the Worlds.* New York: Ballantine, 1981.

Bragdon, Claide. *Explorations into the Fourth Dimension.* Lakemont, Ga.: CSA Press, 1972.

Brinkley, Dannion. *Saved by the Light.* New York: Villard, 1994.

Brown, Courtney. *Cosmic Voyage.* New York: Dutton, 1996.

Bryant, Dorothy. *The Kin of Ata Are Waiting for You.* Berkeley and New York: Moon Books/Random House, 1971.

Budge, E. A. Wallis. *The Egyptian Book of the Dead* (The Papyrus of Ani). New York: Dover, 1967.

————. *Egyptian Magic.* Avenel, N.J.: Wings, 1991.

————. *Egyptian Religion.* New York and London: Arkana, 1987.

———. *Osiris: The Egyptian Religion of Resurrection.* New York: University Books, 1961.

Buhlmann, William. *Adventures Beyond the Body.* Harper San Francisco, 1996.

Burkert, Walter. *Ancient Mystery Cults.* Cambridge, Mass.: Harvard University Press, 1987.

Calasso, Roberto. *The Marriage of Cadmus and Harmony.* Trans. Tim Parks. New York: Vintage, 1994.

Callanan, Maggie, and Patricia Kellet. *Final Gifts.* New York: Bantam, 1993.

Cameron, Julia, with Mark Bryan. *The Artist's Way.* New York: Tarcher/Putnam, 1992.

———. *The Vein of Gold.* New York: Tarcher/Putnam, 1996.

Campbell, Jean. *Dreams beyond Dreaming.* Virginia Beach, Va.: Donning Company, 1980.

Campbell, Joseph. *The Inner Reaches of Outer Space.* New York: Harper & Row, 1988.

———. *The Way of the Animal Powers.* San Francisco: Alfred van der Marck/Harper & Row, 1983.

Carmichael, Alexander. *Carmina Gadelica.* Hudson, N.Y.: Lindisfarne Press, 1992.

Carr-Gomm, Philip, ed. *The Druid Renaissance.* London: Thorsons, 1996.

Cavendish, Richard, ed. *Encyclopedia of the Unexplained.* London: Arkana, 1989.

Cirlot, J. E. *Dictionary of Symbols.* New York: Philosophical Library, 1962.

Corbin, Henry. *Avicenna and the Visionary Recital.* Trans. Willard R. Trask. Princeton: Bollingen, 1990.

———. *Creative Imagination in the Sufism of Ibn 'Arabi.* Trans. Ralph Mannheim. Princeton: Bollingen, 1981.

———. *Spiritual Body and Celestial Earth.* Trans. Nancy Pearson. Princeton: Bollingen, 1989.

———. *Swedenborg and Esoteric Islam.* Trans. Leonard Fox. West Chester, Pa.: Swedenborg Foundation, 1995.

Cott, Jonathan. *Isis and Osiris.* New York: Doubleday, 1994.

Couliano, I. P. *Out of this World: Otherworldly Journeys from Gilgamesh to Albert Einstein.* Boston: Shambhala, 1991.

Crookall, Robert. *The Study and Practice of Astral Projection.* Secaucus, N.J.: Citadel, 1979.

Crowley, Aleister. *Magick.* York Beach, Maine: Samuel Weiser, 1994.

Cumont, Franz. *The Mysteries of Mithra.* Trans. Thomas J. McCormack. New York: Dover, 1956.

Danielou, Alain. *Hindu Polytheism.* London: Routledge & Kegan Paul, 1964.

Daniken, Erich von. *Gods from Outer Space.* New York: Putnam, 1970.

Daumal, Rene. *Mount Analogue.* Reprinted in *Parabola* 13, no. 4 (1988).

De Becker, Raymond. *The Understanding of Dreams.* Trans. Michael Heron. London: Allen & Unwin, 1968.

Doore, Gary, ed. *What Survives?* Los Angeles: Jeremy P. Tarcher, 1990.

Dundas, Paul. *The Jains.* London and New York: Routledge, 1992.

Egyptian Mysteries: An Account of an Initiation. York Beach, Maine: Samuel Weiser, 1988.

Eliade, Mircea. *A History of Religious Ideas.* 2 vols. Chicago: University of Chicago Press, 1984.

———. *Rites and Symbols of Initiation.* New York: Harper & Row, 1975.

———. *Shamanism: Archaic Techniques of Ecstasy.* Princeton: Bollingen, 1974.

———. *Yoga: Immortality and Freedom.* Princeton: Bollingen, 1973.

Elkin, A. P. *Aboriginal Men of High Degree.* New York: St. Martin's Press, 1977.

Evans-Wentz, W. Y. *The Fairy Faith in Celtic Countries.* New York: Citadel, 1990.

———. *The Tibetan Book of the Dead.* London: Oxford University Press, 1960.

———. *Tibetan Yoga and Secret Doctrines.* London: Oxford University Press, 1967.

Fanning, Patrick. *Visualization for Change.* Oakland, Ca.: New Harbinger, 1988.

Faraone, Christopher A., and Dirk Obbink, eds. *Magika Hiera: Ancient Greek Magic and Religion.* New York: Oxford University Press, 1997.

Ferris, Timothy. *The Mind's Sky: Human Intelligence in a Cosmic Contex.* New York: Bantam, 1992.

Fortune, Dion. *The Cosmic Doctrine.* London: Society of the Inner Light, 1995.

———. *Moon Magic.* York Beach, Maine: Samuel Weiser, 1990.

———. *The Sea Priestess.* York Beach, Maine: Samuel Weiser, 1993.

———. *Through the Gates of Death.* Wellingborough, England: Aquarian, 1987.

Fox, Oliver (Hugh Callaway). *Astral Projection.* Secaucus, N.J.: Citadel, 1962.

Garfield, Patricia. *Creative Dreaming.* New York: Ballantine, 1976.

———. *Pathway to Ecstasy.* New York: Prentice-Hall, 1989.

———. *Women's Bodies, Women's Dreams.* New York: Ballantine, 1988.

Gawain, Shakti. *Creative Visualization.* New York: Bantam, 1985.

Gendlin, Eugene T. *Focusing.* New York: Bantam, 1988.

Ghiselin, Brewster, ed. *The Creative Process.* Berkeley: University of Californina Press, 1952.

Ginzburg, Carlo. *Ecstasies: Deciphering the Witches' Sabbath.* Trans. Raymond Rosenthal. New York: Penguin, 1992.

Grasse, Ray. *The Waking Dream: Unlocking the Symbolic Language of Our Lives.* Wheaton, Ill.: Quest, 1996.

Green, Miranda. *Symbol and Image in Celtic Religious Art.* London and New York: Routledge, 1989.

Greer, Mary K. *Women of the Golden Dawn.* Rochester, Vt.: Park Street Press, 1995.

Grosso, Michael. *Frontiers of the Soul: Exploring Psychic Evolution.* Wheaton, Ill.: Quest, 1992.

Guss, David M., ed. *Language of the Birds: Tales, Text & Poems of Interspecies Communication.* San Francisco: North Point Press, 1985.

Guthrie, Kenneth Sylvan, ed. and trans. *The Pythagorean Sourcebook and Library.* Grand Rapids, Mich.: Phanes, 1987.

Guthrie, W. K. C. *Orpheus and Greek Religion.* New York: Norton, 1966.

Harner, Michael. *The Jivaro.* Berkeley: University of California Press, 1984.

———. *The Way of the Shaman.* Harper San Francisco, 1990.

Harper, George Mills, ed. *Yeats and the Occult*. Toronto: Macmillan, 1975.

Harpur, Patrick. *Daimonic Reality*. London and New York: Arkana, 1995.

Hillman, James. *The Dream and the Underworld*. New York: Harper & Row, 1979.

———. *Facing the Gods*. Dallas, Tex.: Spring Publications, 1988.

———. *The Soul's Code*. New York: Random House, 1996.

Hogart, R. C. *The Hymns of Orpheus: Mutations*. Grand Rapids, Mich.: Phanes, 1993.

Holzer, Hans. *The Psychic Side of Dreams*. New York: Doubleday, 1976.

Houston, Jean. *The Passion of Isis and Osiris*. New York: Ballantine, 1995.

———. *The Possible Human*. Los Angeles: Jeremy P. Tarcher, 1982.

Hughes, Robert. *Heaven and Hell in Western Art*. New York: Stein and Day, 1968.

Hultkrantz, Ake. *Conceptions of the Soul among North American Indians*. Stockholm: Ethnographical Museum of Sweden, 1953.

Iamblichus. *On the Mysteries*. Trans. Thomas Taylor. San Diego: Wizards, 1984.

Idel, Moshe. *Studies in Ecstatic Kabbalah*. Albany, N.Y.: SUNY Press, 1988.

Idowu, E. Bolaji. *Olodumare: God in Yoruba Belief*. New York: Wazobia, 1994.

Ingerman, Sandra. *A Fall to Grace*. Santa Fe: Moon Tree Rising, 1997.

———. *Soul Retrieval*. Harper San Francisco, 1991.

———. *Welcome Home: Following Your Soul's Journey Home*. Harper San Francisco, 1993.

Jacobs, Louis, ed. *The Schocken Book of Jewish Mystical Testimonies*. New York: Schocken, 1996.

Jamal, Michele. *Deerdancer: The Shapeshifter Archetype in Story and Trance*. New York: Arkana, 1995.

Jung, C. G. *Aion*. Trans. R. F. C. Hull. Princeton: Bollingen, 1979.

———. *The Archetypes and the Collective Unconscious*. Trans. R. F. C. Hull. Princeton: Bollingen, 1980.

————. "Flying Saucers: A Modern Myth of Things Seen in the Skies." In *Civilization in Transition*. Trans R. F. C. Hull. Princeton: Bollingen, 1970.

————. *Memories, Dreams, Reflections*. Ed. Aniela Jaffe. New York: Vintage, 1965.

————. *Mysterium Coniuntionis*. Trans. R. F. C. Hull. New York: Bollingen/Pantheon, 1963.

————. *Psychology and Alchemy*. Trans. R. F. C. Hull. Princeton: Bollingen, 1968.

————. Selected Letters. Ed. Gerhard Adler and Aniela Jaffe. Princeton: Bollingen, 1984.

Kaku, Michio. *Hyperspace*. New York: Oxford, 1994.

Kaplan, Aryeh. *Innerspace: Introduction to Kabbalah, Meditation and Prophecy*. Jerusalem and Brooklyn: Moznaim, 1991.

————. *Meditation and Kabbalah*. York Beach, Maine: Samuel Weiser, 1982.

Kardec, Alain. *The Spirits' Book*. Albuquerque, N.M.: Brotherhood of Life, 1995.

Kaufman, William J. *Black Holes and Warped Spacetime*. New York: W. H. Freeman, 1979.

Kerenyi, Carl. *Eleusis*. Trans. Ralph Mannheim. Princeton: Bollingen, 1991.

Kharitidi, Olga. *Entering the Circle*. Harper San Francisco, 1996.

King, Francis, ed. *Astral Projection, Ritual Magic and Alchemy: Golden Dawn Material by S. L. MacGregor Mathers and Others*. Rochester, Vt.: Destiny, 1987.

Kingsley, Peter. *Ancient Philosophy, Mystery and Magic: Empedocles and the Pythagorean Tradition*. Oxford: Clarendon Press, 1995.

Knight, Gareth. *Experience of the Inner Worlds*. York Beach, Maine: Samuel Weiser, 1993.

————. *The Magical World of the Inklings*. Shaftesbury, England: Element, 1990.

————. *A Practical Guide to Qabalistic Symbolism*. York Beach, Maine: Samuel Weiser, 1991.

————. *The Treasure House of Images*. Rochester, Vt.: Destiny, 1986).

Kubin, Alfred. *The Other Side: A Fantastic Novel*. Trans. Denver Lindley. New York: Crown, 1967.

Kübler-Ross, Elisabeth. *Death, the Final Stage of Growth*. New York: Touchstone, 1986.

———. *On Death and Dying*. New York: Macmillan, 1969.

Langer, Jiri. *Nine Gates to the Chassidic Mysteries*. Trans. Stephen Jolly. New York: Behrmann House, 1976.

Lawlor, Robert. *Voices of the First Day: Awakening in the Aboriginal Dreamtime*. Rochester, Vt.: Inner Traditions, 1991.

Lawrence of the Resurrection, Brother. *The Practice of the Presence of God*. Trans. Donald Attwater. Springfield, Ill.: Templegate, 1974.

Leadbeater, Charles. *The Devachanic Plane*. Adyar, Madras: Theosophical Publishing House, 1987.

———. *The Inner Life*. Wheaton, Ill.: Theosophical Publishing House, 1978.

Le Braz, Anatole. *The Celtic Legend of the Beyond*. Trans. Derek Bryce. Felinfach, Wales: Llanerch, 1991.

Le Goff, Jacques. *The Birth of Purgatory*. Trans. Arthur Goldhammer. Chicago: University of Chicago Press, 1984.

Lewis, C. S. *Chronicles of Narnia*. London: Fontana, 1980.

———. *The Cosmic Trilogy: Out of the Silent Planet, Perelandra and That Hideous Strength*. London: Pan, 1989.

Lewis, James R. *Encyclopedia of Afterlife Beliefs and Phenomena*. Detroit: Visible Ink, 1995.

Loyola, Saint Ignatius. *The Spiritual Exercises*. Trans. Thomas Corbishley. Wheathampstead, England: Anthony Clarke, 1987.

The Mabinogion. Trans. Jeffrey Gantz. London: Penguin, 1978.

Mack, John E. *Abduction: Human Encounters with Aliens*. New York: Scribner's, 1994.

Manguel, Alberto, and Gianni Guadalupi. *The Dictionary of Imaginary Places*. New York: Harvest/HBJ, 1987.

Marinus of Samaria. *The Life of Proclus*. Trans. Kenneth S. Guthrie. Grand Rapids, Mich.: Phanes Press, 1986.

Matthews, Caitlin. *The Celtic Book of the Dead*. New York: St. Martin's Press, 1992.

———. *Singing the Soul Back Home*. Shaftesbury, England: Element, 1995.

Matthews, John. *The Grail Tradition*. Shaftesbury, Dorset: Element, 1990.

Mavromatis, Andreas. *Hypnagogia*. London and New York: Routledge, 1991.

McKenna, Terence. *The Archaic Revival*. Harper San Francisco, 1991.

McMoneagle, Joseph. *Mind Trek*. Charlottesville, Va.: Hampton Roads, 1993.

Mead, G. R. S. *The Doctrine of the Subtle Body in the Western Tradition*. London: John M. Watkins, 1919.

———. *Thrice Greatest Hermes: Studies in Hellenistic Theosophy and Gnosis*. York Beach, Maine: Samuel Weiser, 1992.

Meditations on the Tarot: A Journey into Christian Hermeticism. Shaftesbury, England: Element, 1993.

Mellick, Jill. *The Natural Artistry of Dreams*. Berkeley: Conari Press, 1996.

Mellon, Nancy. *Storytelling & the Art of Imagination*. Rockport, Mass.: Element, 1992.

Meyer, Marvin W., ed. *The Ancient Mysteries: A Sourcebook*. New York: Harper & Row, 1987.

Monroe, Robert. *Far Journeys*. New York: Doubleday Dolphin, 1987.

———. *Journeys Out of the Body*. New York: Anchor, 1977.

———. *Ultimate Journey*. New York: Doubleday, 1994.

Moore, Robin. *Awakening the Hidden Storyteller*. Boston: Shambhala, 1991.

Moss, Robert. "Blackrobes and Dreamers: Jesuit Reports on the Shamanic Dream Practices of the Northern Iroquoians." In *Shaman's Drum* 28 (1992).

———. *Conscious Dreaming: A Spiritual Path for Everyday Life*. New York: Crown, 1996.

———. *The Firekeeper*. New York: Forge, 1995.

———. *The Interpreter*. New York: Forge, 1997.

———. "Missionaries and Magicians." In Peter Benes, ed., *Wonders of the Invisible World: 1600–1900*. Boston: Boston University Press, 1995.

———. "What Your Dreams Can Tell." In Louise Carus Mahdi, ed., *Crossroads: The Quest for Contemporary Rites of Passage*. Chicago and La Salle: Open Court, 1996.

Mudrooroo. *Aboriginal Mythology*. London: Aquarian, 1994.

———. *Master of the Ghost Dreaming*. North Ryde, NSW: Angus & Robertson, 1991.

Murphy, Michael. *The Future of the Body*. Los Angeles: Jeremy P. Tarcher, 1992.

———. *Jacob Atabet*. New York: Jeremy P. Tarcher, 1977.

Murray, Margaret A. *The Witch-Cult in Western Europe*. London: Oxford University Press, 1921.

Myers, Frederic W. H. *Human Personality and Its Survival of Bodily Death*. 2 vols. London: Longmans, Green, 1903.

Myss, Caroline. *Anatomy of the Spirit*. New York: Harmony, 1996.

Narayan, R. K. *Gods, Demons and Others*. Mysore: Indian Thought Publications, 1967.

Oppenheim, A. Leo. *The Interpretation of Dreams in the Ancient Near East*. Philadelphia: American Philosophical Society, 1956.

Osis, Karlis, and Erlendur Haraldsson. *At the Hour of Death*. New York: Avon, 1977.

Ouspensky, P. D. *A New Model of the Universe*. New York: Random House, 1971.

———. *Strange Life of Ivan Osokin*. London: Arkana, 1987.

Ozaniec, Naomi. *The Elements of the Egyptian Wisdom*. Shaftesbury, England: Element, 1994.

Peach, Emily. *The Tarot Workbook*. New York: Sterling, 1990.

Phillips, Stephen M. *Extra-Sensory Perception of Quarks*. Wheaton, Ill.: Theosophical Publishing House, 1980.

Philostratus. *The Life of Apollonius of Tyana*. 2 vols. Trans. F. C. Conybeare. Cambridge, Mass.: Harvard University Press, 1969.

Plato. *Collected Dialogues*. Ed. Edith Hamilton and Huntington Cairnes. Princeton: Bollingen, 1989.

Plutarch. *Concerning the Face Which Appears in the Orb of the Moon*. In *Moralia*, vol. 12. Trans. Harold Cherniss and William Helmbold. Cambridge, Mass.: Harvard University Press, 1995.

———. *Isis and Osiris and the Obsolescence of Oracles*. In *Moralia*, vol. 5. Trans. F. C. Babbitt. Cambridge, Mass.: Harvard University Press, 1993.

Poortman, J. J. *Vehicles of Consciousness*. 4 vols. Utrecht: Theosophical Society, 1978.

Powell, A. E. *The Astral Body and Other Astral Phenomena*. Wheaton, Ill.: Quest, 1992.

———. *The Etheric Double*. Wheaton, Ill.: Quest Books, 1969.

Prem, Sri Krishna. *The Yoga of the Kathopanishad*. London: John Watkins, 1955.

Priestley, J. B. *Man and Time*. London: Aldus Books, 1964.

Proclus. *The Elements of Theology*. Trans. and ed. E. R. Dodds. Oxford: Clarendon Press, 1992.

The Quest of the Holy Grail. Trans. P. M. Matarasso. London: Penguin, 1969.

Regardie, Israel. *The Golden Dawn*. St. Paul, Minn.: Llewellyn, 1988.

Richardson, Michael, ed. *The Myth of the World: The Dedalus Book of Surrealism 2*. Dawtry, Cambridgeshire: Dedalus, 1994.

Richelieu, Peter. *A Soul's Journey*. Wellingborough, England: Aquarian, 1989.

Ring, Kenneth. *Heading toward Omega*. New York: Morrow, 1984.

———. *The Omega Project*. New York: Morrow, 1992.

Rogo, D. Scott. *The Infinite Boundary*. New York: Dodd, Mead, 1987.

———. *Leaving the Body*. New York: Fireside, 1993.

Ross, Anne. *The Folklore of the Scottish Highlands*. New York: Barnes & Noble, 1993.

Rucker, Rudy. *The Fourth Dimension*. London: Penguin, 1986.

Ruderman, David B. *A Valley of Vision: The Heavenly Journey of Abraham ben Hananiah Yagel*. Philadelphia: University of Pennsylvania Press, 1990.

Saint-Denys, Hervey de. *Dreams and How to Guide Them* (1867). Ed. Morton Schatzman. London: Duckworth, 1982.

Schachter-Shalomi, Rabbi Zalman, with Howard Schwartz. *The Dream Assembly*. Nevada City, Calif.: Gateways, 1989.

Scholem, Gershom G. *Major Trends in Jewish Mysticism*. New York: Schocken, 1971.

Schwartz, Howard. *Gabriel's Palace: Jewish Mystical Tales*. New York: Oxford, 1993.

Sitchin, Zechariah. *Divine Encounters*. New York: Avon, 1995.

Smith, Morton. *Jesus the Magician*. Harper San Francisco, 1981.

Sögyal Rinpoche. *The Tibetan Book of Living and Dying*. Harper San Francisco, 1992.

Song, Tamarack. *Journey to the Ancestral Self*. Barrytown, N.Y.: Station Hill Press, 1994.

Steinbrecher, Edwin C. *The Inner Guide Meditation.* Wellingborough, England: Aquarian, 1985.

Stewart, R. J. *Robert Kirk, Walker between Worlds: A New Edition of* The Secret Commonwealth. Shaftesbury, England: Element, 1990.

———. *The Underworld Initiation.* Wellingborough, England: Aquarian, 1985.

Temple, Robert K. G. *The Sirius Mystery.* Rochester, Vt.: Destiny, 1987.

Teresa of Avila, Saint. *Interior Castle.* Trans. E. Allison Peers. New York: Doubleday Image, 1961.

Thompson, Keith. *Angels and Aliens: UFOs and the Mythic Imagination.* Reading, Mass.: Addison-Wesley, 1991.

Thompson, Richard L. *Alien Identities.* Alachua, Fla.: Govardhan Hill, 1995.

Twitchell, Paul. *Eckankar: The Key to Secret Worlds.* Golden Valley, Minn.: Illuminated Way, 1987.

Ulansey, David. *The Origins of the Mithraic Mysteries.* New York: Oxford, 1989.

Vallée, Jacques. *Dimensions: A Casebook of Alien Contact.* New York: Ballantine, 1989.

Vaughan, Frances E. *Awakening Intuition.* New York: Anchor, 1979.

———. *The Inward Arc: Healing in Psychotherapy and Spirituality.* Nevada City, Calif.: Blue Dolphin, 1995.

Veggi, Athon, and Alison Davidson. *The Book of Doors: An Alchemical Oracle from Ancient Egypt.* Rochester, Vt.: Destiny, 1995.

von Franz, Marie-Louise. *The Golden Ass of Apuleius.* Boston: Shambhala, 1992.

———. *On Dreams and Death.* Boston: Shambhala, 1987.

———. *Projection and Re-Collection in Jungian Psychology.* La Salle, Ill.: Open Court, 1990.

Wang, Robert. *The Qabalistic Tarot.* York Beach, Maine: Samuel Weiser, 1987.

Watkins, Mary. *Waking Dreams.* Dallas, Tex.: Spring Publications, 1984.

Watson, Sam. *The Kadaitcha Sung.* Ringwood, Victoria: Penguin, 1990.

White, John. *A Practical Guide to Death & Dying*. Wheaton, Ill.: Quest, 1988.

Wilber, Ken. *Eye to Eye: The Quest for the New Paradigm*. Boston: Shambhala, 1996.

Wilhelm, Richard, with C. G. Jung. *The Secret of the Golden Flower*. New York: Harves/HBJ, 1962.

Wilkinson, Richard H. *Symbol and Magic in Egyptian Art*. New York: Thames and Hudson, 1994.

Williams, Charles. *All Hallows Eve*. Grand Rapids, Mich.: Eerdmans, 1981.

———. *Descent into Hell*. Grand Rapids, Mich.: Eerdmans, 1981.

Wilson, Colin. *Afterlife*. London: Harrap, 1985.

Wolf, Fred Alan. *The Dreaming Universe*. New York: Simon & Schuster, 1994.

Wright, Machaelle Small. *Dancing in the Shadows of the Moon*. Jeffersonton, Va.: Perelandra, 1995.

Yeats, W. B. *Essays and Introductions*. New York: Macmillan, 1961.

———. *Memoirs*. New York: Macmillan, 1972.

———. *A Vision*. New York: Collier Books, 1966.

———. "Witches and Wizards and Irish Folk-Lore" and "Swedenborg, Mediums and the Desolate Places." In Lady Gregory, *Visions and Beliefs in the West of Ireland*. Gerrards Cross, England: Colin Smythe, 1992.

Zaleski, Carol. *Otherworld Journeys: Accounts of Near-Death Experience in Medieval and Modern Times*. New York: Oxford, 1987.

Resources

≈

Audio Programs

My nine-hour audio training program, "Dream Gates: A Journey into Active Dreaming," is available from Sounds True. It includes shamanic drumming as well as several inductions into conscious dreaming. In the United States, call toll-free (800) 333-9185. Or contact:

Sounds True
413 S. Arthur Avenue
Louisville, CO 80027
Tel: (303) 665-3151
Fax: (303) 665-5292
E-mail: SoundsTrue@aol.com

Workshops

For information on my Active Dreaming workshops and training programs, and on future publications, please write to:

Robert Moss
Way of the Dreamer
P.O. Box 215
Troy, NY 12181
Fax: (518) 274-0506

I would welcome your account of any personal experiences you wish to share.

Index

~~~

About the Author

≋

Robert Moss is a lifelong dream explorer, a shamanic counselor, a best-selling novelist, and a student of the Western Mystery traditions. He has also been a professor of ancient history and philosophy, an actor, a magazine editor, and a war correspondent in Vietnam. His fascination with the dreamworlds springs from his early childhood in Australia, where he survived a series of near-death experiences and first encountered the ways of a dreaming people through his friendship with Aborigines. He has worked with his personal dream journals for more than thirty years. For more than ten years, he has taught and practiced Active Dreaming, an original synthesis of dreamwork and shamanism. His many books include *Conscious Dreaming: A Spiritual Path for Everyday Life* (Crown) and the novels *The Firekeeper* and *The Interpreter*. He has recorded a nine-hour audio workshop, "Dream Gates: A Journey into Active Dreaming" (Sounds True). He teaches innovative programs in dreamwork, shamanism, and creativity in Europe and Australia as well as across the United States. He was guided by dreams to his present home near Albany, New York.